Broken In
The Right Place

■ ■ ■

ALAN E. NELSON
Foreword by Eugene Peterson

THOMAS NELSON PUBLISHERS
Nashville

Published in Nashville, Tennessee, by Thomas Nelson, Inc.

Unless otherwise noted, Scripture quotations are from the NEW KING JAMES VERSION of the Bible. Copyright © 1979, 1980, 1982, Thomas Nelson, Inc., Publishers.

Scripture quotations noted TLB are from *The Living Bible* (Wheaton, Illinois: Tyndale House Publishers, 1971) and are used by permission.

Scripture quotations noted NIV are taken from the HOLY BIBLE, NEW INTERNATIONAL VERSION® Copyright © 1973, 1978, 1984 by International Bible Society. Used by permission of Zondervan Bible Publishing House. All rights reserved.

The "NIV" and "New International Version" trademarks are registered in the United States Patent and Trademark Office by International Bible Society. Use of either trademark requires the permission of International Bible Society.

Library of Congress Cataloging-in-Publication Data

Nelson, Alan.
  Broken in the right place / Alan Nelson.
    p. cm.
  Includes bibliographical references.
  ISBN 0-8407-7648-9
  1. Spiritual life. 2. Consolation 3. Nelson, Alan. 4. Spiritual
formation. I. Title
BV4501.2.N435 1993
248.8'6—dc20   93-29847
                                     CIP

Printed in the United States of America
1 2 3 4 5 6 7 — 99 98 97 96 95 94

Contents

Dedication

This book is lovingly dedicated to my dream girl, forever friend, co-minister, and wife, Nancy.

Thanks also to Jack Maxwell and my friends at West Coast Church, who endured and benefitted from my times of brokenness.

Foreword

It's odd that a religion that carries the cross as its central symbol should require a crash course in suffering. But it does. Oh, how it does.

We have somehow ended up with a country full of Christians who consider suffering, whether it comes from a broken body or a broken heart, a violaton of their spiritual rights. When things go badly in body or job or family, they whine and complain endlesly. Sometimes they protest vehemently. In between complaints and protests, they seek out the company of those who anesthetize them with soothing words and soft music. They have no difficulty finding such anestheticians—pain-killing spiritualities are a glut on the market. The only cross they seem to have any acquaintance with is a piece of cheap jewelry.

Can anyone get their attention long enough to convince them that suffering must not be avoided, but embraced; that brokenness does not diminish a life of faith but deepens it?

I think Alan Nelson can. I think this book, *Broken in the Right Place,* can convince the person who reads it that suffering is not evidence of God's absence, but of God's presence and that it is in our experience of being broken that God does His surest and most characteristic salvation work. I think that the person who considers the evidence presented in these pages, evidence both biblical and personal, can be persuaded that there is a way to accept, embrace, and deal with suffering that results in a better life, not a worse one, and more of the experience of God, not less.

Alan Nelson is a pastor true to His calling, showing us that God is working out His salvation in our lives the way he has always worked it out, at the place of brokenness, at the cross of Jesus, and at the very place where we take up our *cross*. We can, of course, refuse to pick it up. We will suffer no less, but the suffering will be wasted, dribbling into whine and litigation. But if we accept his counsel and let ourselves be informed by his teaching, we can again become the people whose name we bear, *Christians*, who can turn the world upside down—right side up!—and become the revolutionary presence of the Kingdom of God on this continent.

Eugene H. Peterson
Professor of Theology
Regent College
Vancouver, B.C., Canada

Preface

God has a celestial sense of humor. I'm convinced of it. I do not base this belief on the studies that show Jesus used humor among his teachings. And I do not mean to imply it is a malicious sort of comedy that laughs at our expense. But I'm sure that He sees things somewhat differently than we do, probably most of the time. Good humor usually employs twists, unexpected turns in logic or cause and effect, so that we are caught off balance. It is sort of a cerebral surprise. I'm convinced He has a sense of humor because He had me write this book.

This is a spiritual book, a serious book. I feel a bit hypocritical in that this work would appear to be written by one who is inclined toward monastic solemnity. I can imagine a monk, cloistered away in a monastery, committed to a life of poverty, celibacy, and the lifelong search for spiritual truths. Most of us appreciate, but do not relate to such personalities. You know what I mean, holy men, saints . . . those people you meet who do not seem to get caught up in the lusts of the world, those who have a propensity toward the deeper life, the eternal, the sublime.

Myself, I'm more of a mundane man. I find myself staring at the mirror too often, wondering how others view me. Like most, I'm more prone to enjoy having my ears tickled with "and they lived happily ever after," versus being shocked by the news that "the patient is terminal." I tend to be more motivational in my style of communication. Brokenness is pretty hard to talk about that way. It's sort of like laughing at a joke while walking into a funeral home, only to discover a memorial service is under way. Brokenness is about death; the cessation of the unbridled spirit. Anyone who is in a time of brokenness, or who vividly remembers the pain and disillusionment of the process, knows it as a time of solemnity.

I prayerfully hope that God will use these thoughts and words to expand your capacity for Him, to make sense of the seemingly paradoxical events which transpire in times of breaking, and most of all, that you understand the processes through which He seeks to tame your soul. The pain of childbirth and the pain inflicted by terrorists may feel similar to the person experiencing them, but they are responded to in different ways. Why? Because the former pain has a beautiful result, the emergence of new life. The latter pain is burdensome and embittering, because it seems senseless. Understanding the process of brokenness will not necessarily impede the pain, unless it quickens one's responsiveness to God, but it will make the pain much more bearable. So it is with excitement and a sort of sanctified trepidation that I commit these next pages to you.

Acknowledgments

I thank God for supplying the clay to throw this literary pot. This is a book I never intended to write. Thanks to the contemporary and ancient writers, whose thoughts helped mold the vessel. Thanks also to those who helped fire it, by reading early manuscripts, and by supplying endorsements and personal testimonies. Finally, thanks to the glaziers at Thomas Nelson for adding the finishing touches. I am truly grateful for everyone's part.

Christianity did not come in order to develop the heroic virtues in the individual, but rather to remove self-centeredness and establish love.
—Søren Kierkegaard.

CHAPTER
ONE

■

Taming of
the Soul

■ ■ ■

BREAKING THE WILD STALLION

The rust-colored stallion stood regally in the sun, the coat on his muscular thighs shimmering in the light. The magnificent horse paced the length of the corral fence and then threw his head over the top fence board. He scouted the hillside with a lonely look in his eyes and snorted. Moments later, the steed darted across the dirt lot, his mane blowing in the gentle Midwestern breeze.

As a young adolescent I stood on the fence and gazed upon the majestic beast. Admiration and fear churned within me. The animal's wild, untamed spirit caused me to keep a safe distance. The horse's defined muscles and flowing gait transfixed my attention for what seemed like hours. I had no desire to ride this undisciplined creature. No one had ever sat upon his strong, lean back . . . until today.

1

From across the barnyard I watched a man carrying a saddle walking toward the corral. He was a middle-aged cowboy with a ten-gallon hat, cowboy boots, and bow-legged stance. His blue jeans were covered in front by leather chaps. A light-blue denim shirt with imitation pearl buttons extended into his leather gloves. This sauntering image from the West seemed out of place on an Iowa farm where workers wore t-shirts, overalls, round-toed work shoes, and maybe a cap from the local feed store. We primarily raised livestock and grew corn and alfalfa to feed our hogs and cattle. Our general tools were tractors and machinery, not stirrups and lassos; but ever since we moved from the farm to Creston the previous year, this cowboy had run the place with a touch of the West.

Today was the beginning of the end of the stallion's self-centered life. His unbridled neck would soon be bound by the tightness of leather. His belly would constrict as the cinch fastened to hold the saddle in place. He would taste a metal bit for the first time. Today would mark a noticeable change in the animal's behavior.

As the cowboy neared the fence where I stood, I heard the jingling of his spurs. Although the fence was not high, the man grunted as he flung the saddle onto the top board. He relaxed noticably after he unloaded his burden.

The horse stopped his nervous pacing. He looked at the cowboy and seemed to sense that something was about to change. From around the corner, the cowboy brought out a five-gallon bucket half full of shelled corn. As the man held up the bucket, the horse trotted over to the concrete deck below the fence. The horse stuck his long nose into the feed bucket, and the cowboy gently approached him and gingerly placed a rope halter around his head, sliding it behind the tall ears. The horse stepped back hesitantly, but returned quickly for more corn.

The cowboy spoke softly to me. "He's been halter broken for several days now. Yesterday, we started bridle-breaking him."

"When can you ride him?" I asked.

The cowboy grinned, a seasoned grin. "We're gonna try him today," he said with a Texas drawl. "Once they get familiar with a bridle, you can usually put a saddle on them and finish breaking them soon after that. It's been easy up to now."

The cowboy turned around and removed the halter from the horse's head. He then took a leather bridle from off the fenced saddle. He comforted the jittery stallion by putting his arm around the horse's thick neck. He quietly and smoothly placed the constellation of leather straps on the horse's head and fitted the steel metal bar into his mouth. The tall steed resisted.

"Easy boy. Good boy," the cowboy said reassuringly. "Good boy."

He held the reigns and began slowly walking the horse around in a big circle in the corral. The horse responded nervously, taking anxious steps to the left and to the right. The cowboy continued to speak encouraging words to the animal. As he returned to the fence, he tied the reins to the post and replaced the bucket of corn under the horse's nose.

Then the short man lifted the saddle from the fence and walked alongside the tall stallion. He patted the horse on the back with one hand. "Good boy."

The cowboy bent over, and with one hand on the saddle horn and the other grabbing the back edge of the seat, he gently tossed it onto the horse's back. The horse jolted forward. "Easy boy, easy. Good boy. Good boy." He carefully let down the stirrup on the opposite side as the horse returned to the grain. The cowboy reached under the animal's high belly and grabbed the cinch. The man slowly but confidently slid the straps through the appropriate rings. He stroked the horse's back. "Good boy." Then in a swift, strong gesture, he pulled the cinch strap, securing the saddle to the untamed animal's back. The inexperienced animal reeled against the tightness. "Easy boy, good boy."

The horse pulsated with nervous energy. The cowboy stepped back. He continued to encourage the beautiful beast but gave the horse some space. After a few snorts and half-hearted bucks, the horse returned to the almost empty bucket.

From my precarious perch on the fence, I wondered what the cowboy would do next. Just like in the movies, he untied the reigns from the post and cautiously approached the wild stallion. Swiftly he placed one boot in the left stirrup and swung his right foot over the tall horse. For the first time the stallion carried a rider. The horse turned ninety degrees and began running and kicking to the far end of the corral. In spite of the cowboy's verbal affirmations, the stallion continued to resist the rider's invasion. He bucked and snorted and bellowed. The twisting jumps threw the cowboy off balance. His rodeo style of riding with one hand in the air was not enough to keep him in the saddle. Two bucks later, the cowboy tumbled to the churning dirt below. Like a seasoned veteran, he brushed himself off, picked up his hat, and watched as the horse ran away, free from its unwanted passenger. As he walked toward the fence he said, "We'll try it again as soon as he gets calmed down a bit."

Sure enough, several minutes later, the steed's frantic pacing subsided and he returned to the replenished corn bucket. The cowboy patted the horse's neck and whispered more affirmations. "Good boy. Good boy. That's it." Suddenly but smoothly, the cowboy remounted the horse. Again, the stallion jumped left and then right as he arched his back. This time it was a little less violent. Several more times the horse trotted and bucked, trotted and bucked, but soon the majestic beast ran smoothly, carrying his passenger.

The cowboy practiced turning, galloping, and stopping. "Whoa, thatta boy." The horse gave some rebellious snorts and reared up a few times. But within the hour the cowboy was riding the once wild-spirited, now domesticated animal. The horse was authentically broken.

■

BREAKING THE SOUL

The last definition for the word *broken* in my dictionary reads: "reduced to submission; tamed."

The human soul is much like an untamed stallion with his unbridled energy. Sometimes it is majestic and powerful, and at other times it is stubborn and destructively dangerous. Regardless of its potential, the untamed soul has limited capacity for constructive use. Just as the unbroken horse cannot be ridden for enjoyment or used to herd cattle, a person's unbroken spirit is confined to the sheer beauty of its potential productivity. An unbridled soul restricts God's work in a person's life. That kind of soul cannot be guided. Energy cannot be harnessed in the untamed state.

This book explores the taming of the soul. I once believed that when a person had a personal experience with God, all that was left was to learn more and "grow in grace." However, I continue to discover, often painfully, that there is a silent, but common and active process in the building of the Christian called brokenness. I doubt that people who have ever achieved significance for a long period of time, or who have been used productively by the Holy Spirit in ministry, have eluded this process. The soul of a person, in its early and natural state, is wildly undisciplined. Whether it aggressively rebels against God's harnessing like a bucking bronco, or passive-aggressively resists guiding like an old, stubborn mule, the human spirit resents the influence of God's Spirit.

At the same time the wild stallion avoids the saddle, he gazes longingly at the smooth gallup of another horse being ridden. He yearns for the care and affection granted the harnessed horse but resists the process needed to achieve that status.

An unbroken person refuses to accept difficult challenges and questions unexplained events with frustration. This poor soul seeks success and achievement, but, as master of himself, risks depression, disillusionment, failure, and suicide in order to "do it myself." This same person fights reliance on God in an effort to go "my own way." This unbridled orientation seems natural and acceptable, but it inevitably results in hurt and alienation. The person who demands to follow himself, or others, and not God alone, is destined to a future of futility.

I have noticed three parallels between breaking a horse and taming the soul.

The first is that the world has little use for a wild, unbroken soul. An unbroken soul is primarily a consumer. It occupies space and carries on many of the functions of a broken soul; but it performs little good. Its activities are not very useful in the eternal view of things. Like the horse, an unbroken soul can have natural beauty, but it tends to be one of latent potential and not pragmatic beauty.

The second observation is that the breaking process ultimately strengthens the bond between the cowboy (owner, rider, caretaker) and the horse. Prior to being broken, all that exists is admiration from a distance, and the basic maintenance of life (feeding, watering). Once brokenness occurs, there is bonding and affection. The love relationship is able to grow as trust is manifested. Until a person's soul experiences brokenness, it can do little more than admire God and acknowledge His sustenance. At this stage, intimacy tends to be shallow and sporadic, if it occurs at all. Having three boys, I have noticed that an old, worn, "broken-in" teddy bear is usually preferred over a new, fluffy one.

Third, one would think that the breaking process would sap the spirit, drive, and energy of the horse. It does not. The horse is just as strong after breaking as before, but his abilities multiply many times over and his energy is no longer wild, but directed. Dull listlessness does not fill the broken beast's eyes. The gallop emerges just as quick, the steps are just as high as before. The process of being broken in the right place is not a matter of becoming passive, unmotivated, or lackluster. Rather, it is a catalyzing process which ultimately helps the soul reach its potential. All too often we Christians feel that to follow Christ wholeheartedly means to hang up some of our dreams and aspirations. We feel a sense of settling for second best in worldly terms if we allow the breaking process to turn us into true followers of Christ.

A breaking process which results in bitterness, cynicism, or low self-esteem is not the right process. A horse can be broken by beatings, poisons, and drugs, but that animal will not be helpful for a creative cause. When people become broken in the wrong places, they do not grow into people who are mature, productive, and Christlike.

All metaphors have their shortcomings and this one is not intended to portray God as a spur-digging cowboy riding on our backs. Rather, the breaking process, as it emerges in these pages, allows us the often painful opportunity to grow and reach a level of maturity which cannot otherwise be achieved. You will not here find a book of platitudes and tired cliches. Vain repetitions are all too common in the lives of those who claim to follow Christ, but who lack the power and integrity God desires. Hopefully, in the following chapters you will recognize a process you have experienced, but perhaps haven't completely understood or have not fully gained from the intended results of God's transforming work.

■

QUESTIONS FOR REFLECTION

1. Discuss the analogy of comparing the untamed soul to a wild horse. How is that metaphor helpful? How is it limited?

2. What good is an untamed soul in the world?

3. How could a breaking process enhance one's relationship with God?

4. Can you think of someone who has undergone what could be called a breaking experience and who grew stronger and matured through it? What changed?

5. Silent thought: What areas in your life need some taming?

The world breaks everyone and afterwards many
are strong at the broken places.
—Ernest Hemingway

■

CHAPTER TWO

Falling Behind to Get Ahead

■ ■ ■

*Those trials which do not break us make us stronger.
Scottish patriarchs looking for walking sticks, always
passed over the untried wood of the lower slopes, climb-
ing to the weathered heights to search for rods made
strong by storm and wind. For these young trees once
fought the icy Northers and with each fight they bent and
twisted and broke a bit inside. But gradually each inner
scar became the steely fiber, brought by every storm that
they endured.*

These are the Rods of God!

Ask Moses!

*Such Rods can speak to a threatened Pharaoh, or order
Suez water-walls to let the children pass. Such rods will
make a cobra. Lightning rises off their knobby heads.*

*But do not let their majesty delude you! These mighty
rods were once just spindly trees. Bless not the rod, but
rather bless the gales that broke their sinews, lacing them
with stone, 'till the storms they so despised had changed*

them into scepters: such maces make Midianites and shepherds to be Kings.

So all real saints are fashioned in the crucible of God. They are broken—even crushed—between mortar and pestle; then their soft nothingness is changed to granite, from which God fashions monuments to himself. Thus, a Jew of Tarsus was beaten, stoned, shipwrecked, imprisoned (2 Cor. 11:23ff), and yet he speaks out in praise, of the brokenness that forged him! Paul does not brag of being strong! He boasts only of his weakness and praises the storms (2 Cor. 12:10). For in his heart he knew that simple grace has little volume in its soft authority. But when such grace is battered by the storms, the gales do their transforming work. Thus grace and brokenness together can take a frightened Asian Jew and name him Thunder, the Lion of God.

From my little promontory of 30 years of parenting and 35 years of pastoring, I now look back and bless the seasons of my brokenness. Some of these seasons punctuate my recent years with the pain-purchased counsel of God. But for my best lesson of life, I must move back, back, back—through the decades—to old despair.

In college I read incessantly from those atheist philosophers and existentialists who dominated Humanism. I glutted my hunger to understand life by reading mostly those who never knew life: Meade, Russell, Unamuno, Sartre, etc. Throughout seminary I continued my fascination with this pursuit of emptiness and in the process became as hollow as those I read.

Thus, I arrived at my first full-time pastorate, with all the academic credentials I needed, but faithless and confused. I despaired of ever preaching with any certainty, steeped in the dark scholarship of my ghoulish academics, I had no light to see God: Was he there? Was he real? Was he loving? My congregation was so spiritually hungry that they waited each week for bread I could not break. I met their hunger with my own, my Sinai held no manna. Our famine was severe.

I said what they expected, but every sermon left me with the brown taste of my hypocrisy filling my mouth. I did not need to tell them of my confusion. It was self-proclaiming! Like Nazareth we were (Mark 6:5,6); God did not many mighty works there "because of our unbelief." Just when I felt that my own confusion would destroy me, I broke!

I cried out to God to slay me or make me an honest man with an authentic word. My intellectual pride dissolved in utter need. I broke! My brokenness—like all brokenness—had for its sweet fruit, simple fluent tears. Those tears were sheer acetylene. A torch that cut away, at first, my pride, and then my doubt.

With arrogance and doubt both gone, the scales fell from my eyes. I saw God! High and lifted up! His train filled the temple (Isa. 6:1ff.) He took a live coal from off the altar with tongs; he did it for great was the burning and white was the heat! And when my brokenness was complete, I said, "Who art thou, Lord?" (Acts 9:5).

He didn't answer, but I knew.

It was the first time I had felt the fire of God on my tongue. It would not be the last. It was a welcome fire made warm by my own brokenness. Since that first flame came to me, I've found that brokenness and fire are always friends, and those who learn to say within their soul "I'm sorry, God," carry fire within their neediness. Thus only the broken bring the flame.

—Calvin Miller

■

PILGRIM'S PROGRESS OR PILGRIM'S DIGRESS?

Riding in the back seat of a friend's car with my wife en route to a San Diego Padres baseball game, I poured out my frustrations with God. "I feel like God is dumping on me," I lamented. "It seems like God has given up on me."

The previous year, I had finished my master's degree in

communication/psychology and had since invested hundreds of hours into creating a personal growth seminar ministry for pastors and laymen. I was determined to become the next great motivator of the Christian community, exhorting people to seek excellence in their lives. My notebooks bulged with life-changing information, and the initial responses from the seminars assured me that with some work this ministry would be a success. But then, following a move to San Diego where my wife went on staff at a large church, things started to go awry. Sensing a ministerial call from an early age, and believing God was directing me into this itinerant work, I felt desperately confused when, one by one, my speaking engagements began canceling on me. I traveled throughout college, speaking in churches and holding revivals, and was one of the few students allowed to speak in our college chapel services. My ministry was supposed to be enlarging, not decreasing. I knew Christians needed to know this information on personal growth that I had researched. I could not understand what God seemed to be doing in my life, leading me straight to an apparent dead end.

"I feel like God is beating me down," I mourned to my friends in the front seat, who were on staff with my wife at the church.

"You mean you're going through a wilderness," Tim suggested.

I had not heard it put that way before, but I liked Tim's more positive approach better than my image of God beating me. "Yeah, I guess you're right," I agreed. By the end of that year, I was folding sweaters in a men's department store for the Christmas season. There I was, a young visionary with a master's degree, living off my wife's income, feeling abandoned by God. It was the worst year of my adult life. I began praying and seriously seeking God and His desire for my life. That year in the wilderness caused me to realize that God was redirecting my ministry goals and plans toward starting a new church in Orange County, California. My wife and I realized that the wilderness journey, though unpleasant, had been valuable.

The move to Orange County stimulated and fulfilled us. We began the church from scratch, harboring no doubts that God wanted us there. I jumped into the work at full speed, hopscotching the nation, attending church growth seminars. If I were called to be a pastor, I would be a great one. I lined my bookshelves with "how to grow a church" books and seminar binders. I talked to the professionals regarding church growth.

West Coast Church was destined to be one of the hottest new churches in Southern California. We started gloriously. The publicity was top notch. People came and brought their friends. My speaking gifts provided a contemporary flare, linking the biblical with the practical. According to the consultants, we had a textbook church.

But just before the third year, we began experiencing symptoms of burnout. The church had plateaued, and I faced the realization that West Coast Church would not be a stellar success. The new Christians coming to church lacked the depth and commitment to carry the ministry load with us. After the church's third anniversary, I was tired, crabby, and wondered what I could do well for God.

What do you do when you're doing the right things, but results just don't seem to happen? Why don't the seminars talk about that? We took a month sabbatical during which I began learning about prayer in a deeper dimension, and God began taking me on a journey of studying the concept of brokenness.

This period of burnout was similar to my wilderness experience three-and-a-half years earlier. I began pondering brokenness. Why hadn't my professors brought up the subject during my schooling? I took our church staff to Fuller Seminary to spend a day in the library. After a computer search, we found that little had been published on the subject of brokenness. I could count on two hands the number of published articles and books covering the subject. We checked similar topics such as heart allegiance, surrendered living, wilderness experiences, and the like, but the computer screen listed no entries. Afterward I began talking to other pastors about this concept. Several of them related vivid stories of their times of brokenness.

Psalm 51:17 says that the Lord delights in "a broken spirit, a broken and a contrite heart." These are called the "sacrifices of God." Now if God delights in this, and our chief aim in life is to serve and please him, why weren't more people writing and talking about this concept? I found several authors who alluded to the idea and many examples of the process. I saw it mentioned among the classics, including several Catholic works. But no one explored the idea in depth. I realized the great need for a work that would explain, in practical yet spiritual ways, this very challenging process of pruning, brokenness, dying out, crucifying the old self, and going through the wilderness times.

During this time I spoke with a church consultant who expressed great interest in the subject. His theory is that heart-allegiance and brokenness are related to a leader's effectiveness in a ministry. Brokenness seems to be a prerequisite that God demands before doing lasting work through a person. Apparently, numerous historical and present leaders have recognized this very private and extremely revealing passage I call brokenness.

The remainder of this book discusses the unique—at times mystical—process of taming the soul. Much of this process deals with pain, pain that can be physical, financial, relational, emotional, or spiritual. However, this is not a recovery book. It is about making sense of times which seem senseless. The term *broken* is almost always perceived as negative. Viktor Frankl said, "Despair is suffering without meaning." Brokenness helps us avoid despair when our dreams do not come true and when we suffer, because it gives us meaning when we need it most.

If you are presently in a state of brokenness, you will readily understand these pages. If you are not going through this process now, you may be able to remember times of great personal challenge that seemed to have a spiritual reason behind them. For you, this book will explain that what you went through had a purpose, and show you that many other people have shared your feelings. Hopefully, it will also help prepare you for future times of pruning and brokenness.

Only after we are broken in the right place can we be truly healed and experience wholeness. We are born with clenched fists, but we die with an open hand. Life, specifically the process of brokenness, is where we learn to open our hands, hopefully before death. There is a unique sense of freedom that only comes from going through a breaking time. Scripture tells us that God has a special place in His heart for those experiencing brokenness. "The Lord is near to those who have a broken heart" (Ps. 34:18). "He heals the brokenhearted" (Ps. 147:3). A divine romance exists between the broken and their Creator.

As you look at the Bible, you find many examples of brokenness. Saul went through a breaking process prior to his experience with Christ and being transformed into the Apostle Paul. The disciples experienced brokenness prior to Pentecost and traversed a period of discouragement, disillusionment, and awareness of personal inadequacy. Moses had his wilderness experience prior to leading the people of Israel out of Egypt. The nation of

Israel documented its time in the wilderness prior to entering the Promised Land. Jonah underwent brokenness during the storm and in the fish's belly prior to the Nineveh revival. Samson experienced a degree of breaking before he brought down the house. Hagar and Elijah had their desert experiences. Joseph had to know the feeling as a prerequisite to his leadership in Egypt. David became known as a man after God's heart, even after he had terrible experiences preceding and following his repentance. Abraham prepared to sacrifice Isaac. He underwent many testings and faith trials before being labeled a "friend of God." In the midst of his trials Job said, "Though He slay me, yet will I trust Him" (Job 13:15).

Writing on brokenness is similar to writing on humility. Once you claim to understand it, you know you don't. The process eludes our attempts to box it up and tie it with a neat bow. It is messy. I think one of the main reasons you do not see seminars and workshops on the subject is that it refuses to be confined to three-ring binders. Besides, the only time you can really identify with it and appreciate a close look at it is when you are going through it. As we will discuss later, times of brokenness tend to be episodic. They have beginnings and endings, and when you are not in the process, you may remember past events, but you find it difficult to relate to the pain itself. Much like a mother telling you about the pain of childbirth, unless she is currently in labor, it's only a memory, regardless of how vivid it seems.

The concept of brokenness deals with the process of living and how God tries to make us into strong, dynamic people. While browsing through the library of a Jesuit retreat center, I found some wall plaques for sale. One of them read, "No pain, no gain." At first I found that surprising. I would expect such a motto in a weight-training center or in a locker room. "No pain, no gain" did not seem to fit the typical inspirational platitudes adorning walls and knickknack shelves. But "no pain, no gain" describes the process of life during difficult times and episodes of brokenness. Sometimes to progress you must first digress.

■

BEING VS. DOING

We are product-oriented people, particularly those of us living in Western civilization. We are bottom line people. We attend church growth seminars hoping to increase our numbers. We read self-help books by the dozens trying to multiply our output. All of these activities done within reason are fine and exemplary. Our inclination is to achieve, produce, and do. The common result is that we are human thinkings and human doings, but God has called us to be human beings. Our society, like others, focuses on our mental side and our physical side, but we have lost touch with our spiritual side. Multimillion dollar institutions now provide some of the finest education ever available. Our desire to develop the mind is unequaled.

On the other side of the spectrum is our doing side. We greatly esteem those who master this facet. Some of the highest-paid people in the world are those who can hit, run, pass, catch, and throw better than anyone else. Each year we invest billions of dollars in athletic endeavors. But unlike past societies, which emphasized the development of the soul, we keep soul expansion to a minimum. Until we see God's desire to impact our minds and actions through our spiritual lives and development of our souls, we will not only be frustrated with these aspects, we will fail to understand the episodes of difficulties and brokenness in our lives.

God is primarily process-oriented, not product-oriented. ✗
In John 15, Jesus tells us to abide in him in order to bear

fruit. It is the abiding that is the process. If we do this, we will naturally be fruitful. I've yet to walk through an orchard and hear the trees grunting, groaning, and straining to bear fruit. They do not. Fruit producing comes naturally, as long as the roots are watered, the leaves receive sunlight, and the weather conditions prevail. Our natural inclination is to focus on the fruit bearing. We read books, go to seminars, and listen to cassettes on better fruit bearing. What we need to think about is <u>better abiding</u>. When we improve the process, the fruit will come naturally. <u>Brokenness is a process issue</u>. It is a part of God's character building process.

"Almost every one of us," says Gordon MacDonald, "will encounter some issue that introduces us to brokenness at a far greater intensity than we ever thought possible. . . . Broken worlds are a significant part of living; we must be vigilant enough to avoid the avoidable, but prepared and disciplined enough to persevere when facing the unexpected or the unavoidable." [1]

■

QUESTIONS FOR REFLECTION

1. Have you gone through specific wilderness periods you could refer to as times of brokenness? What were they?

2. What did David mean when he said "God does not delight in sacrifice, but in a broken spirit, a broken and contrite heart" (Ps. 51:16–17)?

3. Do you agree with the weight-room slogan "no pain, no gain" when it comes to spiritual growth? Discuss the pros and cons.

4. In what ways does society reward us for what we do (behavior) versus who we are (character)?

5. What do we mean when we say God is process oriented? Where do we find balance between who we become and what we produce as Christians?

When I invited Jesus into my life, I thought he was going to put up some wallpaper and hang a few pictures. But he started knocking out walls and adding on rooms. I said, "I was expecting a nice cottage." But He said, "I'm making a palace in which to live."

—C.S. Lewis

■

CHAPTER THREE

What Is Brokenness?

■ ■ ■

"For Pride is spiritual cancer: it eats up the very pos-
sibility of love, or contentment, or even common sense."
Suddenly, I felt naked and unclean, my bravado defenses
gone. I was exposed, unprotected, for C.S. Lewis's words
were describing me. This passage seemed to sum up what
had happened to all of us at the White House. As I drove
out of the driveway, the tears were flowing uncontrollably.
There were no street lights, no moonlight. The car head-
lights were flooding illumination before my eyes, but I was
crying so hard it was like trying to swim underwater. I
pulled to the side of the road not more than a hundred
yards from the entrance of my friend's driveway, the tires
sinking into the soft mounds of pine needles.
I remember hoping that my friends wouldn't hear
my sobbing, the only sound other than the chirping of
crickets that penetrated the still of the night. With my face

cupped in my hands, head leaning forward against the wheel, I forgot about machismo, about pretenses, about fears of being weak. And as I did, I began to experience a wonderful feeling of being released. Then came the strange sensation that water was not only running down my cheeks, but surging through my whole body as well, cleansing and cooling as it went. _They weren't tears of sadness and remorse, nor of joy—but somehow, tears of relief._

And then I prayed my first real prayer. "God, I don't know how to find You, but I'm going to try! I'm not much the way I am now, but somehow I want to give myself to You." I didn't know how to say more, so I repeated over and over the words: Take me. I stayed there in the car, wet-eyed, praying, thinking, for perhaps half an hour, perhaps longer, alone in the quiet of the dark night. Yet for the first time in my life I was not alone at all.

That is my introduction to knowing God personally, but I believe that most believers must go through a period of breaking as they come truly to know God's grace. Isn't that what our faith is about—we must know the wretchedness of our sinful state before we turn to the Lord for rescue. For many of us, God's mercy must be of the severe sort that allows us to come to the end of our abilities—the end of our rope—in order to see our need of Him. Certainly my life has been an example of God's severe mercy in breaking those He loves.

—Chuck Colson[1]

■

PARADOXES OF LIFE

A begonia . . . I'd never take that plant home to my wife. It was ugly. There they sat, rows of pots with stubs poking out of the soil, a heap of beautiful leaves, hacked off from the young plants, lying in a pile. They sure didn't look beautiful to me. They looked more like my son's hair after his first self-haircut at age two. Where was the

beauty? It was purely latent at best. And this was a nursery. The name itself evokes an image of cradling and
nurture and new life and tender care, not a place for
cutting, pruning, and whacking off leafy appendages. This
was a nursery, the incubator where plants get their start in
life, where they are coaxed into reaching for the sky. So
who cut off their green arms raised upward? I did not care
who. "Why?" was my question.

The answer was very simple. In the first year of a begonia's life in the nursery, it goes through a dormant season, a time of year when the leaves become liabilities
versus assets. If the begonia was ever going to grace the
front yard of a family's beautiful home, or have its blos-
som's color a school teacher's classroom, or glorify the
centerpiece on a dinner table, it needed to go through
this process. In fact, as I walked through the hundreds of
acres of nursery surrounding the retreat center I was at, I
saw giant piles of branches and leaves harvested from the
sprawling nursery. Most of them did not appear to be the
ugly, dead material I would perceive to be the target of
pruning. There was too much green there. But the hor-
ticulturists and groundskeepers knew their trade. They
were obviously successful at it.

In the nursery of life, where we grow up, a significant
amount of pruning goes on within the nurturing process.
What we often fail to understand is that in our development, what feels like a loss or a cutting back of our per-
sonage, really is only an exercise to make us stronger and
more beautiful down the road. The begonias will come
out of their pruning experience. They will grow back,
stronger and better than before. When we are broken in
the right place, we too grow back. That is a part of the
maturing process. We often are tempted to think that this
hacking away at our soul's appendages is better fit for a
grotesque, chain-saw massacre movie than a divine pro-

cess. It feels more like a war zone or a mortuary than a nursery. But regardless of our age, many of our breaking processes occur in a nursery, where we are groomed to grow better.

A few years ago, someone tampered with a few bottles of a widely used pain relief medicine. Because of one death and other scares, the manufacturers of over-the-counter medications redesigned their products with tamper-proof seals. On scores of containers you will read these words, "Do not use if seal is broken." Breaking the seal allows you to get to the contents, the good stuff, the stuff that makes you better. The broken seal, the broken stallion, the feeling of loss and even pain that can occur when something breaks; these are all examples of why I prefer the term *brokenness* for the spiritual process I am describing. In addition, David, whom God referred to as his friend, used it in Psalm 51, referring to it as the condition that God delights in and expects from His people.

So what are we talking about when we talk about brokenness? How is it similar and different from other terms and concepts in Christian life and growth? Unfortunately, simple definitions are difficult to derive.

Brokenness is one of those things that is easier to recognize when it's experienced, but is often difficult to describe. Because brokenness has to do with life and Christianity—both complicated subjects—it is not a simple concept to explain, yet, hopefully through familiarization you will recognize the process when you see it. It is a spiritual process.

I saw a bumper sticker on a van once that read, "If you ain't cowboy, you ain't." I would never say, "If you ain't broken, you ain't a Christian." Brokenness tends to be more of an advanced lesson rather than a basic requirement. However, it is not solely a threshold for being spirit-filled or for major life changes. God uses it in our lives at all levels, sometimes even for conversion (remember Paul?). He basically implements it whenever He needs our attention, wherever we happen to be in our walk with Him. It may or may not be during a time of sin, rebellion, or apathy. Although I am excited about researching and explaining the concept of brokenness, I do not try to see it everywhere in Scripture. Brokenness occupies just one piece in the mosaic of Christian living, but it is an important piece, one that will answer a lot of painful questions if we understand it better.

Psalm 51:16–17 says, "You do not desire sacrifice, or else I would give it; You do not delight in burnt offering. The sacrifices of God are a broken spirit, a broken and a contrite heart—these, O God, You will not despise." Surely God does not care what kind of sacrifice we bring Him, as long as it's sincere, right? Wrong, in chapter four of Genesis we read the story of Cain and Abel. Abel brought fat portions from among the firstborn of his flock, but Cain brought some of the fruits of the soil as an offering to the Lord. The Lord looked with favor at Abel and his offering, but on Cain and his offering He did not look with favor.

In essence, God is picky about His sacrifices. Romans 12:1 says "Present your bodies a living sacrifice, holy, acceptable to God." We can sacrifice objects to God out of good motives and honest intentions, but they do little to delight God. What does he want? What makes our gifts acceptable? He wants a broken spirit and a broken heart.

But how does brokenness relate to what seem to be our natural desires for success and reaching our potential? The answer is revealed in the many truth-packed paradoxes of the Bible. Luke 9:24–26 says that if you want to save your life—and who wouldn't?—then you must lose your life. If you want to be lifted up and exalted—and who doesn't?—then you must humble yourself (Matt. 23:12). If you want to be the greatest—I sure do—then become a servant and be like the youngest (Matt. 23:11 and Luke 22:24–27). If you want to be first—okay—be last and be slave to all (Matt. 19:30 and Mark 10:44). If you wish to rule—sometimes I do—then you should serve (Luke 22:26–27). If we want to live—nothing wrong with that—then put to death the deeds of the body (Rom. 8:13). If you want to be strong—that's me—then boast about your weaknesses (2 Cor. 11:30; 12:9–10). If you want to inherit the Kingdom of Heaven—count me in—then become poor in spirit (Matt. 5:3).

Amazingly God takes our most driving urges and re-directs them. Many of us feel that following Christ means giving up on our dreams and potential and settling for second best, mediocrity, and pious ho-hum. Shelve our ambitions, we perceive. But time after time Christ speaks to those core feelings, those inner voices that long for first place, for strength, for power, for life. I don't think He's manipulating our emotions when he mentions these urges. He knows how dear they are to us and how strong they are. In fact I think He put many of them there. But the Kingdom of Heaven is a paradox to the earthly kingdom. The rules are different. We can have these same urges, but in sanctified form. And the route to obtain them is often the antithesis of the world's advice. "Win by intim-idation." "Look out for #1!" "Pull Your Own Strings." "Get rich quick!"

Malcolm Muggeridge said, "We are henceforth to wor-ship defeat, not victory; failure, not success; surrender, not defiance; deprivation, not satiety; weakness, not strength. We are to lose our lives in order to keep them, to die in order to live."[2]

Because God's ways are different than ours, we should not be surprised to hear that God's process of helping us develop character involves being broken and requires the taming of the soul. This methodology does not make sense in our world's value system. "For the message of the cross is foolishness to those who are perishing, but to us who are being saved it is the power of God" (1 Cor. 1:18).

Natural human strategy tends to be self-indulging, self-asserting. Heavenly strategies involve self-denial. "Then Jesus said to His disciples, 'If anyone desires to come after Me, let him deny himself, and take up his cross, and follow Me'" (Matt. 16:24). "And he who does not take his cross and follow after Me is not worthy of Me" (Matt. 10:38). All too often, joyless Christians make remarks like, "that's my cross to bear," but the cross was never intended to be an instrument of burden. It was an instrument of death.

■

THE GOAL OF BROKENNESS

So what is the goal of brokenness? When Jesus began attracting more attention, someone asked John the Baptist whether he was concerned. John gave his inquisitor an answer that fits all of us. "A man can receive nothing unless it has been given to him from heaven. . . . He [Jesus] must increase, but I must decrease" (John 3:27–30). That is the goal of brokenness—denying oneself, becoming less—so that Christ can become more.

This process is the realization that apart from Christ, we can do nothing that has eternal value. In John 15:5, Jesus says, "I am the vine, you are the branches. He who abides in Me, and I in him, bears much fruit; for without Me you can do nothing." Our natural tendency even as Christians is to work to bear fruit, to try to act good, be loving, be patient, etc. This is the wrong approach. Our job is to abide, to stay in the Lord. When we do so, the fruit will come naturally.

On the farm, occasionally we would have ears of corn

that would grow on tall stalks. But as soon as you pulled back the shucks, you would find no kernels of grain. Good deeds and achievements that are done out of our own power and spirit, regardless of whether they are done with God-given gifts or not, are much like that corn stalk. They look good, but they produce little. "But we have this treasure in earthen vessels, that the excellence of the power may be of God and not of us" (2 Cor. 4:7).

Samuel Logan Brengle, a commissioner of the Salvation Army, was once introduced at an engagement as "the great Dr. Brengle." That day, Brengle penned in his diary, "If I appear great in their eyes, the Lord is most graciously helping me to see how absolutely nothing I am without Him, and helping me to keep little in my eyes. He does use me. But I am so concerned that He uses me and that it is not of me the work is done. The axe cannot boast of the trees it has cut down. It could do nothing but for the woodsman. The moment he throws it aside, it becomes only old iron. O that I may never lose sight of this."[2] A. W. Tozer wrote, "Save me from the curse that lies dark across the face of the modern clergy, the curse of compromise, of imitation, of professionalism. Save me from the error of judging a church by its size, its popularity or the amount of its yearly offering. Help me to remember that I am a prophet, not a promoter, not a religious manager but a prophet."[3]

What hinders or stops this progress toward self-surrender which eventually requires brokenness? In Revelation 3:17, Jesus talks to a church which had become self-sufficient. "You say, 'I am rich, have become wealthy, and have need of nothing'—and do you not know that you are wretched, miserable, poor, blind, and naked." The comment is more interesting when you know that the recipient of the letter was the church in the city of Laodicea, which was the center for banking (poor), for a special eye ointment (blind), and for clothing (naked). These people prided themselves in their accomplishments, but God tells them their self-sufficiency means little.

■

BROKENNESS IS NOT . . .

Marketing companies use a technique called *positioning* with new products. When consumers are unaware of a new product, the strategists intentionally compare their item with other better-known products or brands. The positioning gives the consumer a quick identification for the new item by providing reference marks. Positioning the term *broken* against more familiar concepts will offer us a deeper understanding at this point.

Brokenness is not humility or repentance.

. . . but usually results in both. Humility is a frame of reference that perceives all of life as a gift from our sovereign and gracious God. First Corinthians 3:4–6 says, "For when one says, 'I am of Paul,' and another, 'I am of Apollos,' are you not carnal? Who, then, is Paul, and who is Apollos, but ministers through whom you believed, as the Lord gave to each one? I planted, Apollos watered, but God gave the increase. So neither he who plants is anything nor he who waters, but God who gives the increase." Humility is one of the traits of brokenness, but brokenness goes beyond humility.

The breaking process is that which convicts a person of his or her sin, or stubbornness, or insensitivity to God. It renders the soul responsive. It is the circumstantial confrontation that exposes the truth and results in repentance. Repentance is seeing our sin the way God sees it. Brokenness may find its way into our hearts as a gentle doorbell ring, or it may storm the front gate with a battering ram. Nevertheless, once truth gets inside our hearts, our response determines whether we resist being broken altogether or in the right place or become broken in the wrong place. Emotional and spiritual humility along with repentance tend to be results of the process, and emerge as the first fruits of being broken in the right place, but they are not the same as being broken.

Brokenness is different than being Spirit-filled.

Brokenness calls attention to personal emptiness and weakness. Being Spirit-filled refers to God's fullness and power. A cup cannot be filled with fresh, pure water until it has been emptied. Brokenness is the emptying process required before the Spirit can fill our lives. The breaking process reveals an area of unreleased control and seeks to tame the soul in that place, turning over the reigns to God.

Upon receiving Christ into our lives, we receive His Spirit. The Bible says that if we do not have God's Spirit, we are not one of His (1 John 4:13). The Spirit is an entity, not a quantity. As you grow in maturity you do not receive more and more of the Spirit. You have received all of Him. When a woman becomes pregnant, she is fully pregnant. No one says she gets more and more pregnant just because the baby is growing. However, the baby, as it grows, takes up more and more space, and it is more and more evident that the woman is pregnant. As a person lives in the Spirit, it will become more and more evident that he or she is full of God.

Henri Nouwen tells the story about a university professor who came to a Zen master to ask him about Zen. "Nan-in, the Zen master, served him tea. He poured his visitor's cup full, and then kept pouring. The professor watched the overflow until he could no longer restrain himself. 'It is over-full. No more will go in!' 'Like this cup,'

Nan-in said, 'You are full of your own opinions and spec-
ulations. How can I teach you Zen unless you first empty
your cup?'"[4]

Brokenness is the emptying of selfish ambition so that
we are willing and able to be filled with God's Spirit.

If you grip one end of a sponge and dip the other into a
bowl of water, the end you are holding will absorb very
little water. You are keeping the water out. If you let go of
the sponge, water seeps into that section, too. The sponge
as a whole did not receive more water. The water was just
free to fill the area once you took your hand off of it.

Brokenness, voluntary or involuntary, requires that we
release our grip on a certain area of our life. This process
releases new areas in a person's heart to receive Lordship of the Spirit. In addition, being Spirit-filled typically
refers to a Christian who is established in his faith. It
presumes an existing relationship with God. In contrast,
brokenness can occur in the life of a believer or un-
believer, as God strives to tame, tenderize, and expand
our souls.

Brokenness is different than personal holiness.

Brokenness reflects the attitude of a person who recognizes his or her lack of righteousness and his or her open-
ness to it. So often we speak of holiness in terms of
behaviors. "Good Christians don't drink, or smoke, or go
to movies, or curse." Someone joked, "You know why
(name of a church) are against fornication? Because they
believe it will lead to dancing." Behavior-centered holiness will always fail. It is like tying store-bought apples
onto the branches of your oak tree. Even though apples
are hanging from the tree, it is still an oak. The apples will
rot quickly because they are not receiving sustenance
from the inside. Spiritual fruit comes from living on the
Vine. Brokenness is the process of pruning, where the

Vinedresser clips the branches and leaves in your life that are sapping your energy and preventing effective growth. Holiness, on the other hand, is a natural emergence of one who is led and filled by the Spirit upon releasing his or her life to Christ.

Brokenness is different than sanctification.

Brokenness is the willingness to yield everything to God. Sanctification is God's response of separating and cleansing. Not too long ago, I put a new floor in our kitchen. Pulling out the old flooring was different than laying, grouting, and sealing the new tile. Both processes were a part of creating a new floor, but they required different techniques. Brokenness involves demolition. Sanctification, in this limited metaphor, is better seen as the grouting, sealing, and maintaining. Traditional views of sanctification refer to it as an experience or process based on an existing relationship with Christ. Brokenness transcends those parameters. Hopefully you are beginning to understand that the breaking process is often the doorway to other results. It is the kindling for the fire. It is the starter for the engine. It represents the starting blocks, not the finish line. It is God's way of preparing us, getting us ready so that He can do a significant work in our lives. Brokenness is not so much an end, as a means to an end.

Brokenness is not necessarily suffering.

Many books discuss going through difficult times: "Why do bad things happen to good people?"—divorce recovery, facing cancer, hospice ministry, handling addictions, step-parenting, parenting teens, when your dreams die, on death and dying, depression, anger, etc. As a society, we are keenly in touch with our various pains. This is mostly good. But even counseling for the pains and issues we deal with is limited unless we also consider the soul development which should result from our suffering. While this is not specifically a book on suffering, understanding and embracing brokenness can actually help you avoid suffering. While voluntary brokenness does not necessarily involve suffering, involuntary brokenness often results from suffering. You can suffer without being broken in the right place. Conversely, brokenness can occur with little or no suffering when your heart is sensitive to God's growth initiatives.

Suffering is more generic than brokenness. Suffering may be experienced in the life of a person who already has an attitude of submission and therefore needs no further breaking at that time. Paul's thorn in the flesh served to keep him humble, but it continued beyond his episodes of breaking. John Wesley often assumed a posture of prayer and sometimes stayed on his knees because of his wife's antagonism. Even though emotional or psychological breaking can result in spiritual brokenness, I am not addressing those types in this book. On the other hand, suffering can result in mental, physical, and relational breaking without impacting one's spirit.

■

BROKENNESS IS . . .

In attempting to define brokenness we may benefit from looking at some related concepts. "Heart allegiance" could be a cousin to brokenness. Joseph provides us with a good example of heart allegiance. All our readings of his life reveal him as a man committed to God. We have no biblical evidence that he needed breaking even though we see him through numerous character building situations, which some people suggest were breaking points for him. Meshack, Shadrack, and Abed-Nego demonstrate heart allegiance. Daniel, too, gives us a wonderful example of that quality. However, heart allegiance might be better seen as an intended outcome of the breaking process itself.

"Pruning" is a biblical analogy for the process. God is referred to as the Husbandman who prunes His trees and vines so they will produce better fruit. The pruning process is another seeming paradox. You cut back a tree so it will give more and better fruit. Fruit growers understand this metaphor vividly. Pruning describes God's hand in the process, while brokenness points to the intended result in our hearts. John 15 tells us that God cuts off the non-productive branches, and he also prunes the productive branches in order for them to bear more fruit. Some people assume that if they are being fruitful they can avoid being "cut," but Jesus seems to say everyone is going to be cut at times, some for their lack of fruitfulness, and others for their enhanced fruitfulness. You cannot avoid it.

"Crucified living" is another theological phrase related to brokenness. Several times the Bible talks about being crucified with Christ, and taking up our crosses to follow Him. As we will see in a later chapter on the attitude of brokenness, the concept of death is very common and very strong in brokenness.

Another similar concept is the idea of surrender, chiefly "total surrender." In war, soldiers who are surrendering hold up their hands in a universally understood gesture saying, "I surrender. I give up. Look, I've dropped my weapons. I've quit fighting." It is not a proud action, but a humble one. It is not a holy gesture, but one of repentance. It is not a sign of victory, but rather one of defeat.

When my youngest son was about to turn two years old, he communicated his desire for mom or dad to carry him by holding out his hands and saying, "Upple, Momma, upple. Upple, Dadda, upple." In essence, "I'm tired. I'm afraid. I'm weak. I'm too little. Pick me up. Carry me. Help me." The spirit of brokenness helps us reach out our arms to the Father saying, "Upple. Carry me. I am weak. I am too little to do it on my own." I surrender.

Something inside us despises the thought of surrendering, of quitting. Ah, but surrendering and quitting are two different concepts. Quitting says, "I don't care." Surrendering says, "I care." Quitting says, "I can't." Surrendering says, "I can't. God can." Quitting is often repressed or expressed anger. Surrendering is expressed love. The mate who quits files for divorce. The spouse who says I surrender seeks counseling and accountability. The person who quits becomes an agnostic or atheist, and leaves the church. The individual who surrenders says, "God, whatever it takes for my will to break, do it." The quitter says, "To hell with God. If He won't tell me, I'll do it my way." The person who surrenders asks, "Where is the hell in me? What do You want? Here I am. Speak Lord, Your servant listens."

You may have heard about a unique way to trap monkeys, where the natives hollow out gourds that have long narrow necks. They place fruit in the bottom of the gourds and stake them to the ground. When the monkeys come out of the forest and reach into the gourd to grasp the fruit, they are unable to get their fists surrounding the fruit out of the gourd. The natives casually walk out of their hiding place and catch the monkeys, who could have easily run away, but were unwilling to let go.

Many of us feel that if we surrender, we are being irresponsible. This syndrome drives a person to need to be needed. Certainly slothfulness and irresponsibility are to be avoided, but letting go is not equal to being mediocre or irresponsible. Letting go is an expression of faith. Mediocrity and irresponsibility are expressions of laziness. Letting go is a decision of the will. Irresponsibility is often due to indecision. Letting go is risking failure. Irresponsibility welcomes failure. Letting go says, "I depend on you, God." Mediocrity and irresponsibility say, "I don't depend on anyone, and I don't care." Surrender is responsible irresponsibility.

Children and parents seem to have a universal rule. "You can play with the toy as soon as your brother lays it down." In essence, while the other sibling has it, it is his. In spiritual terms, God does not use us significantly until we take our hands off our lives, and lay them down. Then we truly become His.

■

WHAT INITIATES BROKENNESS?

What promotes brokenness? How does it come about? Through what instruments or processes does it usually transpire?

Brokenness often occurs during a close encounter with God.

Isaiah talks about going into the temple when suddenly the glory of the Lord filled the place. In that instant, he realized how insignificant and unholy he was in comparison to God. "I am a man of unclean lips, and I dwell in the midst of a people of unclean lips" (Isa. 6:5). Saul met God on the road to Damascus through a bright light and voice from heaven. This dynamic leader suddenly broke down and changed directions 180 degrees. Moses in the wilderness, upon recognizing God in the burning bush, fell on his face. No one ever gets close to God without an overwhelming sense of impurity and frailty. In these unique moments, people become fully aware of what is not right in their lives. Historically, special times of revival when the Holy Spirit falls on a group of people or an area, result in great conviction, repentance, and a broken attitude. No one ever comes very close to God and remains proud.

Brokenness often occurs when a person voluntarily and passionately seeks God's blessing in a specific situation.

When Jacob wrestled with God's messenger during the night, Jacob would not let him go until God blessed him. When you have a strong yearning for God to bless your life or ministry, you cross the line of commitment and basically say, "Whatever it takes, bless me." At that time, you need to be ready, for God rarely leaves us as He finds us after such a request. Something in our lives nearly always can use some changing, so when we plead for a blessing or moving, we voluntarily submit to accepting God on His terms.

The breaking process often emerges after moral failure.

Time after time we see biblical events where there is sin, then turmoil, then conviction and guilt, and finally repentance and restoration. The breaking process takes place sometime during the turmoil, brought on by feelings of guilt, or conviction of the Holy Spirit, or even negative elements such as an approaching enemy, the plague, illness, or other calamity. For David, it occurred after Nathan the prophet confronted him. For the city of Nineveh, it was after Jonah's message of pending doom. The Old Testament bulges with stories illustrating the sin cycle of the Children of Israel. Time after time, sin followed by brokenness results in a spiritual homecoming and a person finds himself experiencing a deeper, more intimate communion with the Father.

Circumstances that threaten to defeat us often promote brokenness.

The story of Job is an intense poem about a man tortured, but not defeated, a man truly broken before God. Jehoshaphat called all his people to pray when they discovered enemy troops surrounding their nation. John

Donne, the English minister and poet who penned "No man is an island" and "Never send to know for whom the bell tolls; it tolls for thee," was sick much of his later life. He realized that those times of affliction, the periods of sharpest suffering, had been his greatest opportunities for spiritual growth. Trials had purged sin and developed character; poverty had taught him dependence on God and cleansed him of greed; failure and public disgrace had helped cure worldly ambition.

Although brokenness can be brought on suddenly by crises as in the life of Job, for many people it is a drawn out process with seemingly little or no productivity. A divorce, heart attack, financial setback, or the death of a loved one, can all produce a softened heart. But the plateau syndrome can make many of us realize gradually, and ultimately deeply, that we do not have what it takes to fulfill our dreams. When our dreams appear to be on hold we recognize the lack of control we have over our lives.

This control factor is important to understanding brokenness. We often experience breaking in areas where we think we have control. A businessperson may lose what was once a successful business. A dear relationship, thought to be secure, ultimately fails. Our lack of control in life reveals our need for God and hopefully results in our submitting to his Lordship.

> Unshakable faith is faith that has been shaken.
> Unquenchable joy is joy that has been quenched.
> Unbreakable love is love that has been broken.

A fervent love for God can promote brokenness.

A person who maintains his first love (the love God calls His people to have for Himself) is willing to change and go through incredible things to be available for Him. I remember doing some amazing feats for the sake of chivalry while I was courting my wife-to-be, Nancy. I even let her give me some suggestions on how I should dress and get along with people better. I have learned to seek her opinion, because I love her and I know that she loves me, and therefore I can trust her to want what is best for me. Love is always the best way to become vulnerable to the Father. It always hurts less in the long run, and provides the least risk for thwarting the Holy Spirit and losing precious time and productivity.

■

SOFT AND FLEXIBLE

My young boys love Play-Doh, that squishy manmade clay that comes in beautiful colors. For hours they will mold it, pound it flat, and cut out figures with cookie cutters and other kitchen tools. I've rolled awkward lumps into round balls numerous times for them when their little hands could not manage the clay. We have gone through dozens of cans of the stuff, because my boys have a recurring challenge—they forget to put the Play-Doh back into its containers, or fail to put the lid on properly. Play-Doh dries out. It gets so stiff and hard that you cannot mold it into various shapes or roll it in your hands.

The older we get, the less flexible we naturally become. Arthritis sets in; we feel stiffer. At midlife we realize that we take longer to recuperate from the previous day's exercise. We need more time to loosen up to jog that three miles. Mentally, the older we get, the more we tend to enjoy routine. We have a harder time coping with different ideas and cultures and ways of looking at life.

The same tendency for decay occurs spiritually. There is the temptation to lose our flexibility. That's when breaking occurs. Jesus warns us about putting new wine in old wineskins. New wine creates a chemical reaction resulting in an expansion of gas. Old wineskins are brittle and inflexible. When new wine is poured into them they burst, wasting the wineskin as well as the wine. Jesus talks about the foolishness of applying a new patch to an old garment. The new patch will shrink and tear an even bigger hole into the clothes that needed mending (see Matt. 9:16–17).

Consistently we see Jesus' disdain for those who were inflexible. The Pharisees and scribes refused brokenness in their legalistic, empty religiosity. On the other hand, the adulterous woman responded with humility to being broken. Jesus esteemed the man praying out of a broken attitude in the temple, but condemned the proud Pharisee flaunting his self-righteousness. Jesus turned down the man who wanted to follow Him, but who would not give his riches to the poor. Peter received more than one rebuke from the Lord when he refused to be sensitive to the Spirit and boldly took a rigid stand. Peter eventually learned brokenness, and only then was he able to be used mightily after Pentecost. Jesus associated with the tax collectors and other sinners because they responded to Him with flexibility. They were willing to change, to let Him be Lord of their lives.

Someone closed the sliding door of a van on our boy's fingers when he was young. Nancy rushed him to the doctor. Although the pinch was bad, the doctor reassured us that infants and toddlers seldom break their bones since they are so pliable. Old people break their bones frequently because they are brittle. Such is our spiritual tendency as we age. Jesus calls us to come as little children, pliable.

Hebrews 5:7 says, "During the days of Jesus' life on earth, he offered up prayers and petitions with loud cries and tears to the one who could save him from death, and he was heard because of his reverent submission." Reverent submission reflects the attitude of brokenness.

Although the breaking process tends to precede this intended result, the attitude of submission is still very strong.

Dr. Albert Schweitzer had earned doctorates in science, medicine, music, theology, and philosophy besides dozens of honorary degrees from leading universities around the world. At his Lambarene, Africa, hospital site, an expansion project called for heavy, tiring manual labor. Seeing a man of the country reading a book, Schweitzer asked him to help with the work. Offended at the suggestion the man replied, "Oh no, since I have become an intellectual I no longer do manual labor." At this Dr. Schweitzer observed, "I tried to be an intellectual, but I didn't make it," whereupon Schweitzer picked up some heavy timbers and went on with the work. Jesus said, "Learn from Me; for I am gentle and lowly in heart" (Matt. 11:29). John in his Gospel quotes Jesus saying, "The Son can do nothing of Himself" (5:19); "I can of Myself do nothing. . . . I do not seek My own will" (5:30); "I do not receive honor from men" (5:41); "I have come . . . not to do My own will" (6:38); "I have not come of Myself" (7:28); "I do nothing of Myself" (8:28); "I do not seek Mine own glory" (8:50); "I speak not of myself" (7:17). Jesus' life constantly focused on the Father.

Our self-sufficient culture is one of our biggest barriers to reaching our potential. We are steeped in the idea that "If I work harder, if I learn more, I can achieve whatever I desire." Roberta Hestenes said, "In our day which emphasizes self-confidence, self-assertion and self-fulfillment, we need to learn again the lessons of brokenness—of humility and gentleness before God and each other. This 'brokenness' speaks not of self-worthlessness nor a malformed personality, nor deep clinical depression. It points toward a deeper reality, the response to a prompting of the Spirit in certain circumstances of need, demand, or spiritual yearning and hunger. Brokenness is a yielded heart open before God, a heart emptied of pride and self claims, of all arrogance, knowing our sin, our self-deception, our frailty, weakness and inadequacy. We discover ourselves again to be hungry and thirsty, poor and needy, when we had thought ourselves full and needing nothing. Along with this awareness comes a rediscovery of God's love, mercy and forgiveness—His affirmation of us, care for us, and claim upon us. . . . Brokenness is not the opposite of wholeness; it is the continuing precondition for it."[5]

■

QUESTIONS FOR REFLECTION

1. Can you think of examples of sacrifices we give to God which may not please Him, even though we are earnest?

2. What does it mean in the real world, to become less, so that He (God) can become greater?

3. Explain in your own words the difference between brokenness, humility, and repentance, and being Spirit-filled.

4. How is brokenness different from suffering? Or is it?

5. What are the four sources out of which brokenness is usually initiated? Have you seen this in any other people in the Bible or history?

Draw me, however unwilling, to make me willing;
draw me, slow-footed, to make me run.
—St. Bernard

CHAPTER
FOUR
■

Understanding
the Process
of Brokenness

■ ■ ■

*In the early 1970's, God called us clearly to leave a very
blessed pastoral ministry we were carrying on in Southern
California to begin a nonprofit ministry which had a particular focus on reaching out and ministering to pastors
and local churches. The new ministry was going exceed-
ingly well. However, the "cash flow" was not. It was virtually
impossible for us to reach out to others and expect com-
pensation in return. Our financial situation became more
and more acute.*

*In addition, the enemy brought other attacks upon us
which brought embarrassment, discouragement, disillusionment—and even humiliation. One of the "final
straws" was when an area hospital named us as one of the
most needy families in the community and presented us
with a food basket for Thanksgiving. The Lord had brought
us down to a point of being totally broken before Him
and, thus, totally dependent upon Him.*

On a given evening, while I was driving alone in my car en route to a ministry engagement, I cried out to God in pain and frustration. In fact, I can honestly say that it is the only time that I remember being angry with God. I rehearsed for Him all of the sacrifices that we had made for Him in obedience to Him: I reminded Him of the embarrassment and humiliation which we had experienced. Finally, in utter despair I cried out, "Lord, why don't you just take my life!" Immediately, I sensed He was speaking to me in a loving, tender way like a faithful father wanting what was best for His son. I sensed Him saying to me, "Son, I already have taken your life."

Immediately, I was broken before God. I pulled over to the side of the road and sobbed uncontrollably in praise and adoration before God.

Indeed I had given my total life to Him a number of years before. I was His to do whatever He chose to do with. It was at that time on that particular evening that I committed myself anew to die to self and to be alive to God. I so committed my life to Christ that if He chose for me to be a failure, I would attempt to even do that to His glory!

I have yet to meet a servant of Jesus Christ who is being used powerfully and effectively who has not gone through at least one desert experience which has led to brokenness before God.

—Paul Cedar

■

TWO KINDS OF BROKENNESS

Someone said, "Adversity introduces you to yourself." Perhaps the most difficult thing to understand in life is why pain, problems, and suffering are a part of it. If we knew that answer, then we could better handle the question: What can I do with my pain, problems, and suffering? Somehow, pain, problems, and suffering do not fit into our concept of life and success.

My sons, with the help of their mom, have designated places for their belongings. Toys go in specific plastic tubs, clothes in the dresser and closet, and books in the book box. Even when the room is a mess, someone can quickly order it, primarily because everything has its place. But what do you do with an item which does not have an assigned spot? You stand in the middle of the room, holding it, perplexed, unsure of what to do with this foreign body. That is how most people handle their pain, discouragements and disillusionment. Their sense of direction halts. They stall as they search in vain for a place to put it, to make it fit into their orderly lives.

If we did have some place for pain, problems, and suffering to fit, we would not curse them so much or act surprised when they pop up. If we had a place for them, we could calmly pick them up and put them where they belong, among the other events of life. But no, we curse the pain, scream at problems, get depressed over unkept promises, stress about frustrations, and yell at others to help us fix things. Or we do drugs, have sex, or work on other diversions to help us avoid our perplexing problems. "Why in the world do bad things happen to good people?" We can understand why they happen to bad people. Bad people deserve bad things. It's the risk of being bad. But somewhere we learn that good things should happen to good people, and of course, we're on the good people list. That's why we often do not deal well with obstacles and turmoil; we have no place to put them in our "good person" scheme of things. However, problems and pain are elemental ingredients in the process of brokenness.

There are two basic types of brokenness, voluntary and involuntary. Voluntary brokenness allows God to do whatever He desires with your life. It is an attitude that responds to good and bad challenges with faith and love. It is reflected in a Spirit-filled, Spirit-led life. I will discuss voluntary brokenness in more detail later, but first I'll focus on involuntary brokenness because it is the brokenness that enters our lives uninvited and shows us areas of weakness that need pruning and pinning back and is more difficult to cope with than voluntary brokenness.

Involuntary brokenness often follows unexpected difficulties—financial, physical, relational, emotional, mental, or spiritual. It comes on the wings of events that go awry. Just as Christian, in John Bunyon's *Pilgrim's Progress*, survives one challenge and believes the rest of the road is clear until the Kingdom, something else pops up. Involuntary brokenness often comes via events like a car wreck, burnout, the death of a loved one, divorce, loss of job, acute illness, failure to attain a goal, or other similar scenarios. You can choose one of three responses when involuntary brokenness comes your way. You can rebel and grow bitter. You can gradually give in under constant nagging and increased pressure. Or you can respond positively to it and mature. In essence, you can go through it, or you can grow through it.

People who go through brokenness, but rebel against it usually end up bitter, cynical, and brittle. Brokenness sometimes comes via spiritual warfare and in spiritual lessons, but usually the episode of brokenness comes by way of typical earthly trials and temptations. That's why James tells us how to handle difficult situations, to make the mundane sublime, and the secular sacred.

■

FINDING JOY IN TROUBLES

One of the most expansive sections in most bookstores is the self-help section. The 1970s had such a plethora of personal growth, you-do-it books, that a book exists on nearly every subject. The post-World War II generation has promoted this market. We like to do it ourselves. ATMs, self-serve gas stations, computer shopping, and self-serve food and drink stations all represent this new mentality. Church growth experts tell pastors that if they want to draw people from this generation, the sermons need to be practical and how-to. Here's how to reduce stress, improve your marriage, get more out of work, find fulfillment, use your time better, and the list goes on ad nauseam. James talks about "doing" Christianity. If any single issue dogs the faith of the normal person, it is the effective handling of trials, problems, things that keep them from their goals and from their desired fulfillment. If the book of James came out today, you would probably find it in the self-help section.

James 1:2–4 says "Consider it pure joy, my brothers, whenever you face trials of many kinds, because you know that the testing of your faith develops perseverance. Perseverance must finish its work so that you may be mature and complete, not lacking anything." It is important to realize that pleasure is not synonymous with joy. Christians can have joy in all sorts of unpleasureable circumstances, and yet not be masochistic. Masochists find pleasure in pain. James is not telling us to fake it 'til you make it, or to repress our pain, which often pops back to the surface through anger, guilt, or misbehavior. We are to consider it joy, pure joy. In essence, he is saying to change your attitude and you will change your life. When you change your attitude about trials, they will change your life for the better.

Trials are examinations. A young bird learning to fly tests its wings. In the school of life, problems are the trials. When events go wrong or differently than you planned, it is nothing more than a pop quiz. Your response to that quiz will determine your grade. The attitude you have toward life (in general) and brokenness (in particular) will determine how you develop as a person. Self-esteem is your attitude about yourself. Love is your attitude toward another person. Faith is your attitude toward God. Hope is your attitude toward the future. Forgiveness is your attitude toward the past. The Bible is a book on attitudes. James would say your attitude is everything.

We do some silly things as parents. Some turn to their cantankerous, misbehaving child and ask, "Do you want a spanking?" What do you expect the little kid to say? "Sure Dad, right back here where it will hurt." This is a rhetorical question; a certain answer is assumed. Another rhetorical question is, "Do you ever have tough times?" Well, of course. So how do you respond? Can you meet the tough times like James, who says to meet them with joy? What does he know that we don't?

We can enjoy a test because we know that the testing of our faith produces perseverance, and persevering in our faith always pays off. Nearly all challenges have spiritual overtones. Isn't it true that when we are challenged, it usually results in a faith challenge? We are tempted to become discouraged, get angry, hate, depend on ourselves (instead of trusting God), and give up on God altogether. All of these responses are faith issues, brought about by seemingly non-spiritual circumstances. Although James may have been addressing Christians facing persecution for their faith, everyday challenges are, in and of themselves, faith challenges because they tempt us to respond to them out of our humanity rather than out of our faith in God.

Romans 5:3 says, "We rejoice in our sufferings, because we know that suffering produces perseverance, and perseverance character, and character hope, and hope does not disappoint." You see, if you persevere, everything works naturally. The results are maturity, completion, and wholeness. Therefore, our goal must be to persevere in faith, not get rid of our problems. That brings us back to the process versus product idea. We are product-oriented: solve the problem, cure the sickness, get rid of the obstacle. But God is interested in character development, the growth of the soul. He is concerned primarily with how we face our dilemmas. In essence, we fulfill our potential through tough times, not in spite of them.

In dam safety, the federal government takes concrete core samples from the middle of dams and places them under various stress tests to determine how the dam will hold up under great strain. Nearly always, the stress applied is many times greater than that which would occur naturally. They test the character of the concrete. Problems serve as the stress test of our character, revealing our strengths and showing where we must grow. They are revealers of weaknesses.

I grew up on a farm, and working around farm machinery makes your hands incredibly greasy and dirty. To clean ourselves we used a special soap which scraped the oil and dirt off our hands, often along with one or two layers of skin. Problems are like that. They wear us down or shine us up, according to how we are made from the inside out. Don't curse your trials; embrace them. They will make you stronger if your attitude is right.

In James, God tells us to take joy in our trials. Then He seems to change the subject and says that if we lack wisdom, ask Him for some and He will give it to us. This is no change of topic. The greatest need in facing trials is wisdom. When we first confront a problem, we have difficulty seeing what good can come of it because our initial impression is that the problem will keep us from success, or happiness, or balance, or progress. The need for wisdom comes in answering questions like: "What good can come out of this trial?" "Which way should I go from here?" "What is God's will?" This wisdom does not come primarily from experience or age. It is divine. God gives it. Try hard to avoid the fault-finder solution and strive to accept the trial and learn from it, grow from it, by facing it with the right attitude. First Corinthians 1:25 says, "Because the foolishness of God is wiser than men, and the weakness of God is stronger than men."

By enduring tough times we can eventually develop strong self-confidence. In spiritual terms, those times ultimately reveal our inadequacies so we can develop God-confidence. When we are unable to fix a problem, we suddenly realize that we are finite, limited, mortal. Every trial has within it the seed of brokenness, even though most of our significant problems do not produce a broken spirit because we fail to respond to them as God designed us to confront them. When we eventually face a situation that our education, skills, money, network, or hard work cannot fix, we confront our weaknesses, and that prepares us to consider God. When we go through difficult issues without developing an awareness of our inadequacies and God's love for us, we become broken in the wrong places. All too often Christians with a personal faith in God come to crises that could result in brokenness, repentance, and utter submission to God, but instead they rebel and become bitter or angry. Elton Trueblood said, "An empty, meaningless faith may be worse than none." James tells us to trust God for this wisdom. When we do not absolutely depend on His gift, we express doublemindedness. Kierkegaard said, "Is not despair doublemindedness? For what is despairing other than to have two wills."

I remember a car maker that was trying to demonstrate the durability of the transmissions of its cars by showing a driver dramatically shifting the car from drive to reverse to drive to reverse. . . . The doubleminded, literally two-souled, person is like that in all he does. Like trying to walk on a water bed, the person is unstable. When we face difficult times with a fickle faith that tries to consider God, but ends up doubting, we wonder why we have such a difficult time reaching our spiritual potential. We're like Mr. Facing Both Ways in *Pilgrim's Progress.*

■

FILING FOR SPIRITUAL BANKRUPTCY

James 1:9 says, "Let the lowly brother glory in his exaltation." Try selling that to Madison Avenue. God is telling us to consider the wealth in our humble, difficult circumstances. In problems there are nuggets of gold that go undiscovered, every day, all the time. When we are wealthy, we easily trust in our own resources. But when we are in a humble condition, we turn to God's resources and we have no choice but to trust Him.

Sociologists who study societal movements and changes note that before a culture is likely to pursue a more excellent solution, it is likely to come to a point of desperation. "In order for a critical theory to fulfill its practical task it must be the case that the people whom it is supposed to liberate will at some stage be willing—indeed ready—to listen and to act on its message. But it is highly unlikely that this will be the case unless the level of discontent they are experiencing is really quite high."[1] On a personal level as well as a social level, unless something is broken and causing a certain degree of discomfort, we probably won't be motivated to change it. "Ya gotta wanna" and the strongest "wanna" is developed through pain, whether it be confronting the need for weight reduction, to exercise, to seek an education, or whatever. In this context, Ecclesiastes says,

Sorrow is better than laughter,
For by a sad countenance the heart is made better.
The heart of the wise is in the house of mourning,
But the heart of fools is in the house of mirth.

(Eccl. 7:3–4)

A theoretical explanation of brokenness from the viewpoint of one studying large groups of people from a nonspiritual viewpoint goes like this, "For a social theory to be critical and practical as well as scientifically explanatory, the conditions described in it must be met. Specifically, these are: first, that there be a crisis in a social system; second, that this crisis be at least in part caused by false consciousness of those experiencing it; third, that this false consciousness be amenable to the process of enlightenment."[2]

Mahatma Gandhi said that seven things will destroy us: wealth without work; pleasure without conscience; knowledge without character; commerce without morality; science without humanity; religion without sacrifice; and politics without principle. Life has a certain balance. If we avoid the principles which season the success and the victories, we are apt to reap rewards gained too easily. It is not a negative to think we must suffer prior to having fun; rather, it is positive to have sufficient character strength to endure and enjoy the fruits of our labors. When we avoid the difficult, that which creates strengthened character, we harm ourselves.

In our humble circumstances, whether emotional, financial, spiritual, or other, we discover the strength of God. Brokenness is the process by which we come into awareness of our inabilities and need for His great ability. The Sermon on the Mount is the best description of Kingdom living, and the beatitudes head up that description. We often look at the beatitudes as commandments we have to keep. I think they are better understood as descriptions of how we will live if we have a heart for God. The very first point of Jesus' Sermon on the Mount is, "Blessed are the poor in spirit, for theirs is the Kingdom of Heaven" (Matt. 5:3). "Poor in spirit" means being utterly empty, incapable of experiencing what God has for you. Although I hate to admit it, sometimes I start to think that God is quite lucky to have Alan Nelson on His team. "Isn't He fortunate that I'm willing to forego my adventures and strive to do His will. It is lucky for God and for my church that I'm so compliant and loving." That kind of human attitude is exactly what this beatitude warns against.

Being poor in spirit does not mean having low self-esteem. It does mean being aware of my spiritual inadequacies. Romans 7:18 says, "I know that nothing good lives in me, that is in my sinful nature." Paul also says, "Christ came into the world to save sinners, of whom I am chief" (1 Tim. 1:15). Paul is not advocating a worthless soul theology, but rather is teaching us about our abilities. I am unable to manifest anything of spiritual good on my own. I am spiritually poor. When we learn this, we stop asking the "why do bad things happen to good people like me" question because we, like Isaiah (64:6), realize that our righteousness is as filthy rags. That attitude is a result of an experience with brokenness. Prior to brokenness, we're ready to show God our good works and suggest that "I'm just as good as the rest of the people and no good God would send me to hell."

Brokenness creates repentance and humility, not feelings of pride or superiority. Reinhold Niebuhr talked specifically about an American problem—we are blind as long as we do not see ourselves as sinners. We Americans, whether we go to church or not, hate to see ourselves as sinners. "We cannot expect even the wisest of nations to escape every peril of moral and spiritual complacency;

for nations have always been constitutionally self-righteous. Repentance is the true source of charity; and we are more desperately in need of genuine charity than of more technocratic skills."[3] It is tempting, once you are in a church for awhile, to look down your nose at those whose growth has not matched your own. When a person goes to Alcoholics Anonymous he introduces himself by saying, "My name is John Smith, and I'm an alcoholic." When Christians come to church on Sunday, they ought to say, "My name is Alan Nelson, and I am a sin-aholic." I may not be practicing. Perhaps I've been "dry" for awhile. But as soon as I start to think I am rich in spirit, I have lost the proper attitude. "By assuming control of our lives, we are left with the responsibility of justifying ourselves and establishing our own worth. The poor in spirit know they have lost control, should never have tried to take control, and never again want control."[4]

Charles Colson relates a story he heard while researching his book, *Loving God.* Mike Wallace, of the news show "60 Minutes," introduced a story about Nazi Adolf Eichmann, a principal architect of the Holocaust. Wallace posed a central question at the program's outset: "How is it possible for a man to act as Eichmann acted? Was he a monster? A madman? Or was he perhaps something even more terrifying: was he normal?"

The most startling question came in an interview with Yehiel Dinur, a concentration camp survivor who testified against Eichmann. A film clip from Eichmann's 1961 trial showed Dinur walking into the courtroom, stopping short, seeing Eichmann for the first time since the Nazi had sent him to Auschwitz eighteen years earlier. Dinur began to sob uncontrollably, then fainted, collapsing in a heap on the floor as the presiding judicial officer pounded his gavel for order in the crowded courtroom. Was Dinur overcome by hatred? Fear? Horrid memories?

No; it was none of these. Rather, as Dinur explained to Wallace, all at once he realized Eichmann was not the god-like army officer who had sent so many people to their deaths. This Eichmann was an ordinary man. "I was afraid about myself," said Dinur. "I saw that I am capable to do this. I am . . . exactly like he [is] . . ." Our vulnerability to sin makes our striving for holiness more pleasing to God than if we were immune to sin. The power of God to sustain is shown more clearly in the lives of tempted and tested people.

One who is poor in spirit loses self-preoccupation. The "mirror-mirror-on-the-wall" syndrome nags us. I wonder what people are thinking about me. Should I wear this or that outfit? I wish my church would grow as fast or faster than his. Maybe we need a bigger home or a newer car so the neighbors will be impressed. When we become broken in the wrong places, the focus of our lives turns inward. When you are properly broken, poor in spirit, the focus shifts outward and upward.

The Greek word for *poor* means literally to cringe and cower, referring to the desperately poor, not just those who wish they had more. Poor people are often beggars. When you realize you have nothing, you beg, plead, and cajole others to give to you. When you are poor in spirit, you turn to God and plead with Him to sustain you. Prayer changes from a practice of piety to a pleading for survival. And when we are poor in spirit, we have an attitude of praise and thankfulness to God for His love, because we do not deserve what we have or receive, rather it is His gift. When we are poor in spirit, we accept God on His terms because we do not have the power to force Him into our terms. All who enter the Kingdom of God do so in the same posture, on their knees. In the Kingdom of God, filing for bankruptcy is just the beginning, not the end. At an ashram, E. Stanley Jones asked people in a group to write down their needs. One man said, "What if I have no need?" Jones responded, "I think if you feel you have no need, that's your need."

■

SOURCES OF TROUBLES

In 1:16–18 James says, "Do not be deceived, my beloved brethren. Every good gift and every perfect gift is from above, and comes down from the Father of lights, with whom there is no variation or shadow of turning." One sign of being deceived is thinking God does bad things to people, when He really only does good. It is important to recognize that we serve a good God. "All things work together for good to those who love God, to those who are called according to His purpose" (Rom. 8:28). The beauty of God is that when junk happens to you, regardless of the junk, He can create something good out of it. He recycles our trash. He can salvage gold from the garbage—if we let Him—by His loving response to us when we call to Him out of our brokenness in the right place, the soul.

I want to reiterate that not everything that happens to you is an episode of brokenness. There are definite times when God tries to prune some of the dead wood that may be stopping the Spirit from producing fruit in your life. However, even small problems have the potential of breaking and making us. If we respond to even silly, minuscule events with an attitude of humility and dependence and submission to God, we can maintain (voluntarily) a spirit of brokenness.

The Bible is filled with reasons for suffering: sins (Heb. 3:15–19; Gen. 19:24–25); so that the power of Christ may dwell in you (2 Cor. 12:9); for righteousness' sake (Phil. 1:29–30; 2 Thess. 1:4–5); so that we might fellowship with others who are in affliction (Rom. 12:15); so that one might glorify God (Ps. 50:15). However, I believe we have four main sources of trials, tough times, and challenges.

Normal life problems.

Flat tires, car wrecks, job losses, rebellious children, snagged pantyhose, twisted ankles, bounced checks, miscommunications, and deaths are just a few of the seemingly endless list of normal life occurrences. They vary in degree and in duration and are a result of living in an imperfect and sinful world. The rain falls on the just and the unjust. God does not cause these problems. Satan does not cause them. You may not cause them. They just happen! These challenges can provide opportunities to experience brokenness if you should need it in your life. The apostle Paul's thorn in the flesh may have been an ongoing health problem which served to keep him humble and dependent on God. Yet, his attitude toward this frustration was one of brokenness instead of consternation and doubt.

The letter of Colossians was written while Paul was in jail, literally in chains. In chapter four he says, "And pray for us, that God may open a door for our message, so that we may proclaim the mystery of Christ, for which I am in chains" (4:3). Paul's attitude is not, "Get me out of here. Pray for my release. Go to Rome and hire a lawyer or at least help me make bail." Paul does not seek prayer for his escape, but rather that he could be used. He considered difficulties as possibilities for God to do good things. When we are externally oriented, we want our circumstances to change more than we are willing to change our hearts and our characters to match our circumstances. When we are broken, we pray for strength to match the situation. As one commentator noted, Paul was chained but not contained. The result of a broken attitude is an inability to be controlled by external circumstances, whether they be people, health, finances, or others. When we pray for strength to match the challenge instead of a different challenge, we become the miracle.

Life upheavals can occur in sudden, traumatic turn-arounds, such as a job loss, heart attack, financial disaster, and the like. Someone said, trouble always happens at the same time, when you need it least. Often the shock of the event itself adds to the impact. Other problems occur with a gradual decay of circumstances. Perhaps it is a stalled dream, a business that deteriorates, a relationship malaise, or a worsening health condition. Sometimes the gravity of the process is just the day-to-day awareness that life is not getting better, and you are not sure how to change it. Both types of processes remind us that we ultimately are not in control. They show us our limited power to run our lives.

The result of sins.

Watchman Nee wrote, "God allows that soul to fall, to weaken, and even to sin, that he may understand whether or not any good resides in the flesh. This usually happens to the one who thinks he is progressing spiritually. The Lord tries him in order that he may know himself. It is altogether a most difficult lesson, and is not learned within a day or night. Only after many years does one gradually come to realize how untrustworthy is his flesh."[5] G. K. Chesterton said, "The one spiritual disease is think-ing that one is quite well. If the Spirit of God has given you a vision of what you are apart from the grace of God, you know that there is no criminal who is half so bad in actuality as you know yourself to be in possibility."[6] "A disrespect for the power of evil is a major step toward a broken personal world."[7] Psalm 51 vividly records David's attitude of brokenness when he confessed his sin of adultery and murder/manslaughter to the prophet Nathan. Saul of Tarsus went from the proud patriot of the Christian-haters to zealous apostle via a conversion experience that would soften even the hardest heart. The Children of Israel repented of their sins after seeing the ten spies drop dead and after being sentenced to forty years in the wilderness.

Jonah the prophet profited from some divine discipline as well. He initially ran from God's leading, a sign that he needed to experience brokenness. Because of his sin, the storm came, causing the sailors to reluctantly throw him into the water. Although we usually see the great fish as a part of the punishment, it was also his salvation. He would have surely drowned had it not been for this aquatic limousine service. Jonah allows us to read about what went on in his life while entombed in this oversized holy mackerel. Jonah, chapter two, is a prayer of repentance and brokenness. "I cried out to the Lord because of my affliction" (Jonah 2:2). He had already learned that you cannot run from God. Distress is the soil where brokenness can grow. "You cast me into the deep . . . all Your billows and Your waves passed over me. Then I said, 'I have been cast out of Your sight; yet I will look again toward your holy temple'" (Jonah 2:3–4). Jonah felt his life was over. He figured God had given up on him, much like Job felt, but still, he turned back to God. This part of Jonah's prayer expresses the various emotions we feel when we are in over our heads.

"I have been cast out of your sight" (Jonah 2:4). Like Jonah, the Psalmist regularly cried out "Where are you, God?" in times of turmoil. Jesus screamed from the cross, "My God, my God, why have You forsaken me?" (Matt. 27:46). Job is another one who felt lost. Feeling alone is one of the most common feelings during a crisis. No one understands your circumstances. No one cares. When you need Him most, God seems to slip out for lunch. These are real and common thoughts and feelings. He had been banished from God's sight.

"The waters surrounded me," said Jonah (Jonah 2:5). During times of crisis, we feel insecure. I remember almost drowning in a swimming pool when I was seven or eight years old. I did not know how to swim, and my cousins and I were jumping into five-feet-deep water. I jumped out too far from the side and could not reach back to it. After that experience, I was afraid of water until my senior year in high school. Crises inevitably threaten us and make us feel insecure. They also make us feel vulnerable, weak, and without confidence.

"The deep closed around me; weeds were wrapped around my head" (Jonah 2:5). In the midst of crises we feel suffocated. We sense an inability to find the answers we need. We cannot seem to find enough leverage to get out of the situation. When a prominent businessman who has worked deals all his life is faced with cancer, he suddenly realizes he can't buy or deal his way out this time. He begins to feel like the problem is suffocating him. He has no escape. He feels trapped.

"I went down to the moorings of the mountains" (Jonah 2:6). Depression is a true sinking feeling. The feeling of helplessness often moves to a feeling of hopelessness. Despair emerges as a dominant theme as you read the Psalms which depict crisis after crisis. That sinking feeling, when you have to look up just to see the bottom, is a universal problem in the midst of dilemmas.

"The earth with its bars closed behind me forever" (Jonah 2:6). "Help! I can't move. Let me up! I'm dying!" Jonah felt like all help was gone. The cavalry was not on its way to rescue him. There was no solution. He was pinned down. This emotion is also common during crises. You see no exits. You feel destined to fail. The options have not come through for you.

Jonah's prayer continues with a twist. Normally you would think that a man breathing his last breath, and seeing his life pass quickly before him, would shoot up a typical foxhole prayer. "God, if you get me out of here, I'll do whatever you want." But the prayer of brokenness transcends a plea for escape. Jonah says, "But I will sacrifice to You with the voice of thanksgiving" (Jonah 2:9). Here we know Jonah has seen the error of his ways. True repentance goes beyond seeking an end to the suffering. It cares more about worshiping God than ending the pain. Instead of seeking release, he wants to thank God and sacrifice to Him. His focus of worship moved from Jonah to Jonah's Creator. Thus the cycle of brokenness was complete. Only then did God have the fish spit out Jonah. Interestingly, God often allows us to be in a holding tank, a sort of present purgatory, where we can experience brokenness. We often stay there until we break. What would have happened to Jonah had he not broken? Who knows? At times, God puts things on hold, waiting for us to yield our will while we wander in the wilderness.

Spiritual warfare.

Most people believe that Job's suffering came at the hands of Satan. Obviously, God limited the amount of temptation and suffering, as 1 Corinthians 10:13 tells us. However, Job responded to this testing as a trial from the Lord himself, yet he held his ground. His attitude allowed him to emerge unscathed by the enemy, and he reaped bountiful blessings.

According to the story, Job already had a great attitude. In fact, God presented him to the enemy as a model man. We have no reason to suspect that God needed to take Job through a period of brokenness. Although we may never know the source of our trials, we must consider that we may be experiencing spiritual warfare. Ephesians 6:12

says that we do not wrestle "against flesh and blood, but against principalities, against powers, against the rulers of the darkness of this world, against spiritual wickedness in high places." The best counter to the attacks of the evil one is brokenness before God. In spite of all he went through, even feeling God might slay him, Job held strong to his faith. That kind of faith emerges out of character, not mental assent. Job said, "When he has tested me, I shall come forth as gold" (Job 23:10). God's gold-mining process is rarely pretty. You have to move a lot of rock to get a little gold. But that's what makes gold so precious.

God Himself.

God is sovereign. James tells us that God tempts no one. A temptation is a challenge designed to make us weaker. A testing is a challenge designed to make us stronger. God tested Abraham when He asked him to leave his homeland and eventually sacrifice his only son. God needed Abraham to prove he had the character necessary to carry on the promise of Israel. Jesus tested His disciples from time to time with questions. However, just as we shouldn't look for demons behind every bush during spiritual warfare, we also shouldn't look for God's hand behind every challenge or obstacle. "God, what did You mean by that last light turning red? Are You trying to tell me something by my running out of gas?" He might say, "Yes, silly. Fill your tank." Over-spiritualization leads to paranoia. Be open and receptive to God's hand, but test the spirit and see if God may be trying to tell you something, or if it is just a circumstantial happening. Many pastors I have spoken with report seeing God's direct hand involved in trying situations, teaching them lessons of dependence and humility. Many decide that it does not matter whether negative circumstances are caused by God or not. Our goal is to trust God, to maintain a proper fear of the Lord. When we fail to fear the Lord appropriately, we run the risk of needing to be broken and tamed. "The fear of the Lord is the beginning of wisdom" (Prov. 9:10).

The difficulty with analyzing life challenges is that often we are not aware of their source. We may accuse God when really the source is spiritual warfare, a consequence of sin, or even just a result of chance. It is dangerous to always point to demonic activity for negative situations. It is foolish to automatically blame God for problems and barriers. In fact, as you look at biblical examples, the source of the challenge often makes little difference. What matters is your response, your attitude toward your trouble. Does it make you better or bitter? Does it draw you closer to or drive you further from God? Does it create a spirit of brokenness or an attitude of hostility?

■

THE WHITE FLAG

One significant sign that the soul has been broken is when you are able to pray a sincere prayer of surrender, when you relinquish the struggle at hand. Just as a white flag signals the end of the battle, such an attitude or prayer prevails when the victory is on the horizon. In Matthew 26:39, Jesus' prayer in the garden communicates His desire to pass up the cross, but nevertheless "God's will be done." In 2 Samuel 12:16–23, David ends his prayer and fasting as soon as he discovers his child has died. His servants are confused. David tells them that when the baby was sick there was hope for healing, but now he has given it to God. In 2 Samuel 16:5–13, David is harrassed by a member of Saul's family. The angry man yells at David, curses him, and throws rocks at his men. The soldiers urge David to let them kill this "dead dog." David says, "No, perhaps I deserve this, or God will bless me through it." David gave up his need to defend his reputation and silence his enemy. In Luke 1:38, when the angel announces to Mary her role in bearing the Messiah, she responded, "Let it be to me according to your word." In Acts 2:1 we find the disciples together in "one accord." Apparently they had ended their competition for head disciple. In 2 Corinthians 12:7–10, Paul shares how he has accepted his "thorn in the flesh." In John 17:6–18, Jesus turns over the care of the disciples to God. Whether you are a pastor, parent, or friend, one of the most difficult things to do is release those around you to God's care. In all of these and similar examples, the people let go and gave ownership to God. They willingly surrendered for the sake of bringing glory to God.

Patsy Claremont once pointed out that God wants cracked pots. If you place a light in a pitcher or pot, and put your hand over the top, the only way you can see light is through the cracks. These fissures which we often strive to fill and cover are actually the portholes through which God shows Himself. Paul celebrated his weaknesses, recognizing that through the cracks he could see the good stuff. Even our best falls far short of God's mediocre. Brokenness allows us the opportunity of dropping our guard, of putting our best foot forward, and allowing Him to protrude out of our shortcomings. God is a gentleman. He does not force himself upon us. But when we willfully drop our emotional and spiritual guard, He will demonstrate His grace.

Margaret Clarkson put it this way, "Perhaps the greatest good that suffering can work for a believer is to increase the capacity of his soul for God. The greater our need, the greater will be our capacity; the greater our capacity, the greater will be our experience of God. Can any price be too much for such eternal good?"

■

QUESTIONS FOR REFLECTION

1. What is a trial or testing of your faith right now in which you can find joy? Where can joy come from it?

2. Do you believe stress reveals character or builds character? Discuss the options.

3. What is the difference between low self-esteem and humility (poor in spirit)? Why is it important to distinguish between these traits?

4. Of the four sources of situations leading to brokenness, which describe your brokenness experiences?

5. How does suffering potentially increase the capacity of one's soul for God?

Brooks become crooked from taking the path of least resistance. So do people.

—Harold Kohn

■

CHAPTER FIVE

Bucking Brokenness

■ ■ ■

My gait had lost its characteristic energy and I often appeared downcast. If church attendance was up, I was up; if it was down, so was I. And the numbers had been going down for a long time. A covert, unarticulated animosity had crept through my soul. It was hidden from all. Years of honestly cultivated Christian civility served me well—for inside I was a very angry man.

The focus of my resentment was God Himself, the one who had called me to this. I had given everything—all my time, all my education, years of ministry and true Christian devotion (He knew!)—and now I was failing. God was to blame.

So as I walked up my driveway on this hot summer day, after more than a decade of ministry, I began to lose my equilibrium. My long-established world of bright prospects and success had melted around me. Beneath my pastoral veneer, dark thoughts moved at will. Inside I was embarrassed and fearful. At night, as I drifted off to sleep, the benevolent faces of my well-wishers would slip in and out of focus—always smiling. They seemed benignly to watch me sink into a pit of miserable despair. I wanted to quit. I was in the darkest, deepest depression of my life. My memory of this time is of a gray, horizonless sea.

My wife and I made a covenant to search the Scripture and learn what God had to say about success. What we learned was our liberation from the success syndrome.

—Kent Hughes

■

WHOLE LOTTA BREAKING GOIN' ON

My boys are at the age when they like gliders, the cheap, balsa wood airplanes. The thin, light wood is pre-stamped so that you punch out the airplane and attach the wings to the fuselage. The balsa wood is supposed to break off at the grooves. Sometimes it does not. Occasionally you splinter or break off part of the airplane by accident. When this happens, the planes don't fly as well as they are designed to. Life is delicate, like the balsa plane. When we break in the right areas we will fly higher and smoother than when we break in the wrong places.

In the last chapter we discussed the process of brokenness and the ways God uses difficult challenges to prune us, refine us, and strengthen us. We discussed the importance of attitude. However, we should spend a little more time talking about what happens when we fail to respond to the breaking process with an attitude of surrender.

There is much brokenness in the world. Broken people and broken lives fill counseling centers, bars, and urban gutters daily. They clog the freeways. Many show up nicely dressed at Sunday church. We rarely find someone who is either not in a state of brokenness or who has no vivid memories of such a time, unless the memories are repressed. There are positive and negative responses to the breaking process, whether it is natural, God-directed, or a result of spiritual warfare. The goal is not just to be broken, but to be broken in the right place.

I remember growing up in Iowa, working for my father and uncle, walking the rows of crops and pulling weeds. They spent time teaching me the difference between weeds and the early stages of the crop. The purpose of this lesson was to keep me from walking down the rows and pulling up soybeans or corn. Just because a person goes through a time of breaking does not mean the result will be good. Most people end up broken in the wrong places. They benefit little from the process because they pulled up the good sprouts instead of the weeds.

While researching this book, I interviewed many national and local church leaders around the country. One pastor expressed concern that my concept of brokenness referred to a psychological state rather than a spiritual one. Having a degree in psychology, I know how tempting it is to psychoanalyze Scripture and try to make the Bible out to be primarily a counseling source when it is foremost a spiritual guide. Many Christians languish in their spiritual walk because of psychological barriers, preventing God's Spirit from bringing about the maturity and manifestations He desires. They cannot show unconditional love, patience, kindness, and other spiritual fruits, and are often unaware of their apparent immaturity. They equate Bible knowledge and faith longevity with maturity. However, the process of brokenness, as discussed here, has little to do with psychological brokenness. The truth is that the Bible does talk about spiritual brokenness. A person who experiences a mental breakdown or emotional burnout does not necessarily have a spiritual breaking, a taming of the soul. A person can even emerge from emotional healing without being spiritually whole.

People who go bankrupt, lose their health, are fired

or laid off from a job, experience divorce, suffer from an addiction, burn out, have their teens run away, are depressed, etc., are all experiencing breaking events. Spurned relationships, dreams that never become reality, and disappointments can all break us. However, when we respond ineffectively to these processes, we will end up broken in our will to live, in our emotions, in our self-image, in our finances, and in our relationships. This approach to the breaking results in anger, bitterness, hate, and even suicide, or murder, and requires inner healing. When healing does not take place, people age as empty shells of what they used to be, stagnant and dwarfed. We have all met people like this, people who grow old and cynical. God doesn't want us broken in the wrong places. The negative emotional effects of such a breaking are disastrous.

As Ernest Becker has detailed regarding our denial of death, we construct elaborate means of avoiding crisis altogether. As shown by our exercise regimens and nutrition fetishes, we treat physical health like a religion, while simultaneously walling off death's blunt reminders—mortuaries, intensive-care rooms, cemeteries. We do the same when our dreams, our goals, or a part of our self-image dies. The denial stage becomes a looped tape which plays over and over again.

Our society is a comfort culture. We invest great energies into controlled climate in our cars and homes. We want the latest technology that will increase the fidelity of our stereo or expand our enjoyment of TV and video. So how do we respond to periods of breaking, which very often produce discomfort, and which cannot be muted with a remote control? We feel uncomfortable with discomfort, and other people's pain hurts us. Our feeble attempts to encourage, inspire, soothe, and deflect others' attention only make the broken person feel more uncomfortable expressing his or her true emotions. We set out decoys to deflect the good breaking that could be taking place. Phil Yancey gives an example of this as he discusses our typically negative view of suffering. "It is an interruption of health, an unwelcome break in our pursuit of life, liberty, and happiness. Visit any card shop and you will get the message unmistakably. All that we can wish for suffering people is that they 'Get well!' But as one woman with terminal cancer told me, 'None of those cards apply to the people in my ward. None of us will get well. We're all going to die here. To the rest of the world, that makes us invalids.' Think about that word. Not valid." [1]

■

THE WALKING WOUNDED

Although cancer is a harsh example of what can produce brokenness, the example makes my point. We feel tempted to try to make the cancer victim feel happy and act as if little has changed. But trying to console is not always the best therapy. We often do others an injustice by trying to rush them through a growth process, by diminishing the good that the "bad" thing can do. A breaking event can make you a different person. Let it. Be open to it. Allow it to run its course. Out of our insecurity in helping others we often reveal our own squeamishness with brokenness. What we must learn to do is embrace the pain.

When boxers fight, often one will "tie up" his opponent by coming close to him and hugging him. That way, he has a moment to relax, and he avoids being hit by coming inside the range of his opponent's gloves. The hug is not a sign of affection. The two are still enemies. Rather, it is a strategy. This embrace is contrary to our natural response which says, "run quickly." Embracing our pain first appears to be denial or masochism, but it may just be a wise person's realization that pruning is hurtful and helpful at the same time. This is where experience and discernment make all the difference. When God enables a person to grow from the breaking process, He helps the person overcome the event without necessarily removing the event. The person becomes bigger than the problem. This is all a character-building process.

John Donne discovered that the most growth took place during times of affliction. Some lessons can only be learned by loss, whether a loss of love, or health, or pride, or materialism, or hope, or whatever. The seasoning process requires us to get a little salt into our wounds. Donne realized that "trials had purged sin and developed character. Poverty had taught him dependence on God and cleansed him of greed; failure and public disgrace had helped cure worldly ambition. A clear pattern emerged: Pain could be transformed, even redeemed. He got his mind off himself and onto others."[2] This may help explain the difference between being broken in the right place and being broken in the wrong places, perhaps better called woundedness. There is a difference between being broken and being wounded. The broken person, although feeling wounded and hurt, is truly on the road to healing. The person whose hurts do not result in spiritual breaking becomes a wounded person. Usually, wounded people have emotional sores that resist healing, either because they are infected or because the "victim" keeps reopening them. The neurotic temptation to keep these wounds from healing is motivated by one's desire for an excuse to hate, be angry, or avoid responsibility. Sometimes a person who keeps a wound hidden may still function well in society, but is more likely to become one of the many walking wounded.

The walking wounded are individuals who have experienced some form of physical, financial, emotional, relational, or other breaking, but who have not allowed that breaking to bring them to a realization of their deep need to depend upon God. The walking wounded are all around us, and many of you reading this book suffer from the same maladies as these. We are tempted to allow our circumstances to make us bitter rather than better. You can often detect wounded people because of their anger, whether it is demonstrated toward others or themselves. When focused on themselves it can emerge as low self-esteem, evidenced by a lack of concern about themselves physically (obesity, slumping, drug abuse, promiscuity, etc.), lack of confidence, negativity, whining, or fear. Thomas à Kempis wrote, "A man is hindered and distracted in proportion as he draweth external matters into himself. But many things displease, and often trouble thee; because thou art not yet perfectly dead unto thyself, not separated from all earthly things."[3] When we worry and fret about situations, we have not turned that portion of our lives over to God.

Most anger is directed toward other people. Wounded people constantly feel a surge of frustration with others. Casual interactions with a waitress, fellow driver, pastor, boss, subordinate, spouse, parent, or children are often fodder for reflections of inner hurt. Inner healing will not usually take place, not fully anyway, until spiritual brokenness is realized. I have discovered in pastoring that many of the troublemakers in churches are merely people venting their own pain on others. We often mistake their anger as personal attacks instead of symptoms of inner hurts. Often out of our own woundedness we jump to improper conclusions about others' motivations, and end up doing the very thing that we accuse them of because we simply do not understand their situation.

The walking wounded need healing on the inside. In the last of the 1980s and the first of the 1990s, a large movement began in the field of counseling, addressing this need for healing. The recovery movement seeks to deal with a plethora of manifestations of woundedness. Dysfunctional relationships, co-dependency, alcoholism, drug abuse, etc., all have some similar themes. Someone once said, "People who make life fit into a nutshell belong in one." I would not be so naive as to say that people only need to surrender to God and they will be healed. That's a pious pronouncement with little practical benefit. I am trying to point out that if woundedness results in spiritual brokenness, there is not only a much greater sense of catharsis, resolution, and relief, but also a greater chance that inner healing will take place. Also, we better comprehend what God has in mind when we undergo various breaking circumstances.

Doctors haven't always been aware of the role germs and bacteria play in surgery and the healing processes of the body. Because of the lack of sterile environments, many people died of infections, even though the initial injuries were cured. Spiritual brokenness cleanses our wounds so that healing can take place naturally, and by whatever other means may be necessary. When we are not broken in the right places, infection is likely to enter, and the results are often as bad or worse than the original injury.

When we are broken in the wrong places, we become self-centered. Our broken emotions keep us from loving effectively. We shun future settings where further hurt could take place, like significant relationships, churches, and goal-setting. Or we react defensively to the hurt by overachieving and living a life of abandon. The person who fears to take risks differs little from the person who is reckless with his life because he fails to value his life. When we are broken in the wrong places, we do not see the fruit of the Spirit.

Look around you. The older you get, the more you see people who have lost the twinkle in their eyes. They have endured tough circumstances, but not successfully. There is a wide difference between being weather-beaten and being seasoned and matured. The masses internalize the pain instead of letting it actually be a part of their healing process. Psychosomatic diseases and stress-induced illnesses are often signs of being broken in the wrong places. Agnosticism and atheism can be the result of improper breaking. Other pathological problems such as melancholia, nervous breakdowns, and suicide can be more extensive results of improper brokenness. Being broken in the heart, in the soul, where God can do something with your will and character, is a matter of converting, sanctifying the actual pain, and making it a part of the healing salve. You cannot do it on your own. God must. But you must be willing.

Remember Jesus' question to the poor invalid who was lying beside the pool of Bethesda? "Do you want to be healed?" Jesus was not being cruel. He was not being naive as to the man's daily existence for decades. Jesus was all knowing, and because He is all knowing, Jesus recognizes that each of us has the God-given right to make our own choices. No one can take that prerogative from us. And until we choose to let go and let God have His will and way in our lives, we cannot receive healing. The man became whole, because he was willing. When we say "Yes," we are able to take up our bed and walk. Then Jesus tells us to "go and sin no more" as He so often said to those He healed. Why? Because the greatest sin is the sin of a self-run life. The will to run our lives ruins us more than anything. That is what the process of brokenness seeks to undo.

■

FORGETTING WHO IS IN CHARGE

When Christian leaders fail to grow through submission, they run the risk of losing God's blessing on their ministry. King Nebuchadnezzar's life story illustrates this wrestling with the sovereignty of God. The purpose behind brokenness is to remind us that God is sovereign and that we are not.

In Daniel, chapter two, Nebuchadnezzar has a dream that Daniel interprets. He reminds the king that all he is and has acquired is from God and not through his own prowess: "The God of heaven has given you dominion and power and might and glory; in your hands He has placed mankind. . . . Wherever they live, He has made you ruler over them all" (2:37–38). Daniel reminds him and all leaders, godly or ungodly, that the only reason they have accomplished what they have is by God's allowance, as He alone is sovereign. The king responds to Daniel by saying, "Surely your God is the God of gods and the Lord of kings, and a revealer of secrets" (2:47). Surely, you would think, Nebuchadnezzar had come to realize that God alone is sovereign.

But, in Daniel chapter three, he erects a ninety-foot statue and commands everyone to bow down to it during its dedication. Of course, Daniel's three associates, Meshach, Shadrach, and Abed-nego, refused, were thrown into the fire, and emerged unscathed. "Nebuchadnezzar spoke, saying 'Blessed be the God of Shadrach, Meshach, and Abed-Nego. . . . Therefore I make a decree that any people, nation, or language which speaks anything amiss against the God of Shadrach, Meshach, and Abed-Nego shall be cut in pieces, and their houses shall be made an ash heap; because there is no other God who can deliver like this'" (3:28–29). Then the king certainly recognized the sovereignty of God, didn't he?

In chapter four, Nebuchadnezzar begins by offering to tell of "the signs and wonders that the Most High God has worked for me. . . . His kingdom is an everlasting kingdom and His dominion is from generation to generation" (4:2–3). Then, when Nebuchadnezzar was at home in his palace, contented and prosperous, he had another dream. This dream was of a giant tree reaching for the sky. The strong tree was visible from all the earth. Its leaves gave great beauty, and its branches bore wonderful fruit. It became a shelter for the birds and animals. But a loud voice said, "chop down the tree and cut off its branches, strip off its leaves and scatter its fruit. . . . Nevertheless leave the stump and roots in the earth" (4:14–15). Daniel interpreted the dream. The great tree was the king and the edict for his fall came from God. He would lose his throne and his sanity until "you know that the Most High rules in the kingdom of men, and gives them to whomever He chooses" (4:25). Whenever brokenness comes, God always leaves a stump out of which He can grow another tree. During times of brokenness in the Old Testament, God always left a remnant, from which He could rebuild the dream of His people.

"All this came upon King Nebuchadnezzar. At the end of the twelve months he was walking about the royal palace of Babylon. The king spoke 'Is not this great Babylon that I have built for a royal dwelling by my mighty power and for the honor of my majesty?' While the word was still in the king's mouth, a voice fell from heaven, 'the kingdom has departed from you. . . . seven times shall pass over you, until you know that the Most High rules in the kingdom of men, and gives it to whomever He chooses'" (4:28–31). Nebuchadnezzar's period of brokenness came, as it does for all of us, to remind us of God's sovereignty. The mighty king experienced his own limited power. It took time, living insanely like an animal, to humble Nebuchadnezzar. Brokenness usually takes time.

Finally, he broke in the right place. "At the end of the time, I, Nebuchadnezzar, lifted my eyes to heaven, and my understanding returned to me; and I blessed the Most High and praised and honored Him who lives forever: For His dominion is an everlasting dominion; and His Kingdom is from generation to generation. All the inhabitants of the earth are reputed as nothing; He does according to His will in the army of heaven and among the inhabitants of the earth" (4:35). We are never more sane than when our eyes are raised toward heaven and we praise the Most High. Leaders run the risk of recognizing God's sovereignty in the world without realizing His sovereignty in their personal lives. Even after realizing the latter, they are also prone to forget it. The purpose of brokenness is to remind us who God is, the One in charge. It is easy to forget that He is sovereign when we see power, and productivity, and great blessings come our way. Like the King, we begin thinking our achievements emerge out of our own majesty.

God also breaks us in order to increase our capacity, just as a contractor tears down a wall to build a room addition. "My counselors and nobles resorted to me, I was restored to my kingdom, and excellent majesty was added to me. Now I, Nebuchadnezzar, praise and extol and honor the King of heaven, all of whose works are truth, and His ways justice. And those who walk in pride He is able to put down" (4:36–37). Like Job, Nebuchadnezzar received more than he originally possessed after his period of breaking.

Leaders can go bad. Leaders can lose their focus and fail to see when they have replaced God with themselves. The process is often subtle and self-deceiving, and usually happens as leaders surround themselves with people who encourage the mystique. The first of the ten commandments is, "You shall have no other gods before Me" (Exodus 20:3). The essence of sin is just that, making yourself god of your life. Realizing the sovereignty of God in one's life is the process of salvation and the goal of brokenness. All other sins emanate from this one distortion, to make oneself sovereign.

■

INTIMACY WITH GOD

Eugene Peterson talks and writes a lot about worship, prayer, and the Psalms. He says that we naturally learn three basic Languages in life. When we are born, we use Language 1. It is the language of the cradle. This is the language of intimacy. Babies cry, coo, gurgle, and speak gibberish. Words are not nearly as important as communion. This language is relationship oriented. It expresses things that are pleasurable and painful to us. Healthy humans do not treat infants like animals to be fed. Rather, adults awaken to their compassion and usually respond back to infants using Language 1. Language 1 is typically the language of spiritual intimacy as well. It is not so concerned about content and motivation as it is with fellowship and responsiveness.

As we get older, we learn Language 2, information conveyance. We smile at the two- and three-year-old who is learning names of items: ball, eye, mouth, ear, momma, dadda, etc. This phase starts the endless questions of "why" and "how." Children then learn Language 3, motivation language. This is the ability to get another person to respond to you, to do something he would ordinarily not do. "Could you go get me a glass of water?" "Come here." Preschool children learn this language quickly. They also tend to mix these three types. But when school starts, they tend to focus on Languages 2 and 3, and Language 1 retreats. Language 1 is the language of prayer and the Psalms. It is the Language of intimacy, honesty, and spirituality. We typically regain Language 1 for two or three years during adolescence. This is reflected in the hour-long phone calls, silly gibberish, and the reduction of our vocabulary to just a few words. It is also the Language we often return to at old age. Old people are tired of informational and motivational language. They repeat their stories, talk about simple things, and enjoy pets and babies.

Language 1 also strives to reenter our lives around age forty, midlife. It is a part of the midlife transition, or crisis, where we grow tired of the manipulation and marketing strategies of Language 3. We realize that Language 2 is not fulfilling. During this time some people experiment, though usually only briefly, with Language 1. During midlife we are often ripe to being broken in the right place. We invite God to transform our dreams and undo some things of the first half of life. But if we become broken in the wrong places, and if we resist the spiritual breaking process, we again bury Language 1 and return to Languages 2 and 3, losing out on intimacy with God. Midlife can be a time of great opportunity, a chance to be recreated for a great second half. It can also be a time of upheaval—divorce, affairs, and irresponsible behavior—when we resist the breaking or let it happen in the wrong places. The language of intimacy is most often a result of being broken in the right place. As a result of brokenness, we are more in tune with our soul's true condition, and we strive less to inform and persuade God and more to commune with Him. A faith primarily based around knowledge about God and/or the manipulation of Him is not likely to be highly intimate.

■

RESPONSES TO BROKENNESS

Some responses to brokenness result in a need for healing simply because we are broken in the wrong places. Just because you go through a difficult time, whatever the degree, you have no guarantee that you are growing more mature and developing in character. Many people wander their entire lives like the Children of Israel in the wilderness because they do not learn from their pain. Whether our brokenness results in good things or in being wounded is ultimately determined by our attitude. The good news is, regardless of what happens to us, we have the God-given ability to pick the response which will allow for the greatest outcome. The other side of the coin is that our response can also create further hurt and a festering of our wounds.

One way of responding to brokenness that results in being broken in the wrong place is making excuses for your sin or for your shallowness, defending your actions as right or justifying your attitude because of the circumstances. "It's not that bad." "Everyone's doing it." "Here's why I . . ." This attitude does not result in an acknowledgment of one's own sin or part in the dilemma. It strives to whitewash your part in the situation, or place blame on someone or something else. This attitude refuses to recognize what God may be trying to teach you through the situation. I John 1:9 addresses the solution, "If we confess our sins. . . ." Sometimes, we make justifications sound like confessions, when they really are not. Larry Crabb points out that the man who apologizes in order to reunite with his wife after separating due to an argument, may not really be confessing. "It's clear that the husband apologized to relieve his own loneliness rather than to soothe his wife's hurt. Like most apologies, his included an explanation for the offense, making it into a request for understanding. His was not a true apology. True apologies never explain, they only admit."[4]

In Psalm 51, David not only confesses and repents of his sin, but also acknowledges the role of brokenness. This might be too refined an explanation of the biblical concepts, but I think it might be helpful here to draw some lines between confession, repentance, and brokenness with regard to sin. To confess means to admit and to claim ownership. There is often a lot of denial in the lives of the walking wounded. "Hey, it's not my fault. I didn't do it. They're the ones with the problem." Confession halts denial. When you fly, the airline agent at the counter asks if you have identification tags on your luggage. Confessing is filling out an ID tag and placing it on your attitude or action of disobedience. When a teacher finds a pupil's paper without a name, she is likely to ask, "Who does this belong to?" The owner then raises her hand. As long as you deny your sin, you are avoiding responsibility for it. Confessing is saying, "Yes, I did it. That's mine."

Confessing a sin also implies a certain sense of truthfulness, that is, in calling it what it is. Dr. Menninger asked the question, "Whatever happened to the word 'sin'?" Politicians refer to this concept as being "politically correct." That's where you modify the language to the point that no one is offended. Of course, no one knows what you really mean, either. We are so scared of offending people, we often find ourselves compromising on the gravity of sin. It is so easy to devalue the grossness of our sins by calling them mistakes, bad judgments, poor choices, oversights, or moral lapses. We gossip and call it a story. A woman becomes pregnant outside of marriage and we call it an accident. The problem is one of surrender. Confession involves seeing our sin the way God sees it. We can find a solution to a mistake, but only God can forgive a sin. It takes His blood, not our better judgment.

Perhaps not biblically, but in the everyday concept of confession, a person can confess, claim ownership, call sin for what it is, and yet still not repent. For example, we regularly hear about criminals who admit to a crime and show no remorse. They confess, but fail to repent. Repentance is the next level above confession. Repentance means "I not only admit to the sin and call it what it is, but I am sorry and do not want to do it again." I do not wish to be a repeat offender. It is more grave, more intense. A friend of mine used to pastor an inner-city church in Detroit. He said one young woman, street smart but spiritually simple, came forward one evening during a public invitation. She said, "I'm tired of hurting God." That's a profound definition of repentance.

To take this explanation even further, it is one thing to confess, and another to repent, but we approach the root of sin when we get to the point of brokenness. "We rarely feel deeply broken by our sinfulness. When we admit that we are not broken, we must then notice how strongly we resist seeing our jealousy (or impatience or pettiness) as truly ugly."[5] David was broken in Psalm 51, and he addressed the rootedness of sin in his life: "In sin did my mother conceive me" (51:5). Confession tends to focus on the fruit. In repentance we tend to chop off the limb. But in brokenness we strive to pull up the root of the problem. Brokenness involves both confession and repentance, but goes further to acknowledge one's desperate need for God, and one's inability to respond as God desires, even at full power.

A second response which produces brokenness in the wrong place is the blame game. Adam blamed his sin on Eve, "whom You gave to be with me, God" (Gen. 3:12). Ultimately, most blames eventually end up on God's desk. "I couldn't help myself." "It really wasn't my fault." "That's the way I was created." When people say, "I don't know what it is; they just bring out the worst in me," they need to realize that if "the worst" was not in them already, then it couldn't have come out. It's the chicken and the egg question. Does stress create character or reveal character? We can claim a little of both, but instead of blaming others and situations for our negative and unloving responses, we should acknowledge that they reveal character traits which otherwise go unnoticed. Words show what is in our hearts, and tough times reveal character.

Blame is a common dilemma in marriage counseling and divorce. When each mate is pointing his or her finger at the other person, neither one is able to grow. The pain crescendos until one or both partners take some responsibility in the situation. As long as "he" or "she" is the problem, we will never come to the point of breaking. People blame ex-spouses, present spouses, parents, siblings, pastors, bosses, employees, friends, the church, the government, almost everything but themselves. No one can make you respond a certain way without your giving them a degree of your will.

More than once while driving the freeway in southern California, I have started to make a lane change. I look in my left side mirror. I look in my rearview mirror. I begin crossing the left lane and all of a sudden . . . HONK!!!!!!! I jerk the wheel back over to the right and the driver I nearly crunched glares angrily at me, mouthing who knows what. I did not see him because he was in my "blind spot." Nearly everyone is aware of weaknesses in their lives. What we need to fear more than our weaknesses is our blind spots. In Numbers 14:10, the people of Israel were about to stone their leaders, Moses and his staff, because they were angry at them for disputing the spies' recommendation to avoid entering the Promised Land. The people had a major blind spot, their own lack of faith. We cast stones at others out of our own blind spots. Brokenness allows us to see our own blind spots. "Oh, I didn't know I had that dead wood in my life. I was not aware of my character deficiency in that area." The blame game is a way of avoiding the unveiling process. As long as I can point my finger at others, I don't have to look at myself.

A third response to the breaking process, which can result in being broken in the wrong place, is filling your life with hectic activity, while leaving it empty of God. That is a common technique in our culture. We are the society of the mad dash, the rat race, the daily calendar, the wristwatch alarm, and the goal-planning seminar. We have so much going on that even when we are going through tough times, we often avoid any solitude or spiritual contemplation which would allow us to see clearly what is wrong, and what needs to be corrected. We are doers. One of the elements of the breaking process is getting us to stop, or at least to slow down so that we can take a look at our lives, our priorities, our motivations. When the body experiences extreme hurt, it often goes into a state of shock. When our emotions are damaged, we experience a nervous breakdown. Both of these processes actually enable the organism to repair itself. Shut down the systems to investigate the problem. Brokenness is sort of a speed bump in life. When we fail to slow down we are likely to do some long-term damage to our lives.

During difficulties, some people just spin their wheels faster when they actually need to slow down and see if something else needs to be done. This denial usually results in further damage to your emotional and spiritual health, which may require intensive care later. I believe that our busy paces often disguise our needs for brokenness.

A fourth response which can result in being broken in the wrong place is trying even harder on your own. As we noted in the previous chapter, God's intention is for us to discover our unholy desires to run our own lives. Because His goal is to help us grow and excel, He wants to equip us with His power. He knows the character traits we will need to persevere and overcome. Brokenness in the right place is thwarted when I see the difficulty, feel the pain, and sense the need to reevaluate things, but instead choose to try all the harder. "Hey, if my dreams don't come true, I'll work twice as hard as before. I'll think more positively. I'll use my contacts. I'll put in more time. I'll read more books and get another degree." Our self-help culture has given us the idea that we can fix all our problems. We have become our own gods.

Although I am not one to advocate giving up, laziness, or foolishness, I do believe that much of what we often call "trying harder" is nothing more than preventing God from working more. How many times has a parent taken over the cooking, cleaning, or carrying process of a child, merely out of impatience? "Here, let me do it." With this attitude we become the god of our own lives. Human activity must never be a substitute for godly power. Psalm 127 says,

> Unless the Lord builds the house,
> They labor in vain who build it; . . .
> It is vain for you to rise up early,
> To sit up late,
> To eat the bread of sorrows;
> For as He gives His beloved sleep. (vv. 1–2)

He is reminding us again to cease striving and know that He is God. Our extra striving is often an attempt to avoid what really needs to happen, to abandon more self-effort and submit to God-effort. Our work ethic sometimes ends up being our downfall, so that after a while, we grow cynical and angry because our hard efforts did not solve our dilemmas. What happened is that we failed to allow God to prune us, to change our hearts, where we needed to be broken all along.

You see, if we do not give in to the breaking process, we will not learn. It is best to learn as quickly as possible so that God can get on with your life. If you don't learn, you are likely to go around, and around, and around. In counseling, I have seen people make the same mistakes again and again. More often than stupidity, I see this mistake resulting from an unwillingness to be broken. The forty years of wandering by the Children of Israel in the wilderness was little more than their attempt to escape brokenness. You begin feeling like the scenery is strangely familiar. Your life starts looking like a treadmill. Troubles come and go, but you note little advancement. Each time you failed to learn what you needed to learn for God to take you to the next level of His desired life for you.

Jacob wrestled with God, and God named him Israel, which literally means God-wrestler. In fact, an entire nation was named God-wrestlers. God-wrestlers try to manhandle their lives. They want things done as they deem best. Sometimes God even gives in a bit to the pressure, but this action rarely yields long term productivity. The angel touched Jacob's thigh bone and he was afflicted by it for the remainder of his life. The thigh bone is significant for it is the biggest bone in the body. This was God's way of saying, "Remember where your strength really lies." Someone said, "All of God's chosen men walk with a limp." We are afflicted for the rest of our lives when we wrestle and fail to yield to God as He desires. Sometimes, our unwillingness to be broken in the right place, in the heart and in the will, keeps us from being used for great and noble purposes.

In *A Layman Looks at the Lord's Prayer,* the author talks about watching a potter mold a lump of clay. On the shelves in his workshop stood gleaming goblets, beautiful vases, and exquisite bowls. The potter went to an odorous pit in the floor and took out a lump of clay. The smell was from rotting grass which increased the quality of the material and made it stick better. The potter patted the lump of clay in his hands into a ball. Placing the lump onto the slab of stone with seasoned skill, the potter sat down on his wobbly little wooden stool. Already the master potter could envision the work of art this lump of earth would become. Whirling the wheel gently, the artist caressed the spinning mound. Prior to each touch, he dipped his hands into the two water basins flanking each side of the wheel. The clay responded to the pressure applied by his fingers. A beautiful goblet arose from the pile, responding to each pinch and impression.

Suddenly the stone stopped and the potter removed a piece of grit. His seasoned fingers detected the unpliable aggregate. The stone spun again, allowing him to smooth out the former lodging of the grit. Suddenly the stone stopped again. He removed another hard object from the goblet's side, leaving a mark in the vessel. The particles of grain within the cup resisted his hands. It would not respond to his wishes. Quickly the potter squashed the form back into a pile of clay. Instead of the beautiful goblet, the artisan formed the material into a crude, finger bowl. "What might have been a rare and gorgeous goblet was now only a peasant's finger bowl. It was certainly second best. This was not the craftsman's first or finest intention, rather, just an afterthought."[6] When we resist the Master Potter's hand, we run the very real risk of becoming less than we could become. The process of brokenness is like stopping the potter's wheel, where gritty, grainy, noncompliant attitudes and character traits can be extracted to allow further work on our beauty. But if those pieces remain obstructive, we will surely become a vessel which cannot be used to the extent that He originally intended.

When we are broken in the right place, in the arena of

the soul and the will, we experience great peace and productivity. This condition is the prerequisite for maturity, wisdom, and greater fruitfulness. However, when we resist the breaking process, we become our own worst enemy. In his book, *The Fifth Discipline,* Peter Senge shares a tragic story which illustrates the fight many of us go through in the brokenness process.

Some years ago, while on an early spring canoe trip in Maine, we had come to a small dam, and put in to shore to portage around the obstacle. A second group arrived, and a young man who had been drinking decided to take his rubber raft over the dam. When the raft overturned after going over the dam, he was dumped into the freezing water. Unable to reach him, we watched in horror as he struggled desperately to swim downstream against the backwash at the base of the dam. His struggle lasted only a few minutes; then he died of hypothermia. Immediately, his limp body was sucked down into the swirling water. Seconds later, it popped up, ten yards downstream, free of the maelstrom at the base of the dam. Ironically, it was his very struggle against the forces at the base of the dam that killed him. He didn't know that the only way out was counterintuitive. If he hadn't tried to keep his head above water, but instead dived down to where the current flowed downstream, he would have survived. What he had tried in vain to achieve in the last moments of his life, the currents accomplished for him within seconds after his death.

■

QUESTIONS FOR REFLECTION

1. Can you think of examples of people who experienced being broken but which did not result in spiritual brokenness? What was their response subsequent to this experience?

2. "No pain, no gain" seems like a negative theory for

growth. How do you grow in character without pain? Are there traits you can only gain via painful situations? What are they?

3. Think of some everyday conversations which reflect each of the three language levels: intimacy, information, and motivation. Why is intimacy so challenging for adults?

4. What unhealthy responses to brokenness have you seen in others and/or yourself?

5. Can you think of some times in your life when you have been like stubborn clay and resisted the Potter's hands?

The man who knows his sins is greater than one who raises a dead man by his prayers. He who sighs and grieves within himself for an hour is greater than one who teaches the entire universe. He who follows Christ, alone and contrite, is greater than one who enjoys the favor of crowds in the churches.

—St. Isaac the Syrian

CHAPTER SIX

■

Our Example of Brokenness

■ ■ ■

Normally I would be at my best for a big Sunday like Christmas. In years to come I would look back on that Sunday morning, not remembering what I said, and wonder how I ever stood up, faced the people, and proclaimed the joys of Christmas on the saddest day of my life.

It all happened exactly as my wife had told me months before that it would. According to her pre-planned time schedule, a total stranger handed me those dreadful divorce papers on that fateful Friday a few days before Christmas. Within twenty-four hours I stood at the Portland International Airport, and through misty eyes watched helplessly as the woman I had loved, honored, and cherished since I was eighteen years old led my two children onto an airplane and departed, never to return. Many times as a minister I have heard people talk like they thought there were some things worse than death. At that moment and in the following days, for me, life was worse than death.

I practiced what I call "let go and let God." I took my hands and cupped them in front of me, held them up, and verbally put inside those hands everything I was fretting over and didn't have any answers to. I said out loud as I held up both hands, "There it is, God; I can't change it, I don't know what to do with it, it's all so unacceptable to me. I have been struggling over it. I have been fighting it. I just don't know what to do. There it is, Lord, I give it all to you. I give to you what people think about me." As I talked to God, I turned my hands upside down and said, "There it is, Lord. It's all yours." As I stretched my fingers out as far as I could, turning my hands upside down so that it was impossible to hold on to anything, as I dropped my arms to my side, a wonderful feeling of serenity suddenly spread throughout my entire being. I now had peace in the midst of the storm.

—Dale Galloway

∎

CHILDLIKE, NOT CHILDISH

Jesus said, "Assuredly I say to you, unless you are converted and become as little children, you will by no means enter the Kingdom of Heaven. Therefore, whoever humbles himself as this little child is the greatest in the Kingdom of Heaven. Whoever receives one little child like this in My name receives Me" (Matt. 18:3–5).

The older we get, we naturally become less like children. And according to this progression, we are moving further and further from greatness. Jesus said we must be converted to become like a child. Jesus is full of para-

doxes, seeming contradictions, opposites. He said to experience what He has we must change who we are. What
does He mean? Must I become a kid again? Is this what
they mean when they talk about a second childhood?

When we are broken, we tend to be childlike. When we
are unbroken, or broken in the wrong places, we tend to
be childish. It is the childish part of adulthood that creates all sorts of havoc. Children can be notoriously selfish.
Have you ever tried to get a two-year-old to share toys
with playmates? Forget it. Children actually believe the
world starts and stops according to their lives. When they
go to bed, so does the world. When they get up, the world
is up again. They are the center of their worlds. Adults
who need to experience brokenness tend to be very
myopic as well, self-centered and selfish. That helps explain the sky-high divorce rates and stellar consumer
debts. Many would sooner die than share their time, or
money, or possessions with others. The United States is
perhaps the most individualistic culture on the face of the
earth. We also have the most violent culture in the world,
with a higher percentage of our citizens incarcerated than
any other country on the globe. Children stick out their
tongues and call each other names. Adults curse, gossip,
and litigate. There really isn't much difference.

Paul says when he was a child he thought and acted like
a child, but when he became an adult he did away with
childish ways. Childish ways reveal a need for brokenness. There is little chance you will see a person "grow out
of it" as an adult without going through a breaking process. Avoid investing a lot of energy in childish people.
You are probably not going to see much change until they
are motivated to yield to God and surrender their wills.
What Jesus is commending us to become is childlike, having the good qualities of childhood.

Children are vulnerable.

Many years ago, Art Linkletter had the most popular show on television. The entire program focused on interviewing little children, asking them questions, and responding to their comments. The show was so funny and cute because the children, besides being creative, were incredibly vulnerable. Kids tell it the way it is, or at least the way they see it. It is only as we grow older that we become defensive and withdrawn. We learn the fine art of mask-wearing. We are not born worrying about what others think of us. We have no rights to stand up for or defend. Similarly, a broken person is able to be vulnerable. He has no pretenses. This is not a license to be socially insensitive or crude, but rather it is the quality of being genuine. When you are broken, your inside matches your outside. Your private life and public life are basically the same. Broken people are authentic. What you see is what you get. They don't mind risking vulnerability.

Children are forgiving.

True, kids get into a lot of squabbles, but they have an incredible ability to forgive and forget. As we grow older, our grudge-keeping enlarges. Our boys sometimes pinch, bite, hit, and push each other. Then my wife, Nancy, jumps into the action. "Boys, stop it! Now hug each other." After a few moments the boys wrap arms around each other. Mom and Dad smile—how cute. Less than fifteen seconds later they are back to their games. Why are adults able to carry our offenses for lifetimes? Spouses tell nasty stories about their ex-mates. Middle-agers fume over what their siblings did to them as children. Nations invest billions of dollars for defense because of threats made decades before. Churches split because someone's feelings got hurt. Where there is a lack of forgiveness, there is a need for brokenness. This is one of the surest signs that me-ism still exists. The person who cannot forgive is really masochistic. He or she takes some sort of pleasure in reliving the offense over and over again. Only whole, healthy people can forgive. God tells us to forgive, not just to help others, but because it is a step in healing ourselves. As long as you run the old video in your mental VCR, you are hurting yourself over and over and over and over again. The person who offended you may even be dead, but you just cannot let go of the hurt. Brokenness is often the prerequisite for inner healing.

Children are trusting.

As a toddler, my youngest son had few fears. One evening I was lying on the floor when he suddenly jumped off the couch, over my head, and onto my stomach. He just assumed Dad would catch him. Our boys used to play a game as we would leave the house. Most of our home is upstairs, so as I would get about one fourth of the way down the staircase, they would call for me to catch them. They would leap into my arms, trusting me to save them from falling the other three fourths of the way down, onto the tile entry or through the plate glass window.

Broken people are very trusting, not only of others but also in their faith. People who need to experience brokenness tend to be cautious and reticent in relationships. This can kill a marriage, which requires trust to survive. It has a lot to do with forgiveness as well. As long as our egos and identities are wrapped up in ourselves instead of God, we will be self-conscious. We will avoid vulnerability in order to keep from being hurt by someone else. Our friendships will be shallow and few. Worst of all, unbroken people hold back from God. We withhold our emotions, and have difficulty letting ourselves go in worship. We hold back with our intellect, casting doubts at God. Broken people still question and face discouragement, but they do not keep these emotions from their faith. The Psalms are full of earthy feelings which seem almost anti-spiritual. But when you are broken, you trust God with everything—your anger, fears, and discouragements. You are free to be obedient. You can cry with Him and laugh with Him. He ceases to be a stained-glass icon and becomes an intimate friend.

Children are loving.

One of the greatest joys of parenthood is having a three-year-old come to you multiple times and say, "Daddy, I wuv you!" Hugs, kisses, primitive Crayola drawings, Popsicle sticks, and wrestling matches are all ways my little boys have demonstrated their love for Daddy and Mommy. Kids are natural. They are uninhibited. The older we get, the more difficulty some people have hugging and saying, "I love you." Nearly every year, Nancy and I host a marriage retreat called Marriage Celebration. One of the reasons we began doing this was to keep our own relationship alive and growing. The young couple courting writes notes, talks for hours over the phone, carves their initials and a heart in a tree or park bench, and whispers sweet somethings to each other, oblivious to the world around them. But what happens five, ten, or twenty years later? The same couple stares out the window at breakfast, muttering details about work and bills. They turn on their sides at night, facing the walls, preparing to invest another day in holy matrimony which seems more like unholy monotony.

People who are unloving need some brokenness. They need the ability to love life and appreciate others. The most loving people in life are those who have been broken in the right place. Broken people allow God to fill them. When you are full of God, you ooze love. God is love. Qualities like pride, selfishness, and unforgiveness get in His way. Broken people are sensitive to others as no one else can be.

Children are teachable.

Infants want to experience everything with their senses. They stick whatever is close into their mouths. Many objects end up in ears and other convenient body cavities. Four- and five-year-olds enter the "why?" stage. A little boy asked his father, "Dad, why does it get dark?"

The father answered, "Well, because the sun goes down."

"Where does the sun go, Daddy?"

"The earth is round, and the sun goes to the other side of the earth."

"Why does it do that?"

"Well, if the sun shone all the time, we would get too hot and burn up," Dad responded.

"Why don't we burn up when it's light?"

"Well, because we're far enough away from the sun."

"Daddy," the son asked, "why don't you know why it gets dark?"

Why is the sky blue? Why do birds fly? Why can't we go out for ice cream? Kids' little computer brains are working overtime to learn what life and the world are all about.

The older we get, the greater the tendency to stop learning. We tend to read fewer books, enter fewer philosophical debates, take fewer courses. Likewise, we tend to be more critical of new ideas, tend to stick to familiar restaurants, friends, and hobbies. People who are unteachable need brokenness. How can God help us grow if we are unwilling to learn new lessons, regardless of our age? God says, "See, the former things have taken place, and new things I declare" (Isa. 42:9). God desires new things in our lives. New things require us to learn. We only learn when our spirit is teachable. Broken people are teachable. They can learn from a scholar and from a little child. Pride and ego do not prevent them from saying, "Teach me. I'm willing to learn. I don't know."

Children have simple values.

It never ceases to amaze me. Every parent knows the feeling. You fight the holiday crowds to shop for your little ones. You test drive dozens of toys, scour the sale ads, wait in eternal Christmas lines, bungee strap your gifts in the yawning trunk, fight traffic to get home, sneak in the presents under cover of dark, wrap them up in Christmas paper, and refuse endless requests to open the presents, only to see your child on Christmas afternoon, playing in the box the toy came in while the toy lies lonely under a pile of crumpled paper. Kids like simplicity in their gifts. Young children are unimpressed with designer labels. They do not care whether their clothes are orange or green, or whether they match, or, at times, whether they are even wearing any at all.

People who are and have been broken find they desire a simplicity in life, a childlikeness. Objects that used to be so attractive—the certain model of car, location and size of home, clothes, and gadgets—fall in their priority order. This is not to say that broken people cannot be wealthy, or live in large homes, or possess quality merchandise. But these things fail to own them. They find little joy in them. Unbroken people tend to join the rat race, sprinting toward the symbols of success and "the good life." Broken people are of another culture, the Kingdom of Heaven. Someone said, "With my luck, someday I'll get to a place where I can afford frivolous luxuries, and I won't even want them."

Children are powerless.

They depend upon their parents. Babies need to be changed, fed, dressed, bathed, guarded, and taken to the doctor. It is amazing how much newborns depend on Mom and Dad. They cannot move. They can easily smother or choke or drown. Yet, as we grow older, we become more independent. During our late teens we long for the time when we will be on our own, totally independent from home and rules and parents. As adults we strive to become financially independent, attending seminars on how to invest our money so we need not worry about retirement, and perhaps not even have to work. That is life's tendency.

■

DECLARATION OF DEPENDENCE

The broken person returns to an almost fetal dependence upon God. This is not the neurotic dependence you achieve by spiritualizing every thought and event into some mystical occurrence. Rather, it is a dependence which sustains us. The broken believer comes to view God as his or her source of all that is worthwhile. God is the ultimate source of his or her food, money, healing, and security, even though God might use human tools to supply these needs (Phil. 4:19). Babies are all born alike . . . naked. When Adam and Eve lacked brokenness after their sin, they realized their nakedness and tried to hide. They had become insecure. They needed clothes to provide security. In similar fashion, unbroken people seek to cover their naked souls with people, education, money, or success. Job's brokenness reminded him that, "Naked I came from my mother's womb, and naked shall I return there. The Lord gave, and the Lord has taken away; Blessed be the name of the Lord" (Job 1:21).

It is true, you never see a hearse pulling a U-Haul. You will leave behind as much as Howard Hughes, Rockefeller, and King Tut . . . all of it. Henri Nouwen wrote, "The world says, 'When you were young you were dependent and could not go where you wanted, but when you grow old you will be able to make your own decisions, go your own way, and control your own destiny.' But Jesus had a different vision of maturity: It is the ability and willingness to be led where you would rather not go. The way of the Christian leader is not the way of upward mobility in which our world has invested so much, but the way of downward mobility ending on the cross." [1]

Broken people do not own anything.

They see themselves as gifted stewards. In his brokenness, Job realized that God owned all he had. He gave. He took away. Blessed be the name of the Lord. Unbroken people find it very difficult to praise God when they lose something, because somehow they feel it was "theirs." The ability to praise God amidst times of loss reflects an attitude of brokenness. "Now godliness with contentment is great gain. For we brought nothing into this world and it is certain we can carry nothing out . . . those who desire to be rich fall into temptation and a snare, and into many foolish and harmful lusts which drown men in destruction and perdition. For the love of money is a root of all kinds of evil, for which some have strayed from the faith in their greediness, and pierced themselves through with many sorrows" (1 Tim. 6:6–10).

Independent people plan their lives such that interruptions create intense stress and frustration. "Come now, listen, you who say, 'Today or tomorrow we will go to such and such a city, spend a year there, buy and sell, and make a profit; whereas you do not know what will happen tomorrow. For what is your life? It is even a vapor that appears for a little time and then vanishes away" (James 4:13–14). People who have been broken still have dreams, plans, and aspirations. But these dangle loosely. They are not set in concrete, for the dreamers realize their life is dependent upon God. They are people of the mist. They realize they cannot achieve everything, and they need not. They are able to seize the day and make the most of every opportunity as Paul says in Colossians chapter four. Ironically, this allows them the freedom to be creative, and to work more effectively, because they are free from the bondage of having to "make it." Broken people are called, not driven. Unbroken people tend to have a hard time making the most of every opportunity, because they are so busy working for the future. They are waiting for their ship to come in. The broken person's ship has come in . . . God.

In the same passage where Jesus talks about being childlike, he continues by saying, "If your hand or foot causes you to sin, cut it off and cast it from you. . . . And if your eye causes you to sin, pluck it out and cast it from you" (Matt. 18:8–9). Brokenness means coming to a point in life where you are willing to do whatever it takes to live for Christ. No cost is too high. No action is too drastic.

Growing up on the farm in Iowa, I would sometimes trap muskrats at the pond. The muskrats would dig holes around the pond that were dangerous to our farm animals and to people walking by. Muskrat traps are called "spring traps." They spring up on the animal's leg, because muskrats will chew their leg off in order to escape the trap if necessary. Christ came with such an attitude. He was willing to come as a baby and die on a cross. No sacrifice was too great. He donated His own body, blood, and bones, and did it without a fight. He had no martyr complex or death wish. He became fully obedient to the will of His Father.

This example of brokenness brings people to personal faith in God. In Acts 8:32–36, the eunuch was reading the passage of Scripture: "He was led as a sheep to the slaughter; and as a lamb before the shearer is silent, so He opened not His mouth. In His humiliation His justice was taken away." Just then, Philip came along and explained the passage to this curious reader, who made a commitment and was baptized. It is out of a broken spirit that you can most effectively influence people for Christ. Proud, legalistic, Bible-thumping, hypocritical, apologetic attitudes are impotent for healthy evangelism. When a person is truly broken, he or she becomes authentic. We become honest with our failures and with our faith. People are attracted to that.

Zeal for the Lord is not the same as brokenness. Zeal without the fruits of brokenness—humility, authenticity, integrity, and sensitivity—often makes a person offensive. Being equipped with the truth of God without the tempering of brokenness thrusts you into ministry without the warmth and attraction that disarms others. Jesus was incredibly disarming to the lost. They would talk to him at the well, come out of trees and take him home, and invite him to festivities. We have all met well-intentioned people, enthusiastic for the Lord, who radiated spiritual superiority. In a spirit of condemnation and judgment, they tend to leave a lingering bad taste. Broken people with a zeal for God make you want to be around them. You feel good beside them, even if you recognize the difference in spiritual depth and values. Unbroken people with zeal tend to make you feel unholy, not good enough, intimidated. One of the dilemmas of life is that during college and the early twenties, people often have ambition for life that is second to none. But they tend to lack brokenness. The enthusiasm of idealism can accomplish a lot, but it gets done through force, rebellion, or human strength. The breaking process, if it breaks people in the right place, sanctifies that ambition. You become a better model of Christ, and people are drawn to that spirit in you. Broken people do not even own their own lives.

■

THE ULTIMATE EXAMPLE

The final quality of brokenness is that broken people do not respond defensively when criticized, accused wrongly, or misunderstood.

> Surely he took up our infirmities and carried our sorrows, yet we considered him stricken by God, smitten by him, and afflicted. But he was pierced for our transgressions, he was crushed for our iniquities; the punishment that brought us peace was upon him, and by his wounds we are healed. We all, like sheep, have gone astray, each of us has turned to his own way; and the Lord has laid on him the iniquity of us all. He was oppressed and afflicted, yet he did not open his mouth; he was led like a lamb to the slaughter, and as a sheep before her shearers is silent, so he did not open his mouth. (Isa. 53:4–7 NIV)

Jesus exemplified the life of brokenness. The thought of being punished for someone else's sins makes me cringe. I would never want that. I'd surely stand up for my rights, or hire the best lawyer, or seek revenge. I'm ready to open my mouth if someone even thinks about afflicting me. I do not understand this degree of brokenness. But this is what transformed the disciples from a group of nervous, insecure followers around the crucifixion, to men who faced martyrs' deaths. This kind of behavior is foreign to the natural person. This sort of attitude is of a supernatural type. Broken people are secure and confident and, therefore, can let truth stand for itself. Unbroken people are quick to defend their actions and stand for their rights. Jesus died as he was born, exemplifying brokenness.

I visited Romania not long after their revolution. While visiting an open-air market, I walked through the meat section, which consisted of a couple of small trucks with a few sheep in them. A few of the sheep were lying on the ground, eyes closed, feet tied, motionless. I thought this strange that they would slaughter the lambs before they actually sold them. They had no refrigeration. These poor people could not afford to kill a sheep and then not be able to sell it. Then I looked closer, much closer. There was no blood coming from the carcasses, and no blood around the truck. No, these sheep were still alive. They just looked dead. I then understood the scriptures that refer to Jesus as a sheep to the slaughter. These sheep were at market, to be killed as soon as they were purchased. Yet, they were not kicking, bleating, or trying to run or escape. They lay passively on the ground.

I took a picture of the sheep, had the pictures made into prayer cards and had one blown up into a large picture which hangs in my study. It is a symbol, a pictorial example of brokenness. On the matted photograph is the passage from Romans 8:36–37: "'We are accounted as sheep for the slaughter'. . . . Yet in all these things we are more than conquerors through Him who loved us." We are conquerors when, through the process of brokenness, we are free to lay down our lives. Most of us will never be persecuted to the point of death. But we lay down our life when we lay down our ego, our rights, our money, our personal agendas, our pride, and our will. Suddenly we understand how we can have strength to go the second mile, to give our coats to a person suing us, to turn the other cheek when we are slapped. This is how we can pray for those who persecute us and love those who hate us. In the unbroken state, we fight going to the slaughter. We stand up for our rights and countersue. We go out with a fight, kicking and screaming and throwing a fit.

Jesus was our example of brokenness. His birth incarnated the concept. He defied common sense by coming as a baby, small, helpless, innocent, powerless, simple, poor, uneducated, and dependent. He knew from personal experience when He said, unless you become childlike, you will fail to know what the Kingdom of Heaven is all about. That is why he told the wise theologian Nicodemus that to see the Kingdom of God you must be born again. I'm not sure we evangelicals have kept that verse in context by telling people that to enter the Kingdom of God you must be born again. I believe that. But another variation is that only when we become childlike, infant-like, can we see the Kingdom of God as it is. Although being born again gains us entrance to God's family, once in, it is easy to forget what it really looks like. Look at the world as a child. Jesus did.

At the retreat center where I am writing this, at the end of my dorm is a tile plaque with this well-known story. It reflects the power that resulted from Jesus' life of brokenness.

Here is a man who was born of Jewish parents in an obscure village, the child of a peasant woman. He grew up in another obscure village. He worked in a carpenter shop until he was thirty, and then for three years he was an itinerant preacher. He never wrote a book. He never held an office. He never owned a home. He never had a family. He never went to college. He never put his foot inside a big city. He never traveled 200 miles from the place where he was born. He never did one of the things that usually accompany greatness. He had no credentials but himself. He had nothing to do with this world except the naked power of his divine manhood. While still a young man, the tide of popular opinion turned against him. He was turned over to his enemies. He went through the mockery of a trial. He was nailed to a cross between two thieves. His executioners gambled for the only piece of property he had on earth while he was dying, and that was His coat. When he was dead He was taken down and laid in a borrowed grave through the pity of a friend. Nineteen wide centuries have come and gone and today, he is the centerpiece of the human race and the leader of the column of progress. I am far within my mark when I say that all the armies that ever marched, and all the navies that were ever built, and all the parliaments that ever sat, and all the kings that ever reigned, put together have not affected the life of man upon the earth as powerfully as has that One Solitary Life." (Author Unknown)

Jesus is our example of brokenness.

■

QUESTIONS FOR REFLECTION

1. How would you describe the difference in being childlike versus being childish? Can you think of everyday examples of these?

2. Which of the childlike traits do you find most challenging in your own life experiences?

3. How do the concepts of brokenness and stewardship relate to each other?

4. As you think of the picture of the sheep lying on the ground and the verses that describe Jesus as a lamb to the slaughter, what are some areas in your life which would change if you would live by this picture?

5. How is Jesus' example of brokenness so different from the world's definition of success and fulfillment? How can Jesus' model actually be lived out today?

The grace of God makes a man godly, and then proceeds to make him manly.

—Henrietta Mears

CHAPTER SEVEN

■

Developing the Attitude of Brokenness

■■■

The person I gave Christ when I became a Christian was very insecure. I covered that with a bravado that contradicted how unsure I was of myself and the talents He had given me. To hide my inner emptiness, I polished the exterior. That put people off and kept them from me. I wanted to be adequate. Accepting Christ changed the goals of my life, but I attempted to accomplish them on my own strength, education, and personality prowess. This came across as self-sufficiency, lack of humility, and studied adequacy. It was all a cover-up. Then, in those early years, the Lord began a character transplant and a personality reconstruction. He did it, not by telling me how bad I was, but, by showing me how much He loved me.

Each failure in my relationships broke my false pride and opened me further to the Lord's Spirit. His most valued gift in those days was self-honesty. I was freed of blaming people and began to ask Him what it was in me that had caused the difficulty. He was often more ready to tell me than I was to hear. But the miracle had begun. I wanted to be filled with more and more of His Spirit. Each breaking of the old patterns of my personality allowed Him greater access to me. He wanted to reconstruct the channel through which He could pour His supernatural power. I began to experience the sheer delight of being used and giving the credit and glory to the Spirit.

I do not know of any Christians who have grown in freedom without passing through a time of realizing the futility of putting ultimate trust in their own strength, people's reliability, or dependence on circumstances.

—Lloyd John Oglivie

■

IMPORTANCE OF ATTITUDES

One of my favorite stories is about a balloon salesman who was trying to drum up business. He blew up a blue balloon and let it rise. Then he blew up a yellow balloon and let it go. Next a red one and then a green one. A little black boy walked over to the man and said, "If you filled a black balloon, would it go up too?" "Sure," the man replied, "it's not the color of the balloon that matters. It's what's inside that counts." Of course, with people, that inside ingredient is attitude.

As I grow older, I realize how crucial attitude is to our lives. What separates the haves from the have-nots, the doers from the don'ters, the winners from the whiners, the water-walkers from the boat-sitters, is one word—*attitude.* I know the smell of a motivational talk is foul to a book on brokenness, but for just a moment, let me drive home a salient point about maturity, and Christianity, and life itself. The more years you tuck under your belt, the easier you can see that life seasons some people and ages others. Life chips away idealism and superficiality in people, so that after a while, they drop the emotional facades that require so much energy to maintain. You run out of energy as you get older. But why is it that some wise and gracious individuals, who undergo the same pains and problems as others, emerge so well? The solution is simple, so simple it risks embarrassing the naive and being rejected by the pseudo-sophisticated reader. The million-dollar difference is attitude.

As you study the Bible, you find that most sins really are not behavior based, nor are they external character traits that God esteems. We Christians have been guilty for some time now of emphasizing the *doing* of faith over the *being* of faith. In our striving to apply the subjective, the spiritual, the invisible, we have highlighted certain behaviors. The black list includes items like drinking, smoking, doing drugs, cursing, adultery, etc. I am not in favor of these activities, but they remind me of the Old Testament law and the New Testament Pharisees. Jesus was more interested in attitudes than behaviors, because attitudes go deeper than behaviors, and eventually manifest themselves in action. That is, we can be good at Christian behaviors and still have raunchy attitudes. God's list of quality traits includes things like love, patience, gentleness, peace, hope, joy, forgiveness, etc. Nearly all of these are attitudes and can be manifested in action. God is attitude-oriented. So if you have a bad attitude, if you're full of criticism and complaints and doubts and bitterness, you're on the wrong road.

We are all familiar with our rights. We hear about the Equal Rights Amendment, animal rights, women's rights, our right to bear arms, our constitutional rights, and our right to privacy. Lawyers hound the television, yellow pages, radio, and newspapers telling us to stand up for our rights. Police are told to "read them their rights." The

Miranda Bill covers the right to remain silent and the right to an attorney. But there is one right we rarely hear about these days. It sounds unconstitutional. What we often forget is our God-given right to let go of our rights. The Bible offers little information about rights. It gives us a wealth of insight into sacrifice, giving, and yielding preferences. Those are the attitudes of Jesus, the attitudes of brokenness.

So what does all of this really have to do with brokenness? The answer should be elementary at this point. Brokenness is chiefly an attitude, the attitude of a tamed soul in relationship to its sovereign Creator. Attitude isn't everything; it's the only thing.

Brokenness was the filter through which Jesus lived and responded. It affected His perception of reality and, therefore, His responses. If we want to attempt to do as Jesus did, we must begin to think like Jesus thought and perceive the way Jesus perceived. Philippians chapter two tells us about Jesus' attitude, the attitude of brokenness.

■

GIVING UP OUR RIGHTS

Philippians 2:3 says, "Let nothing be done through selfish ambition or conceit, but in lowliness of mind let each esteem others better than himself." This passage is the appetizer for the main course to follow, commonly known as the "kenosis passage," referring to the word meaning "emptying out". We are each instructed to develop the attitude of Christ. Why? Because we are His followers. We are to emulate our leader.

First of all, Christ did not claim His most basic right, the right to be who He really was. Philippians 2:6–7 says, Jesus "being in the form of God, did not consider it robbery to be equal with God, but made Himself of no reputation." He was God, but did not act on His right as God, even though He was by nature God. This does not mean that Jesus gave up His divinity. Rather, it means He voluntarily gave up the glory, freedom, and honor that was due Him because of His Godness. He was God, but He gave up the right to be Himself when He became a man. Never before had Jesus been confined to just one location. Never before had He intentionally limited Himself to the parameters of a body, requiring food and suffering physical pain and temptations.

Most of us never consider giving up the right to be ourselves. In fact, we often promote that "right" as a necessary requirement to finding fulfillment and self-actualization. But Jesus never sang the song "I've Gotta Be Me." Psychologists counsel us to find ourselves. The Bible says you will not really find yourself until you lose yourself—in God. There is a Ziggy cartoon in which Ziggy is talking to himself in the mirror. "Who are you?" he finally asks himself. Discouraged that he made little progress toward self-discovery, Ziggy walks away. The reflection in the mirror is watching him leave and says, "Get over yourself, Ziggy." That's pretty good theology.

The problem is that we attempt to excuse selfish actions with excuses such as, "That's just the way I am" or "That's my temperament" or "I'm an only child" or "I'm a middle child" or "I came from a broken home" or "I'm a redhead," or "I was born a homosexual." I don't want to appear insensitive to real hurts that need healing, but I am suggesting that we get beyond the popular solution of acting out who we think we are. This type of attitude tends to place our own interests before the needs and interests of others. To put others first out of brokenness is not co-dependency. It is healthy. Some of the most ill and neurotic individuals are those who are stuck on themselves. They can't get out of themselves. "Hey, that's the way I am. Love me or leave me."

Larry Crabb writes, "All our relationship problems spring from one place—the foul well of selfishness. More than anything, what gets in the way of getting along is self-centeredness that seems reasonable [my right]. Poor communication, temper problems, unhealthy responses to dysfunctional family backgrounds, co-dependent relationships, and personal incompatibility—everything (unless medically caused) flows out of the cesspool of self-centeredness."[1] We become particularly self-interested when we are in pain, whether because of a bad mood or problems. "We use our suffering to excuse our self-interest. When our Lord hurt, other-centeredness came naturally: 'Father, forgive them, for they do not know what they are doing.'"[2]

In addition to not demanding His most basic right to be God, neither did Jesus demand special privileges. Jesus never played "Let's Make a Deal." He did not barter with God. The unbroken person tends to be a wheeler-dealer with the Almighty. "Hey, God, if you do this for me, I'll give to the building campaign." "God, if you just get me out of here, I'll start going to church." Our offers often sound like used-car commercials. But Jesus never demanded that God respond a certain way. By the same token, the attitude of brokenness does not demand that the Father respond the way we want Him to respond.

The second major right Jesus gave up in the attitude of brokenness was the right to be something. Philippians 2:7 tells us that Jesus took "the form of a bondservant." We spend a lot of our energy making ourselves something, and trying to keep others from making us nothing. "Be all that you can be!" "Go for it!" "You only go around once in life!" We shouldn't shrivel up and settle for mediocrity, but an unbroken person tends to be humanly motivated, not spiritually motivated. Brokenness purifies our ambitions. If anyone had the right to make something of his life, it was Jesus. And He did, but He did it the broken way, through servanthood.

What motivates you? What sustains you? To understand and apply this attitude, as a pastor I need to disown my ministry periodically. I can easily get caught up in my congregation's "need" for me. This might explain why many people in ministry and the helping professions have co-dependent tendencies, which can be very unhealthy. When you need to be needed, you feed off of others' weaknesses and hurts. The "Messiah complex" is the feeling that you are personally necessary to fix people's lives. Disowning my ministry is not the same as rejecting it out of frustration and anger. It means recommitting it to God. It means stepping back, disengaging a bit, so that I recognize the ministry is God's, not mine. He is the healer. He is the owner.

The same is true of all Christians regarding their families, ministries, and work. When we try to control our families, we are apt to damage them. When we like the power of a certain ministry, it needs to be broken so that we can give it back to God. When we get so involved in our careers that we become unbalanced, so wrapped up in achieving that we get stressed out, so busy we have little time for the Lord, we need breaking. The follower of Christ is one who recognizes that all things are owned by the Father, and we are merely managers of our allotment.

Jesus told a parable about a vineyard owner who rented his vineyard to some workers. The owner sent servants to collect his share of the rent, but the renters started thinking the vineyard belonged to them, so they killed the servants and eventually killed the owner's son too. Stewardship is the concept that all we have is God's, and that He has entrusted us with gifts, resources, and relationships which we are responsible for managing and increasing. Unbroken people start thinking they are owners rather than stewards and strive to make themselves into something with loaned gifts, resources, and relationships.

Abraham went through a very difficult period of bro-kenness when God told him to sacrifice his only son, Isaac. Isaac was supposed to be God's ticket to the prom-ise He had made to Abraham about fathering a powerful nation. Snuffing out the seed of God's people seemed ludicrous. Sacrificing his only son appeared insane. Many things do not make sense when you are being broken. Abraham made the long trek up the mountain, built an altar, tied up his son, and prepared to kill him. He did not whine or wheel and deal with God. He did not doubt the Father. He did not run from God. God was testing Abra-ham, to see which he loved most, his mission or his Mas-ter. God was not supporting murder or child sacrifices. God is not in favor of many of the things we go through during times of testing. But He does need to know our commitments. It is so easy to fall in love with a mission, even a God-given mission, to the point that it becomes our god. The story of Abraham and Isaac is really not about killing Isaac. It has everything to do with the death of Abraham. He died to himself. He was broken, and therefore prepared to carry on the project God had in store for him. Sometimes God does that. He will launch a ministry and then periodically check the loyalties, be-cause loyalties can change. Hearts can turn. Priorities can vacillate.

Scripture says, "The joy of the Lord is our strength." The joy of the Lord needs to be our sustenance. When it is not, we become weak. We may not be unsuccessful, or unproductive, or even unhappy. But we are weak. When our joy comes primarily from something other than serv-ing God, be it a ministry, spouse, family, career, house, or possessions, we are vulnerable. Our driving energy is based on events, and statistics, and things, and people, and situations, all of which are unpredictable.

Much of our life revolves around making ourselves

something. We go to seminars, put in long hours, earn degrees, network social events, and put our best feet forward. These activities are not sinister in themselves, but when you consider how much energy goes into them, you can see how self-promotion can have an overpowering affect on our motivation. When we adopt the popular "winning isn't everything, it's the only thing" attitude, we become unbroken. When this becomes the mode of operation, we must also work hard at keeping others from making us nothing. Office politics at work and one-up-manship become the strategies. We defend ourselves against false accusations or perceptions. Interestingly, Jesus rarely defended himself. He responded to accusations with questions or with simple comments. He was obviously a controversial character, but His attitude of brokenness conveyed security and confidence. His confidence was not the cocky, conceited pseudo-confidence which is usually an overcompensation for feeling inadequate. Rather, He felt at peace before His accusers. Jesus prevailed because He had given up His rights. He was unthreatened by others' attempts to make Him nothing.

The third right we give up when we are broken is our right to win. Philippians 2:8 says, "He humbled Himself and became obedient to the point of death, even the death of the cross." John 1 tells us that Jesus was with God in the beginning, when everything was created. He is the coauthor of life itself, the creator of all living. He had the means and the knowledge and the power to win over death. Our culture says, "If you've got it, flaunt it; if you don't have it, fake it 'til you make it." But emptying ourselves means sometimes not winning (voluntarily) out of humility, even when we have the power to win.

In Matthew 4, Satan tempted Jesus in the wilderness. One of the temptations involved jumping off a high point and calling His angels to catch Him. He was God. He had the power. He had the ability. But He did not usurp His right. An old hymn talks about Jesus on the cross and says, "He could have called, 10,000 angels, but He bled and died, for you and me." We cannot imagine the restraint needed for the Creator of life to allow one of His creations to purposefully end His life. "Do you know who I am?" He could have said. But in a broken attitude, He humbled himself to death—even death on a cross. Jesus hung between two thieves. The association left no question of what the accusers thought of Him. This was death in its worst setting. Crucifixion was a slow, torturous death, used as Rome's crime prevention program. People saw the agony. They would come and mock and vent their anger on criminals who took advantage of their society. Jesus could have won. But He chose not to win, so that we could win, when we deserved to lose.

The broken person does not need to have the last word in confrontations. He or she does not have to burn the bridge in a relationship in order to correct a misunderstanding. The manager need not fire a discontented employee, even when he has that right. A minister does not have to tell everyone the truth and justify himself, in order to ask for forgiveness for something of which he is innocent. This does not make sense to the world. Common sense says if you have the ability, take the promotion, sign the deal, win the race. Broken people realize that you can win and still end up losing.

■

DEATH OF SELF-WILL

Death is often associated with times of brokenness. The kenosis passage refers to Jesus' obedience to death. Jesus said "Unless a grain of wheat falls into the ground and dies, it remains alone; but if it dies, it produces much grain. He who loves his life will lose it, and he who hates his life in this world will keep it for eternal life" (John 12:24–25). The sacraments of baptism and communion are symbols of death. Job refers to death. Paul talks about death several times: "Put to death the deeds of the body" (Rom. 8:13); "Reckon yourselves dead indeed to sin" (Rom. 6:11); "I affirm, by the boasting in you which I have in Christ Jesus our Lord, I die daily" (1 Cor. 15:31); "For you died, and your life is hidden with Christ in God. . . . Therefore put to death your members which are on the earth" (Col. 3:3,5); "For we know that our old self was crucified with him so that the bond of sin might be rendered powerless, because anyone who has died has been freed from sin" (Rom. 6:6–7). I used to think it was enough to kneel at the altar and pray for my concerns and worship God. I have come to realize that is not enough. God wants me on the altar.

Some of the above passages involve more than the concept of brokenness. However, the feel of death is in the air during the breaking process. Jesus gathered His disciples with the simple challenge, "Follow me." But if you follow Him all the way, you see that His destination was the cross, to lay down His life. "I am the good shepherd. A good shepherd lays down his life for his sheep." Believing in Christ is much easier than following him. I can watch my son play, but when he says, "Let's play follow the leader," my task is to copy his lead. Following is all-engaging. Dennis Kinlaw wrote, "We want to manage our lives, because we don't know what Jesus will require from us; but the truth is we're never safe until we've gotten our hands off the last control knob, until we have forfeited our right to ourselves."[3] And it is our own death that we avoid. Dr. Ernest Becker said, "The idea of death, the fear of it, haunts the human animal like nothing else; it is a mainspring of human activity—activity designed largely to avoid the fatality of death, to overcome it by denying in some way that it is the final destiny for man."[4] "Then said Jesus to his disciples, 'If anyone desires to come after Me, let him deny himself, and take up his cross, and follow Me'" (Matt. 16:24). "I beseech you therefore, brethren, by the mercies of God, that you present your bodies a living sacrifice [live as if you've died], holy, acceptable to God, which is your reasonable service" (Rom. 12:1). The act of pruning results in a loss of branches. Even though the end result is good and what was cut was not beneficial, when a part of you dies you still mourn.

Watchman Nee defined death as "the cessation of communication with the environment." It is not so much a lack of existence as it is being rendered powerless. "What is lacking today is not a better living but a better dying! We need to die a good death, a thorough death. We have talked enough about life, power, holiness, righteousness; let us now take a look at death!"[5] Augustine said, "It's only in the face of death that man's self is born." Oswald Chambers wrote, "This fundamental principle must be borne in mind, that any work for God before it fulfills its purpose must die, otherwise it 'abides alone.' The conception is not that of progress from a seed to full growth, but of a seed dying and bringing forth what it never was. That is why Christianity is always 'a forlorn hope' in the eyes of the world."[6]

Elisabeth Kübler-Ross developed a well-known theory of the emotional stages we experience at the loss of a loved one. Initially, there is a sense of shock and numbness. This becomes a stage of denial. "No, this can't be. He can't be dead. She's still alive, this is all a mistake." Next comes anger. "God, why did you do this? This person was too young to die, too good to die, too needed to die." The anger stage is the point at which many people become wounded. Their wounds fester and result in feelings of despair and hopelessness and an underlying cynicism throughout their lives. Hopefully, people work through the anger stage toward acceptance and finally adaptation. Sometimes people say they are over a death, but still dwell on memories and ask "Why?". When this happens, some fixation is present and healing is not yet complete. The end result should be a person who has faced reality and has emerged stronger.

This path is common among all sorts of death, whether it's the death of a dream, a goal, a relationship, a personal interest, or even the death of the old nature. The emotional response during the breaking process often has many similarities to the mourning process. In Matthew 5:4 Jesus said, "Blessed are those who mourn, for they shall be comforted." The word *blessed* there means happy or contented. Happy are the sad? The word for mourning in that verse is the most severe form of the word, as in those who mourn for the dead. It is a gut-wrenching, nauseating, sobbing feeling.

The paradox continues . . . they will be blessed, happy, content. This does not make sense to most people. Jesus knew mourning. When His friend Lazarus died, Jesus knew He had the power to raise him, and that He was the resurrection of life, but He still wept. The shortest verse in the Bible, the one kids memorize in Bible school to get extra points, expresses His grief. "Jesus wept" (John 11:35). It is salient, unhindered by burdensome, flowery words. This is a part of the breaking process as you mourn in varying degrees your own death, the death of the old self or part of it.

As you study adult development, you find that one of the major events in the midlife transition, especially for men, is confronting one's own mortality. Prior to midlife you look at how long you have lived. At midlife you begin looking at how much time you have left. You see that your body is aging, and it fails to respond as it once did. You become more aware of illnesses. You know peers who have suffered heart attacks, cancer, and who have died. Midlife is a transition where you put away your youthfulness and prepare for older age. No one would admit to believing they will never die, but they live like it. Around midlife, we often mourn the loss of youth, as we face our own mortality. We will die. You will die. We will not stay young forever. This experience is often called "midlife crisis" because most men (80 percent) admit to a feeling of loss during this period. It can include elements of mourning like minor depression, the desire for solitude, sadness, and a reflection on priorities. This transition can also be a wonderful time of brokenness.

Paul had a transition of priorities when he said, "I also count all things loss for the excellency of the knowledge of Christ Jesus my Lord, for whom I have suffered the loss of all things, and count them as rubbish, that I may gain Christ" (Phil. 3:8). Job sat in ashes as he mourned his loss and breaking. Jehosaphat called for people to fast and pray when they were about to be attacked by the Moabites and Ammonites (2 Chron. 20). The people of Nineveh put on sackcloth and sat in the dust to convey their repentance. An interesting similarity exists between feeling the loss of a loved one who has died and the conviction of sin and repentance in the Bible. Both involve mourning. Brokenness is similar to both of these events. The death of a dream hurts. If you are like Uncle Remus singing "Zippidy Doo Da," you are not experiencing brokenness. Even as you become aware of what needs to happen in your life, relinquishing selfishness, submitting your goals, or surrendering your rights, you still feel a sense of loss in your life. A part of yourself is being put to death, even if it is a loathsome, fruitless part.

We sometimes perform a disservice to those who are

experiencing this process when we try to make them happy. This happens because we are personally uncomfortable with someone else's pain. We try to make people happy quickly, so that their turmoil does not threaten our own shaky contentment. "Our task is not to offer information, advice, or even guidance, but to allow others to come into touch with their own struggles, pains, doubts, and insecurities—in short, to affirm their life as a quest. All teachers of religion are constantly in danger of becoming like Job's friends, anxiously avoiding the painful search and nervously filling the gap created by unanswerable questions."[7] There is a time to weep, and a time to mourn. God makes everything beautiful in its time.

Feeling loss is perfectly acceptable. It is a part of the healing process. However, a person who cannot escape the mourning process may have become broken in the wrong places, for joy does return in the springtime, as blossoms and fruit appear where there once were bare sticks. Joy comes in the morning. But during the loss, go on walks, cry, talk to God, and let the process run its course. "In the days of His flesh, when He had offered up prayers and supplications, with vehement cries and tears to Him who was able to save Him from death, and He was heard because of His godly fear, though He was a Son, yet He learned obedience by the things which He suffered" (Heb. 5:7–8). Among Jesus' last words before He died were, "Father, into Your hands I commit my spirit" (Luke 23:46). Stephen, at his martyr's death, stated, "Lord Jesus, receive my spirit" (Acts 7:59). These are the last words of everyone who is broken in the right place. Father, into your hands I commit my spirit, my will, my motives, my dreams, my job, my family, my relationships, my body, my emotions, my expectations, my rights. The final surrender is the passing of the spirit.

Aristotle, in his analysis of virtue, says that to truly be virtuous, one must find his or her *telos.* In classical Greek, *telos* referred to an end, a meaning, a purpose in life. Just after Jesus committed His spirit to the Lord, as His lungs exhaled their last breath of air, He yelled, "It is finished!" (John 19:30). This is only one word in the Greek, from the root word *telos.* This was not the desperate cry of a failed Messiah, "Thank God, I'm finally going to die so the pain can stop." This was an exclamation of victory and a sense of completion. Although vastly different in its intensity, it is similar to the sigh of relief a painter gives as he makes the last stroke on his masterpiece. It is the panting of weary affirmation by the mountaineer who has just planted his flag on the rocky summit. It is the joyful cry of fulfillment a mother gives as she sees the newborn infant who just caused her so much pain. "It is finished!!!" Such is the mission of spiritual endeavor, to place our souls into the hands of our Creator. This is not the end. It is just the beginning, the sealing of our purpose.

■

THE RESULT OF OUR INNER DEATH

The paradox continues, for it says in Philippians chapter two that the result of Jesus' emptying Himself, and becoming nothing, and modeling servanthood as God, and becoming obedient to death, is that "God also has highly exalted Him to the highest place and given Him the name which is above every name, that at the name of Jesus every knee should bow, of those in heaven, and of those on earth, and of those under the earth, and that every tongue should confess that Jesus Christ is Lord, to the glory of God the Father" (Phil. 2:9–11). He who voluntarily became the least has become the greatest. A time will come when every person who ever lived will realize that Jesus really is who He says He is, and every single one will kneel before Him. Unfortunately, for many it will be too late, but they will still acknowledge His supreme position. To be broken is to voluntarily accept the inevitable future today. It is recognizing that Christ is Lord, and that someday you will bow down and worship Him. You want to do it now, not later.

To understand this paradox of emptying in order to be exalted, I should also consider what rebelling against the breaking process is going to cost me. Dietrich Bonhoeffer titled his famous book, *The Cost of Discipleship.* He knew and understood the concept of brokenness. But if we understand the nature of the Kingdom of God, we must look at the even higher cost of not accepting brokenness. We will not be exalted. We will not experience intimacy with God. We will not gain what we could have achieved, by clinging and groping desperately to our rights. We will never realize all we have, until all we have is Christ.

The fourth right we give up for brokenness is the right to be respected. Paul continues his writing about Jesus' attitude by describing how it should show up in our lives. "Do all things without complaining and disputing" (Phil. 2:14). Most complaints, arguments, and personal tensions result when people with unsurrendered rights come in contact with each other. Dead people do not complain or argue. In Numbers 14, the people of Israel grumbled and complained about Moses and his leadership in crossing over into the Promised Land. God had to take them through the breaking process and lead them back into the wilderness for forty years of wandering. We often wander aimlessly through life when we are unbroken. Brokenness helps us see God's will and submit to it, giving us direction and purpose.

"Self-centeredness convincingly and continually whispers to me that nothing in this universe is more important than my need to be accepted and respectfully treated.

Nothing is more necessary to understand than my neediness, and all its complexity and depth."[8] When you demand that people respect you, even though it may be your right, your life will be full of contention and disappointment. It is amazing how much stress results because we insist upon standing up for our rights. "I have the right to my opinion!" "I have the right to be served on time!" "I have the right to this lane! I was here first." "It's my right to be loved by you. You need to treat me better." Leonard Bernstein, the great conductor, said, "The most difficult position to fill in an orchestra is second fiddle." We all want to be first chair. I can probably safely say that the basis of most neuroses is our unwillingness to be broken in the right place. The person who voluntarily gives up his or her right for respect out of strength emerges as the more powerful person. This person cannot be intimidated. When we are intimidated by others, we tend to either imitate them or be paralyzed by them.

It takes two to argue, but only one to complain. Arguing is a dialogue of not getting your way. Complaining is a monologue of the same. Basically, sin is placing your choice before the right choice. We tend to argue and complain when we feel we did not get our choice. The broken person does not demand his most basic of rights, to be respected. He or she does not criticize when the service is less than expected. This is not to imply that this person is intentionally masochistic. A masochist seeks abuse and pain out of low self-esteem, feeling he deserves it. Jesus died, but not due to a martyr complex. The broken person does not respond out of his rights, but out of his surrendered rights.

Paul says that out of such an attitude "you may become blameless and harmless, children of God without fault in the midst of a crooked and perverse generation, among whom you shine as lights in the world" (Phil. 2:14–15). The paradox continues. As you give up your rights, you excel. You shine like a star against the cold black backdrop of the cosmos. We think that to stand out, to reach the top, to become a star, we have to stick up for our rights and promote ourselves. God says just the opposite. In putting down our rights we build ourselves up. Why? Because the natural inclination for everyone is to promote oneself and one's rights. When you trust God, you do not need to do your own promotion. Brokenness is letting God take over your public relations department. "For to this you were called, because Christ also suffered for us, leaving us an example, that you should follow His steps. . . . who, when He was reviled, did not revile in turn; when He suffered, He did not threaten, but committed Himself to Him who judges righteously" (1 Peter 2:21–23). Your goal is to be blameless and pure. The self-centered life loves to be noticed by others. God will do your PR. He will blow your whistle. He will advance you, in His time, in His way. He's got your address when it's time for the promotion. The way to shine in life is not seeing how big you can get, or how far you can go, or how much you can obtain. Rather, you shine by taking on the attitude of Christ and living a life enlarged by brokenness.

Oswald Sanders wrote:

> Because we children of Adam want to become great
> He became small.
> Because we will not stoop,
> He humbled himself.
> Because we want to rule,
> He came to serve.[9]

Being broken enlarges your capacity for life. Being unbroken dwarfs your capacity for love and for God. The pruning process appears to make us smaller, but the result is that we become much more productive. The difficult part is realizing that truth and trusting God. Breaking provides some of the pain and motivation necessary to trust Him. Barren parts of your life are draining, burdensome. When you are tired of carrying the load, unload. Christ gave up his rights from the beginning. Most of us must work in stages. Following is a daily checklist for the attitude of brokenness.

■

ATTITUDE CHECKS FOR BROKENNESS

1. Am I willing to let go of my dreams and ambitions if such is God's will?
2. Am I defensive when accused, or criticized, or misunderstood?
3. Am I coveting what others have instead of waiting for heaven's rewards?
4. Am I forgiving when offended, with or without an apology?
5. Am I complaining or arguing out of unsurrendered rights?
6. Am I thinking of others first out of love?
7. Am I proudly appearing that I am always right or know all the answers?
8. Am I practicing the spiritual disciplines (prayer, fasting, solitude, simplicity, etc.)?
9. Am I being silent regarding self-promotion and letting God do my public relations?
10. Am I daily saying, "God, whatever it takes, I'm willing to submit to your leadership?"
11. Am I expressing joy in the difficulties which serve to refine me?
12. Am I taking risks out of obedience to Christ instead of giving in to fear, pride, or denial?

■

QUESTIONS FOR REFLECTION

1. "Attitude isn't everything; it's the only thing." Discuss the pros and cons of that statement. How is attitude underestimated in "the real world"?

2. Of the rights that Jesus gave up, which do you struggle with the most as you consider them?

3. How does the concept of death relate to brokenness? What are the similar emotions and thoughts of the two?

4. As you think of your telos, your purpose and meaning in life, what would it take for you to say, "It is finished"? Another approach to this question is, "What would you like your epitaph to be?"

5. Which of the daily attitude checks do you find the easiest? Which do you find the most difficult?

Where a man's wound is, that is where his genius
will be. Wherever the wound appears in our
psyche, that is exactly where we will give our major gift to the community.

—Robert Bly

CHAPTER
EIGHT

■

Voluntary
Brokenness

■ ■ ■

*I showed up outside the screen door and my little
daughter spotted me. "That's my daddy!" There were hugs
for the little girl but no kissing between parents. My wife
and I sat and stared at each other. My wife saw the tor-
ment in my eyes, and it cut her to the heart. "He's not
well," she thought. "He's done it all, tried everything, and
there's nothing left. He's a truly broken spirit. The cocky
kid who went his own way and blew his mind on drugs is
no more."*

*Later, at a church service, the speaker asked, "Does
anybody here want to receive Jesus Christ as your Savior
and Lord? I want you to stand right now."*

*"I'm not going to join them," I thought. "I know all this. I
couldn't stand if I wanted to. It's just too humiliating. I'm
not a teenager; I'm twenty-six years old." Something was
indeed happening in the universe. It happens every time*

a human being finds his way home. A wandering star was coming back into orbit. The freaked-out flower child, the apotheosis of the lost generation, was about to turn into a servant of the Most High. Whatever my reservations, I knew my moment of decision had come. There on the floor in the remotest corner of the packed church, I surrendered my life to Jesus Christ, not as a boy, but as a man. This time the war was over. I had put down my gun; the capitulation was complete. I was forever changed.

—Mike MacIntosh

■

IN HIS STEPS

As newlyweds, Nancy and I once stayed in a grand, old hotel in Brussels, Belgium. On our jaunt through major sites in Western Europe, we made a hobby of observing the styles and furnishings of various bathrooms from culture to culture. While investigating the Brussels bathroom, we came upon a chain hanging from the ceiling and could not figure out a practical purpose for it. We pulled on it. Nothing happened. We yanked on it several times. No water flushed. No light came on. Nothing seemed to occur. What a strange thing.

On our way out for lunch, I stopped at the front desk and asked, "We noticed a chain coming out of the ceiling and down to the floor. What is that for?" The desk keeper responded, "That is an emergency chain. If you have an emergency, you pull on it. It alerts us and we come to your room to assist you." I smiled sheepishly. "Well, I pulled that chain and no one came." He said, "Oh yes, whenever Americans come we just ignore the alarms because they are always pulling them." How silly I felt.

We do a lot of silly things as humans. We look all over for our reading glasses and find them conveniently propped on our heads. We cannot find our keys anywhere, only to discover them concealed in our hand. For three years I sat in an office chair that was too low for my desk. People commented on it from time to time and I laughed it off, because I had tried to find a height adjuster, but could not. A Mr. Fix-it type fellow in our church doubted my prognosis one day and tipped the chair over. "There you go," he said, turning a screw. Sure enough, within moments I was seated behind my desk as I should have been for the previous three years.

A silly thing we Christians do is to earnestly attempt to live Christlike lives on our own. At best we behave as the people in Charles Sheldon's book, *In His Steps,* who responded to life's scenarios with the question, "What would Jesus do?" The concept is appealing. But we find our behavior consistently appalling. Why? Most Christians cannot live out the answers, even if they know what to do, because they are not empowered to truly do as Jesus did. How silly for us to think we can act like Jesus when we fail to practice the lifestyle which enabled Him to respond to people and circumstances as He did. Society looks at faith today as something that *should* make us different, not as something that *does.*

We are mistaken when we think that following Jesus consists only of going the second mile, loving our enemies, turning the other cheek, and suffering with patience, while we live the remainder of our lives "just like everyone else." G.K. Chesterston said, "Christianity has not so much been tried and found wanting, as it has been found difficult and left untried." Matthew 11:29–30 says, "Take My yoke upon you and learn from Me, for I am gentle and lowly in heart, and you will find rest for your souls. For My yoke is easy and My burden is light." Who is he kidding . . . easy, light? Our common human failing is wanting what is right and important, but not commiting to the kind of life that will produce right actions and an enjoyable existence.

Carl Jung said, "Neurosis is always a substitute for legitimate suffering." If Jung was correct, that might explain why our society is so neurotic. Perhaps we have attempted to avoid the breaking process which, when it happens in the right place, produces health and wholeness. What did Jesus mean when He said His yoke is gentle and his burden is light? How can this be, when Christianity is humanly impossible?

Brokenness is more than just the intellectual realization that human efforts are not enough; it is confronting that truth with our emotions. Consider some of the following thoughts. "We can't free and purify our own heart by exerting our own will. Willpower has no defense against the careless word, the unguarded moment."[1] "Unless the LORD builds the house, they labor in vain who build it" (Ps. 127:1). "Oh Lord, I know the way of man is not in himself; it is not in man who walks to direct his own steps" (Jer. 10:23). "Not that we are sufficient of ourselves to think of anything as being from ourselves but our sufficiency is from God" (2 Cor. 3:5).

■

EMPOWERED CHRISTIANITY

How can we live powerful lifestyles? The biblical response to that question is the power of the Holy Spirit. But before we experience the power of the Holy Spirit, we must experience brokenness. We have to be emptied out so that infilling can happen. Just as the wild stallion needs to be tamed for the rider to have his will, so the human soul needs taming so that God can have His will. Otherwise, we are forever bucking off the Holy Spirit. "For I know that nothing good lives in me, that is, in my sinful nature. For I have the desire to do what is good but I cannot carry it out. For what I do is not the good I want to do; no, the evil I do not want to do . . . this I keep on doing. For in my inner being I delight in God's law; but I see another law at work in the members of my body, waging war against the law of my mind and making me a prisoner of the law of sin at work within my members. What a wretched man I am. Who will rescue me from this body of death?" (Rom. 7:18–24). The solution comes in Romans 12:1, "Present your bodies a living sacrifice." To withhold our bodies from Christianity is to exclude Christianity from our lives. We are to present the parts of our bodies as instruments of righteousness. St. Francis of Assisi called the body "Brother Ass" (donkey). We are to ride it and not have it ride us. Salvation is not just forgiveness. It is also a new order of life. But how do you do something so subjective as "salvation"? It makes for great preaching, but what about pragmatics?

I live in a neighborhood where most of the landscaping is maintained by hired workers. I have noticed that every Friday, the team of men drive up in their trucks, unload lawnmowers, trimmers, and leaf blowers to do their weekly tasks. I also notice that periodically, though seldom, they will make an extra effort to do some major trimming, like cutting back the hedges and pulling out a whole line of plants. The extra effort represents the periods of brokenness that occur in our lives. The regular mowing and clipping are more like the behaviors of brokenness that we implement in our lives. They can also help us avoid the need for those major clippings at times.

Earlier I mentioned the two strains of the breaking process, voluntary and involuntary. The involuntary is that which pops up when we least expect it. It appears in the form of health issues, financial distress, relationship turmoil, job disruption, dream frustrations, aging milestones, and periods of spiritual and emotional dryness. What makes such times difficult is that we discover our finiteness and our need to turn over new parts of our lives to the Lord.

This book focuses on those few, specific episodes in life when we go through a major pruning. These are involuntary life situations which serve to break us in the right place. There are multitudinous events which come our way, involuntarily, which can serve as lessons in brokenness. Whether an illness, a job loss, a frustrating boss or relative, a betrayal by a friend, or just the stress of thwarted goals, these regular bumps and bruises can tenderize us if our attitudes are right. If we respond poorly, we are likely to become critical, cynical, and stressed out. Becoming tender is the way of faith.

The Apostle Paul talked about his thorn in the flesh (2 Cor. 12:7–8) and the long list of hazards he had endured for the sake of the gospel (2 Cor. 11:16–29). No doubt such occurrences would have emotionally broken a person who was not spiritually broken. Instead, they likely allowed Paul to maintain his supple spirit before the Lord by constantly reminding him how much he must depend on spiritual power and not physical or intellectual power. He cheered when the Lord said, "My grace is sufficient for you, for My strength is made perfect in weakness" (2 Cor. 12:9). Paul boasts in his weaknesses. An untamed soul tries to hide its weak spots. "That is why for Christ's sake, I delight in weaknesses, in insults, in hardships, in persecutions, in difficulties. For when I am weak, then I am strong" (2 Cor. 12:9–10).

Many of Paul's trials helped him maintain an attitude of brokenness and a heart-allegiance to God. How do we maintain such a spirit? Most weight-reduction programs demand a somewhat arduous, disciplined regimen to get the first several pounds off. Then, a less strenuous maintenance program is suggested. In a similar fashion, periods of brokenness tame the soul and cause us to respond humbly to God. Voluntary brokenness often serves as a maintenance plan to perpetuate the conditions and fruit of a tamed soul.

■

THE BEHAVIORS OF BROKENNESS

Many people God used in the Bible did not seem to go through involuntary brokenness, or at least we have no record of it. Daniel and his cohorts were sold out for God. John the Baptist presents a lifetime of apparent selflessness. Joseph experienced difficult circumstances and grew in wisdom. It was not brokenness he needed as much as experience that would have taught him not to flaunt his anointing in front of his parents and brothers. But as far as we know, his heart was in allegiance with God's.

Why is everyday Christianity so difficult? For the same reason you cannot go out and run a marathon if you have not been training. The same reason you cannot go out and win a tennis, or golf, or volleyball tournament if you have not been practicing. It is the same reason you cannot bench press 250 pounds if you have been lifting only a fork and a remote control.

Shouldn't there be a way to voluntarily maintain an attitude of brokenness? Wouldn't it be nice if we could strengthen our spiritual muscles on top of the involuntary processes in our lives? The good news is that God has provided a way for us to maintain tamed souls. Voluntary brokenness is the intentional exercise of submitting yourself to God. It is initiating the attitude of surrender as a continuance of prior breaking, and can also serve as a prevention for the need for future breaking. Much of this activity revolves around the spiritual disciplines I have named, the behaviors of brokenness.

"Do you not know that those who run in a race all run,

but one receives the prize? Run in such a way that you may obtain it. And everyone who competes for the prize is temperate in all things. Now they do it to obtain a perishable crown, but we for an imperishable crown. Therefore I run thus: not with uncertainty. Thus I fight: not as one who beats the air. But I discipline my body and bring it into subjection, lest, when I have preached to others, I myself should become disqualified" (I Cor. 9:24–27).

Spiritual disciplines are little different than physical and mental disciplines. Our spiritual muscles require regular exercise for us to be strong, confident, and energetic. Like athletic champions, we must choose a life of preparation, but we prepare the soul. A basketball team conditions, practices, and plays a game. The success of the last two require the first. In the pastorate, we find practicing (administration and sermon preparation) consumes most of our time, leading up to the main event (ministry). All too often, we are less effective than desired because we have failed to condition properly. When you look at a tree, you only see a part of it. Unseen are cumulative miles of roots which serve to not only feed and nourish the tree, but also to anchor it against gravity and other external stresses. During moments of crisis, a person with a strong, developed character will stand firm. We look at Jesus' actions, see His miracles, and read about His responses under pressure. But we need to look at his "off" times to see how He practiced. "The spirit indeed is willing, but the flesh is weak" (Matt. 26:41).

"But to obtain these gifts, you need more than faith; you must also work hard to be good, and even that is not enough. For then you must learn to know God better and discover what he wants you to do. Next, learn to put aside your own desires so that you will become patient and godly, gladly letting God have his way with you. This will make possible the next step, which is for you to enjoy other people and to like them, and finally you will grow to love them deeply. The more you go on in this way, the more you will grow strong spiritually and become faithful and useful to our Lord Jesus Christ" (2 Peter 1:5–8 TLB).

John Wesley wrote, "It was a common saying among the Christians of the primitive church, 'The soul and the body make a man; the spirit and discipline make a Christian;' implying that none could be real Christians without the help of Christian discipline. But if this be so, is it any wonder that we find so few Christians; for where is Christian discipline?" Most of our Christian training centers around giving time, attending services, donating money, praying, reading the Bible, witnessing, and doing ministry. But most average church members have very little confidence in their own abilities for spiritual work. Modest estimates show that over 25 percent of the entire U.S. population profess an evangelical conversion experience. William Iverson remarked, "A pound of meat would surely be affected by a quarter pound of salt. If this is real Christianity, the salt of the earth, where is the effect of which Jesus spoke?" Thomas Aquinas walked among the splendors of Rome and a friend said to him, "We Christians certainly no longer have to say to the world, 'Silver and gold have we none.'" St. Thomas replied, "But neither can we say to the lame man, 'In the name of Jesus of Nazareth rise up and walk.'"

Hebrews 5:8 says that Jesus "learned obedience by the things which He suffered." Brokenness is not necessarily always a removal of carnality or rebellion. Sometimes it is merely an expansion of capacity, a fortification of character, and a seasoning toward maturity. As long as Jesus had a body, He knew He had to practice certain disciplines. These tend to be private and personal, but they are vital. When the Olympic runner steps into the blocks, most of the world has no idea of the training that has been going on for years: early mornings in the cold, while feeling sick, without support, in spite of pain. But we applaud and envy the results. Jesus went into the wilderness forty days before His ministry. After He fed the 5000 He went off by Himself to pray. He entered the Garden of Gethsemane for an evening of prayer prior to His crucifixion. We catch glimpses of His private life which give us insight into the power behind His public ministry.

Voluntary brokenness is the practice of spiritual ascetics. The Greek word from which we get the term *asceticism* simply means exercising. Many of us confuse asceticism with the holy monk, secluded in some distant monastery, oblivious to parenting, traffic, taxes, and the lusts and temptations of the real world. But asceticism differs from monasticism in that the latter refers to an escape from the world. Monasticism came into practice under the belief that if a little solitude and practice of the disciplines was good, a whole life of it would be great. Many believed that forgiveness or merit could be gained by hating the body or suffering. But spiritual discipline is not penance or a way to manipulate God. Macarius of Alexandria ate no cooked food for seven years, exposed his naked body to poisonous flies, did not lie down to sleep for 40–50 years, and went years without speaking a word. When normal Christians hear of such a lifestyle, we offer our congratulatory praise, and then dismiss it as some melodramatic behavior, foreign to our intentions. These sorts of accounts have separated the rest of us from the ascetic "exercise" of spiritual disciplines because we think they are reserved for holy and/or eccentric people destined for a monastery. Surely they are not for a businessperson, homemaker, or student. Mainstream Christians consider such practices fanatical and strange.

A simplistic definition of monasticism says, "Get me

out of the world." A simple definition for asceticism is, "Get the world out of me." Voluntary brokenness and heart-allegiance take the form of several of the ascetic behaviors. The purpose of the spiritual disciplines is liberation from stifling slavery to self-interest and fear. Most involve self-denial, which is a humble dethroning of self. Asceticism for asceticism's sake is like body building or dieting out of self-admiration or self-obsession rather than for health reasons.

A woman came in for counseling after numerous affairs and self-indulgent binges of alcohol and drugs. She broke down in relief when she came to understand that she did not have to continue this lifestyle. She cried, "You mean I don't have to do what I want?" Some people believe the body is evil, sort of a modern gnosticism, but when the body occupies its proper place in the hierarchy of the universe, it is not evil because it belongs to the divine world. The body is evil only when it usurps the place of something higher. Gordon MacDonald said, "An unguarded strength and an unprepared heart are double weaknesses."[2] I have labeled the spiritual disciplines as behaviors of brokenness because they emulate the self-denial that occurs during the breaking process. They condition the soul by reminding the rest of the self that it does not have to give in to its natural impulses and yearnings. This periodic exercising is a voluntary response which creates the feel of loss, pruning, and surrender.

Most people do not practice the piano to practice the piano. They practice the piano so they can learn to play well. Likewise, the behaviors of brokenness are activities carried on to prepare us indirectly for some activity other than itself. They serve as means to an end, namely, the stretching and conditioning of the soul. Even though a horse is broken, the trainer saddles up regularly and takes the steed through given routines. The character development process of spiritual disciplines tones and exercises important aspects of the inner person. Experience tells us that almost anything worth doing in life is very difficult in its early stages. In fact, the more difficult behaviors are the ones that are better for you because they reflect weak areas where you may need breaking.

Several new books, workshops, and articles have appeared in the last decade or two and have inspired a new look at these biblical and early church traditions. Much of the following material is a synthesis of these resources. (I heavily used Richard Foster's *Celebration of the Disciplines* and Dallas Willard's *Spirit of the Disciplines*.)

The disciplines need not be boring, stuffy, or joyless exercises. God doesn't want a bunch of stiff, unfeeling, obsessive, and dissatisfied followers trying to impress people for Christ. Here are some brief descriptions of the behaviors of voluntary brokenness.

■

SPIRITUAL DISCIPLINES

The single most obvious trait of those who profess Christ, but who do not grow into Christlikeness, is their refusal to take the reasonable and time-tested measures of spiritual growth. Church consultant Dan Reeves notes, "I almost never meet someone in spiritual coldness, perplexity, and distress, who is regular in the use of these spiritual exercises that will be obvious to anyone familiar with the contents of the New Testament."[3] (Although some lists of spiritual disciplines include worship and prayer as specific practices, I feel that worship and prayer are basic Christian behaviors. They are not so much disciplines as they are essential ingredients for a basic ongoing relationship with God. Therefore, I have avoided placing them in the following list of the behaviors of brokenness, which tend to be more personalized and less utilized on a daily basis.)

Most writers break up the practices into two major groups, the disciplines of abstinence and the disciplines of activity. The abstinence behaviors represent a withdrawal from certain areas of life—not doing something you may normally do. These practices provide a sense of loss because you are surrendering your natural inclinations. They teach your soul what it is like to not indulge in its wishes, when God would have your surrendered life not participate in something. The body often becomes the workout room in which this conditioning takes place. The disciplines of activity involve intentionally doing things that you would ordinarily find challenging and not do. This teaches us the other side of maintaining a disciplined soul, responding to God when He calls us to do something that would be against our normal inclinations.

Experiment with each of the following disciplines so you are familiar with them and can apply them as needed. You will find times when you need certain exercises. Apply them. You will enjoy three or four of them more than others. Use these periodically. This is a personal practice. Avoid having someone else tell you how often or to what degree you should use them. They are to serve as your conditioning program for a strong, supple soul.

Behaviors of Abstinence

1. Solitude This behavior separates us from social activity for a significant amount of time. Most people hate being alone because we are so conditioned to being busy, doing, listening, talking, and thinking. Solitude is choosing to be alone with yourself, isolated from other humans and hectic activity. Much of our hurried living is lived out of pride, self-importance, fear, or lack of faith. Solitude grants freedom from ingrained behaviors that hinder our integration into God's order. Some research shows that it takes twenty times more amphetamine drugs to kill one mouse than it takes to kill a whole group of mice. Experimenters also found that a mouse given no amphetamine at all and placed in a group of mice that are on that drug will be dead within ten minutes. Western men and women talk a great deal about being individuals, but our conformity to social pattern is hardly less remarkable than that of the mice and just as deadly. We fail to recognize the needs of our souls. Most of us avoid good solitude because it is hard work.

Henry David Thoreau wrote, "The poor fellow who walks away with the greatest number of letters, proud of his extensive correspondence, has not heard from himself this long while." Christian meditation goes beyond the notion of detachment. We must focus on attachment to God and others. "We can cultivate an inner solitude and silence that sets us free from loneliness and fear. Loneliness is inner emptiness. Solitude is inner fulfillment."

Solitude typically ranges from three hours to a multiday event of intentionally withdrawing from the normal pace of life to pray, worship, study, and meditate on your spiritual life and God. For me, a half-day visit to a nearby retreat center once per month is a good solitude discipline. I have also used monasteries and state parks for more prolonged times of solitude.

2. Silence Silence can be experienced in solitude or in community. It is the quiet contemplation of thoughts verbalizing a response. It is hearing your soul talk. Silence goes beyond solitude, and without it solitude has little effect. Henri Nouwen observes that "silence is the way to make solitude reality." Miguel do Unamuno said, "We need to pay less attention to what people are trying to tell us, and more to what they tell us without trying." Silence helps teach us this. Thomas à Kempis wrote, "It is easier to be silent altogether than to speak with moderation."

"Silence is intimately related to trust, because the tongue is our most powerful weapon of manipulation. We are constantly in the process of adjusting our public image. We fear so deeply what we think other people see in us, so we talk in order to straighten out their understanding. Silence allows us to believe God can justify and set things straight."[4] I have found that silence is natural during times of solitude, but it can also be implemented at home and with groups during a silent retreat. Silence withdraws us from most interactions with others and, after awhile, forces us to communicate with our own souls and with the Holy Spirit.

3. Fasting Giving up food or other physical pleasure is a way of showing your free will is functioning and that you prioritize God's sustenance. This practice can humiliate us by revealing how much our peace depends upon the pleasures of eating. Fasting confirms our utter dependence upon God by finding Him to be a source of sustenance beyond food. Fasting before the Lord is therefore feasting on him and doing his will.

Thomas à Kempis wrote, "Refrain from gluttony and thou shalt the more easily restrain all the inclinations of the flesh." Fasting teaches us the ability to say "no" to physical temptations. By not eating, we learn temperance and self-control, as well as moderation and restraint, with regard to all our fundamental drives. Hedonistic people, those who indulge in sex, food, or drugs, have not learned to surrender their appetites to God. Fasting is a hard discipline to practice without having our attention consumed by it, but it needs to be utilized to the point that we stay focused on it rather than preoccupied by it. "Too many are trying to conquer problems such as procrastination, impatience, or pride, while still a slave to their appetites. If we can't control the body and its appetites, how can we ever control our tongue or overcome our passions and the emotions of anger, envy, jealousy, or hatred?"[5]

Fasting can involve appetites other than the desire for food. Paul says, "I beat my body." Typically fasting does mean giving up food. It could also mean giving up sleep for periods of time. Conversely, it could mean physical exercise when the appetites call for rest and relaxation. In our sedentary world, the discipline of intentional physical activity can do wonders in teaching the spirit commitment and self-denial.

John Wesley expected his young preachers to fast one to two days every week. Fasting means feasting on God. Jesus was tempted when spiritually strongest, after fasting forty days. Fasting is a silent form of self-denial and putting to death our drives, many of which are physical. Once you become familiar with what self-denial feels like, you are more likely to do it in other areas when God calls on you to do His will. I have found this a challenging area, but one which I try to practice periodically, typically fasting all solid food for one 24-hour period per week unless a pressing issue requires a longer duration.

4. Simplicity Simplicity refers to abstaining from using money or goods at our disposal in ways that merely gratify our desires or our hunger for status, glamour, or luxury. In our world today, a large part of the freedom that comes from frugality is freedom from the spiritual bondage caused by financial debt. "Our contemporary culture lacks inward reality and an outward lifestyle of simplicity."[6] "Simplicity sets possession in proper perspective. Simplicity rejoices in the gracious provision from the hand of God."[7] For this matter, simplicity is not the same as poverty. "The inward reality of simplicity involves a life of joyful unconcern for possessions."[8]

When you have to have the latest gadget, one more remote control, the latest model or fashion, and need to charge it because saving for it takes too long, your ability to surrender to God is probably very weak in this area. Simplicity not only strengthens your ability for stewardship, it allows you freedom from materialism and peer pressure. Most of us are more attracted to physical goods than we realize. Our wants have become our "needs." Simplicity replicates the attitude of brokenness in that it seeks no security other than that of God alone. Aleksandr Solzhenitsyn observed, "You only have power over people as long as you don't take everything away from them. But when you've robbed a man of everything, he's no longer in your power—he's free again." Simplicity is the freedom from being possessed by possessing things.

5. Chastity This behavior refers to the voluntary abstinence from sexual pleasures in exchange for seeking higher fulfillment. Our sexuality reaches into the essence of our being. Therefore, chastity does not mean nonsexuality, and any emphasis to that effect will certainly do great harm. The suffering that comes from sexuality does come in large part from improper indulgence in sexual thoughts, feelings, attitudes and relations. Improper abstinence in marriage can also create problems (1 Cor. 7:5).

6. Sacrifice This behavior transcends logic. "The cautious faith that never saws off the limb on which it is sitting never learns that unattached limbs may find strange, unaccountable ways of not falling."[9] Here, pure faith is demonstrated as you go beyond the realm of what is rational and humanly possible, and are forced to trust God to intervene. At times it may appear foolhardy and ridiculous, but when done by faith and out of obedience, it enlarges your faith capacity. Sacrifice is the giving of our resources (i.e. time, finances, physical energy) beyond what is convenient and comfortable, for the purpose of reminding us our security is in Christ alone.

7. Secrecy This behavior can be placed in the context of both giving and receiving. Serving in secrecy denies self-promotion. Doing acts of kindness anonymously means we look to God alone for reward. One of the greatest acts of unbelief is the thought that our spiritual acts and virtues need to be advertised to be known. By serving others in silence, without telling anyone, we purify our motives.

The receiving side of silence comes into play when you have a need. Although the Christian community ought to minister to each other, there come times when out of discipline, you make your requests known only to God. You depend on Him to tell others. You thereby see Him as your source and trust Him to fulfill that need should it be in His will. This teaches the ability to trust Him and not rely on your own persuasive skills and network. George Mueller of Bristol, England, was famous for this practice of depending on God to come through for his orphanage ministry.

Disciplines of Activity

1. Study Study behavior refers to the voluntary and intentional reading and contemplation of the Bible and spiritual classics. This behavior often is implemented along with solitude. Here the mind is stretched to focus on interpretation, understanding, and evaluation of the literature studied. Calvin Miller said, "Mystics without study are only spiritual romantics who want relationship without effort." Study disciplines the mind and the soul at the same time, and provides the necessary substance to direct our growth. In a culture where instruction through the mass media and consumerism are rampant, this behavior communicates an earnest desire to focus one's mental energies into spiritual growth.

"A major obstacle is convincing people that they must learn to study. Most people assume that because they know how to read they know how to study." [10] Romans 12:2 says, "Be transformed by the renewing of your mind." 2 Timothy 2:15 says, "Study to show yourself approved unto God, a workman that does not need to be ashamed, and who correctly handles the word of truth."

2. Prolonged Prayer Prolonged prayer transcends our ongoing need for regular worship and prayer and includes the practice of intense prayer over a longer period of time. This is also utilized with solitude. It involves setting oneself apart for a season of prayer without interruptions. This discipline forces us to resist outer disturbances and demonstrates our willingness to spend significant time in fellowship with God. It is like going out on a date with him. It may also take the form of a vigil, denying sleep in order to pray and worship.

Praying beyond devotional prayers is often laborious. The more we pray, the more we think to pray, and we learn to depend on God for all our daily needs. Just as spouses need get-aways to renew their love beyond daily activities, we also need spiritual times of renewal. Richard Foster wrote, "To pray is to change. If we are unwilling to change, we will abandon prayer as a noticeable characteristic of our lives," thus revealing a lack of brokenness. [11]

3. Celebration Celebration refers to dwelling on the greatness of God as shown in His goodness to us. It is sunbathing in God's glory. It may include dancing in the Spirit, applauding for God, or laughing out of joy for what He has done in your life. In the *Screwtape Letters,* the demons get into an explanation of pleasure: "When demons are dealing with any pleasure in its healthy and normal and satisfying form, they are on the enemy's [God's] ground. We've won many a soul through pleasure. All the same, it is God's invention, not ours. He made the pleasures. All our research so far has not enabled us to produce one."[12] Celebration is finding pleasure in God.

4. Service Service is the practice of doing mundane things that help others. It is feet-washing ministry. This discipline might be more important for Christians who find themselves in positions of influence, power, and leadership. It is a statement which tells those who are great how to behave (Matt. 20:25–28). Service to others in the spirit of Jesus allows us the freedom of a humility that carries no burdens of appearance. "If I then, your Lord and Teacher, have washed your feet, you also ought to wash one another's feet. For I have given you an example, that you should do as I have done to you. Most assuredly, I say to you, a servant is not greater than his master" (John 13:14–16). "Nobody is too good for the most menial service. One who worries about the loss of time that such petty, outward acts of helpfulness entail is usually taking the importance of his own career too solemnly."[13]

5. Fellowship Fellowship is intentionally setting aside time for Christian community. In a society which finds itself more and more alienated from intimacy and seeks autonomy, fellowship willingly submits an individual's priorities to those of the group. That costs both time and emotional energy. Fellowship may include times of worship, prayer, Bible study, service, and celebration. Here the diversity of gifts can be seen and implemented. This community demonstrates the Kingdom and family of God and provides for the opportunity to give and receive.

6. Confession Confession involves admitting and taking responsibility for a sin or weakness, and calling sin what it is. This behavior comes out of Scripture: "Confess your sins one to another" (James 5:16). David did this as he wrote Psalm 51. The purpose of this practice is not to gossip or for self-abasement or guilt release. It is letting trusted others know our deepest weaknesses and failures and it then nourishes our faith in God's forgiveness and ability. It is easy to want to appear whole and infallible. Confession communicates your mortality and at the same time usually encourages others who have their own inner, hidden weaknesses. Confession helps us avoid sin. It provides for accountability. Nothing is more supportive of right behavior than open truth. "Anybody horrified by the dreadfulness of his own sin that nailed Jesus to the cross will no longer be horrified by even the rankest sins of a brother."[14]

7. Submission Submission is the highest level of fellowship. In submission, there is complete honesty, transparency, and sometimes confession and restitution. It is intentional and voluntary accountability for our actions before other Christians. It can take the form of mentorship. This submission may be to a group of believers which may or may not be in relation to a sin or moral lapse. Submission is an extension of laying one's will at the feet of Christ and following his recommendations.

This is not a definitive list. We could also mention hard physical work, journal writing, Sabbath keeping, and the like. Rather, this list is intended to be an introduction to the spiritual disciplines. It is good to see their role in the concept of voluntary brokenness and heart-allegiance. As you may have recognized, several of these behaviors are based on ongoing expectations of Christian living. They specifically become spiritual disciplines when they are practiced out of an attitude of willful intention for the purpose of keeping spiritually sharp. This produces the "invironment" (inner environment) for breaking that we have been learning about.

Dallas Willard, in *The Spirit of the Disciplines,* tells us why we are naturally so reserved when it comes to pursuing these behaviors for voluntary brokenness. "We delude ourselves about the sustaining conditions of people's evil deeds because we wish to continue living as we now live and continue being the kinds of people we are. We do not want to change. We do not want our world to be really different. We just want to escape the consequences of its being what it truly is and of our being who we truly are."[15]

A Christian practicing the behaviors of brokenness is the same as a runner who does laps, a football team that scrimmages, and a soldier who keeps his gun cleaned and oiled and ready for when it needs to be used. Although the wild stallion is tamed during an intentional breaking process, he needs to be ridden and taken through the paces periodically to maintain the results of that initial action. "Doing" the behaviors of brokenness are ways of maintaining the "being" of a tamed soul.

The natural temptation in life is to maintain the status quo. Jesus criticized those who were not growing, who had ears that did not hear and eyes that did not see. Change is inevitable; growth is intentional. In spite of what Darwin believed, life in its natural condition is in a constant state of decay. Our bodies begin to sag without intentional exercise and nutritional control. Our streets fall apart and develop potholes. Buildings crumble. Fields erode. Cars rust. The behaviors of brokenness provide an intentional regimentation for spiritual growth and strength. They can maintain results of past breaking processes and, at times, prevent the need for future breaking by creating a sample condition in which the soul is tamed.

■

QUESTIONS FOR REFLECTION

1. Discuss why we find that exhibiting our Christianity and doing as Jesus would do is so difficult according to the chapter.

2. Discuss further the difference between voluntary and involuntary brokenness.

3. What has been your opinion of the spiritual disciplines in the past? Have you practiced any of them? If so, when and under what circumstances?

4. Which of the disciplines of activity do you think you would find most challenging? Most rewarding? Which of the disciplines of abstinence do you think you would find most challenging? Most rewarding?

5. What way could you schedule one or more of these disciplines into your calendar for your spiritual development?

"Come to the edge," he said.
They said, "We are afraid."
"Come to the edge," he said.
They said, "We will fall."
"Come to the edge," he said.
They came. He pushed them . . . and they flew.
                                    —Guillaume Apollinaire

CHAPTER
NINE
■

Results of Brokenness

■■■

The miracle had become a mirage. All of our hopes and dreams had suddenly crumbled. Now, since we had failed to meet our goal, we were in an impossible position financially. Not only could we not write off the debt, but also we would actually lose the property unless God intervened immediately. This possibility seemed rather remote in those bleak moments of discouragement. Furthermore, I would have to write the thousands of friends who had read only a few days before that God had worked a miracle and tell them that there had been no miracle at all. There was personal humiliation involved, of course.

What was I to do? Since the righteous are to live by faith and since "all things work together for good to those who love God," I didn't know of a better way to demonstrate faith than to say, "Thank you." So I got back down on my knees and thanked God for what had happened. I thanked Him through my tears. I thanked Him that in His wisdom and love He knew better than I what should be done and that out of this chaos and uncertainty I knew would come a far greater miracle. There on my knees while I was giving thanks for this great disappointment, God began to give me the genuine assurance that a greater miracle really was going to happen.

—Bill Bright

■

GATEWAY TO GROWTH & MATURITY

Nancy and I thoroughly enjoy traveling. We have the bug to discover new sights and cultures. Some people enjoy driving. But for us, any jaunt over four hours seems too long. For long trips, flying is the only way to drive. Most airports now are so convenient. You check in, walk down the climate-controlled corridors, sit in a lounge, enter the boarding walkway, have a seat, and take off. That description is a bit simplistic, but air travel beats the old stagecoach method. Usually you do not even need to experience the weather or go onto the noisy tarmac. The terminal's telescopic arms reach for the airplane and become the portable sidewalk to enter and exit. It sure beats the "good old days."

The process of brokenness is a lot like those mechanical walkways that telescope to the plane. It is a transitional phase that provides for greater growth and opens the door for new destinations in life. An attitude of brokenness is usually best described in terms of what you see resulting from the breaking process, namely surrender, humility, prioritization of spiritual development, and dependence on the Holy Spirit. Brokenness has numerous results, chief among them is a tamed soul. Although brokenness is not a cure-all, certain qualities will not emerge out of a life which lacks sufficient breaking and submitting. A very important quality is maturity.

■

THE MATURE PERSON

Someone said people go through three stages: youth, middle age, and "you're looking fine." There is a difference between maturity and old age. The question is not are you getting older, but are you getting better? The breaking process brings elements to the maturing process that would not come into play otherwise. Maturity is not necessarily a component of age, experience, education, or status in life. It is predominantly a result of emotional, social, and spiritual growth. I Corinthians 13:11 says, "When I became a man, I put away childish things." You can be a grown-up and not be a mature person.

At the age of two, my little boy was really cute. But if he looked and acted like that at five years old, and fourteen years of age, and as a thirty-one year old, he would not be cute. He would be an oddity, what we call "weird." The word *teleios* occurs seventeen times in the New Testament pertaining to the meaning of "perfect and mature." The breaking process does a lot to inaugurate *teleios* in our lives.

Growing up on a farm, my dad and I would sometimes disappear into the cornfield. I would follow him down the long rows of tall, golden stalks. I watched him stop, pull off an ear, tear back the husks, and push his thumbnail into several of the kernels. "The corn's just about mature," he'd say. "See these dimples in the kernels?" That meant it was time to get the picker on the tractor, because harvest was coming. I didn't see a lot of difference between a mature ear of corn and an immature one, but there was a difference. People look basically the same on the outside. Some of them may look slightly more sophisticated, educated, successful, or sociable. But when you meet people who are truly mature and deep, you see a big difference between them and the rest.

The first thing you notice about mature people is that they keep loving when they do not receive love in return. "Love bears all things . . . endures all things. Love never fails" (1 Cor. 13:7–8). We should start with the most important character trait of the Christian: the ability to consistently love. How quickly does your love stop? Paul said when he became a man, he did away with childish things. The chief difference between a child and an adult is responsibility. Mature people take responsibility for their actions and emotions. Emotional children blame others. "You make me mad." "If you wouldn't do that, I wouldn't get so angry." "I'll get you for hurting me." These statements are from people who have relinquished responsibility for their actions. Broken people tend to be good lovers. They are slow to anger, quick to forgive, reticent to condemn, and swift to affirm.

A second quality of mature people is the ability to maintain a positive joy flow during times of emotional recession. James 1:2–8 talks about this joy during trials and temptations. Christian joy is a kind of activity. My family likes going to the ocean. Sometimes we drive to piers. A pier stands unmoving, whether the tide is in or out, high or low. Likewise, mature people do not base their responses on circumstances. They are emotionally consistent. God is a great recycler. He takes the garbage that happens to us and makes something good out of it. The breaking process has a spiritual ecology. Problems are never wasted. The importance of tough times is not what they do *to* you, but what they do *in* you. Mature people do not rise and fall with their day-to-day emotions. "It is a universal guarantee that life is my servant, if I am His slave. I have one concern and only one—that I be His. I don't belong to my sorrows, troubles, sickness, and death. I belong to Christ. These things belong to me not to bear but to use."[1]

A third quality of mature people is that they live in holiness. Their brand of holiness is not a long list of rules and regulations. It is an inner purity which produces external piety. E. Stanley Jones noted that "outer sins are only fruit—the unsurrendered self is the root; the outer signs are symptoms, the unsurrendered self is the disease."[2] Hebrews 5:12–13 says, "Though by this time you ought to be teachers, you need someone to teach you again the first principles of the oracles of God; and you have come to need milk and not solid food. For everyone who partakes only of milk is unskilled in the word of righteousness for he is a babe." The word used for *babe* refers to a suckling child who cannot talk yet. Mature people learn to feed themselves and do so on a regular basis, instead of having someone spoon feed them God's word.

Most pastors periodically hear the expression, "I want more meat." Ideally, such intentions sound good. Most of the time, that means "I want to grow and study the Bible." But this expression can also be used as an excuse for quitting a church or ministry, as well as an insult to the leader for not sharing deeper truths about God. "But solid food [meat] is for the mature, who by constant use have trained themselves to distinguish good from evil" (Heb. 5:14). According to this passage, the difference between milk (food for spiritual infants) and meat (food for spiritual adults) is the constant use of God's word. In other words, meat is applying milk. It does not say here that meat is verse-by-verse teaching as opposed to topical preaching, or a two-year discipleship curriculum instead of ninety-day growth groups. The bottom line is that meat is "doing the milk." James tells us to be doers of the word, not just hearers.

Belief, in the biblical sense, involves the emotions and will, not just passive mental acceptance. My dissertation looked at the role of leadership training in ministerial preparation. I learned during my research that the method of training pastors has changed from an apprenticeship model to a Westernized classroom version, which tends to be cerebral but not necessarily incarnate.

In biblical times, learning implied application, not just accumulating knowledge. We must move away from the cognitive approach to Christianity, which suggests that if one merely hears more Bible, one will mature. Brokenness raises our level of awareness to recognize the difference between information and application. Although I am all for biblical literacy, I realize our problem is not so much our theological intelligence quotient as it is our obedience quotient. Brokenness confronts the latter. It is always easier to study God's word than it is to obey it, and sometimes we would rather appear holy by hearing the word (milk) than doing the word (meat).

As we grow, we learn to distinguish between what is good from what is evil. Little kids do not understand the difference between ant spray, cough medicine, lipstick, and apple juice. They are liable to stick anything in their mouths. As children grow, they learn to distinguish colors from each other, red from blue, yellow from green. We eventually learn the difference in hues: forest green and kelly green, chartreuse and light green. Likewise, mature people are able to distinguish between what is beneficial to them and what is not.

Immature people do not see the ill effects of certain behaviors, attitudes, habits, impulses, and media. They fail to discern differences in moral influences unless they are very obvious. The immature often rely on external standards because they lack the sensitivity and power to respond effectively to God's Spirit within them. You can see varying examples of this in the different cultural regions within the United States and in different countries of the world.

A fourth characteristic of mature people is that they are not preoccupied with possessions or status. The area in which I live is a very nice, planned community. It is not stuffy, but it contains a significant amount of social awareness and competition. I laughed the other night when I saw a new Mercedes with a pizza wind sock on the antenna, delivering a pizza. There is a strong drive in our culture to have the very best, buy what we want, move up and dress for success. Bigger is better. Nice is neat. Sneakers alone now have hundreds of options, some of which require a second mortgage to purchase. Jesus talked about the seed that fell among thorns and choked, never producing a crop.

You would think that farmers would be good at growing gardens. We weren't. We tried for several years to grow a garden in our backyard, right next to the hog lot and the dutch elm trees that served as a wind block. We eventually realized that the plot near the trees was a bad location. The soil nutrients were deficient and the trees sapped most of the moisture. Like gardens, mature people thrive in different fields than the immature. They are not sapped by the cultural influences to possess and acquire. They may have good taste and enjoy excellence, but they do not find fulfillment in possessions. Brokenness reveals the true value of tangible things. A person is rich in relation to the things he or she can live without.

A fifth characteristic of mature people is that they are consistently service-oriented. Ephesians 4:13–14 talks about becoming "mature, attaining to the whole measure of the fullness of Christ. Then we will no longer be infants, tossed back and forth by the waves." That passage talks about using our various gifts to serve others. Not only do mature people have a refreshing emotional consistency, but they also are willing to get involved in service and to look for needs to fill. Mature people are others-oriented. It is a healthy others-orientation, unlike a co-dependent need to be needed. Immature people can also be others-oriented, but they tend to be consumed by trying to please people. Mature people are not *driven* to serve. They are *called* to serve.

Infants have short attention spans. They are easily distracted. They go from one toy to another to another. We never attain the full measure of Christ by being up and down. Roller coaster Christians vary in their service to God. Some follow Him only when things are good and they can get their minds off of themselves. But if something comes up, or their days turn bad, their attention moves to the person in the mirror. Others stray from God when things go well, only seeking Him when tough times arrive. Broken people give of themselves, for they have let go of much of their fixation on themselves.

A sixth trait of mature people is that they learn from the past, live in the present, but aim for the future. Immature people live in the past, complain about the present, and usually avoid the future. Of course, exceptions exist. Some very immature people only live in the fantasy of the future. They talk about their ships coming in while they are presently falling apart because they have not learned from the past.

However, mature people have a good concept of time. No wonder most people do not get any further in life; they drive looking in their rearview mirrors. Rearview mirrors are good for getting your bearings, but they are not effective for forward movement. When we rely on old trophies, photo albums, and "good-old-days" stories to get us going, we often distort reality. Those broken in the wrong places, wounded people, often fixate on past hurts and painful memories. Paul says, "Not that I have already attained, or am already perfected; but I press on, that I may lay hold of that for which Christ Jesus took hold of me . . . but one thing I do, forgetting those things which are behind and reaching forward to those things which are ahead, I press toward the goal for the prize of the upward call of God in Christ Jesus. . . . Those who are mature should take such a view of things" (Phil. 3:12–15).

Mature people are perpetual learners. They are always growing. They press forward. They are progress-oriented. They use the past to provide wisdom for the future. They get on with life. They do not rest on past laurels. They quit licking yesterday's wounds. The world is full of people bitter over ex-spouses, former pastors, unreasonable parents. Someone ought to tell the complainer to get off his or her cross because we need the wood. People who have been broken in the right place keep their gaze on the future. They exude hope, and hope is always out in front of us—Hanging On to Positive Expectations. There is a contemporariness about them. Yet, they have also learned daily contentment.

A seventh characteristic of a mature person is humility. Humility is one of the major results of the breaking process. It is at the very heart of the process, while its antithesis (pride) is at the root of the need for breaking. Out of pride we rely on ourselves and seek our own satisfaction. Our concern for what others think of us prevents us from obeying God. Our reliance upon our giftedness motivates us to call on our skills, education, and networks, rather than to live by faith.

"And I, brethren, when I came to you, did not come with excellence of speech or of wisdom declaring to you the testimony of God. For I determined not to know anything among you except Jesus Christ and Him crucified. I was with you in weakness, in fear, and in much trembling. And my speech and my preaching were not with persuasive words of human wisdom, but in demonstration of the Spirit and of power, that your faith should not be in the wisdom of men, but in the power of God" (1 Cor. 2:1–5). Pride (arrogance) is a luxury of youth. Adolescents have not had enough failures, let downs, and experience to be seasoned. I never cease to be amazed that the more I learn, the more I realize I do not know. Immature people have a pride in life, an "I can do it; I don't need any help" attitude. Our self-sufficiency is the root of many of our problems and necessitates breaking.

I think men have a harder time with this problem than women. Women are more receptive to following Christ. The women kept their faith during the crucifixion. Women were the first to see that Christ had risen. We men have a more difficult time letting go of our stubbornness and admitting our weaknesses. We would rather drive for miles in circles than ask for directions. We would rather jump right into putting our children's Christmas toys together instead of first reading the instructions. We stammer to admit we were wrong and squeak out, "Will you forgive me?" Our arrogance is why statistics say 90 percent of the men in America do not have close friends, because close friends hold us accountable and require an amount of vulnerability.

■

PRIDE POLLUTION

The process of brokenness frees us from the impurities of pride and enslavement to self-will. A while ago, McDonald's stopped using styrofoam containers and reverted to paper wrappers for their products. Our society is turning green, thinking of the environment, recycling glass, aluminum, and plastic. Anti-pollution laws continue to become stiffer and stiffer. Everyone seems concerned to a degree about nuclear waste, toxic dumps, global warming, and the ozone layer. Brokenness causes us to be ecologically minded in the spiritual domain.

Pride pollutes our relationships. "Where do wars and fights come from among you? Do they not come from your desires for pleasure that war in your members? You lust and do not have. You murder and covet but cannot obtain. You fight and war, yet you do not have because you do not ask. You ask and do not receive, because you ask amiss, that you may spend it on your pleasures" (James 4:1–3). Sin is a paradox itself. It always seeks satisfaction, but never delivers long-term fulfillment. It is like stereotypical Chinese food; it fails to fill you up for long.

Most quarrels come from inner conflicts, not external circumstances. Most interpersonal tensions are merely projections of intrapersonal stress. I remember being in northern Oregon following the Mount St. Helens eruption. Powder ash was everywhere. I did not cause the explosion, but I experienced its fallout. Most anger and relational frustrations are the ashes of exploded pride.

The James four passage tells us that inner conflicts result from unmet desires. Unmet desires result from unanswered prayers. And unanswered prayers result from selfish motives. The word there for *amiss* means, literally, diseased and sick motives. Pride is toxic to our motives and to our relationships.

Pride also pollutes the spiritual life. That is why God tells us, "You adulterous people, don't you know that friendship with the world is hatred toward God? Anyone who chooses to be a friend of the world becomes an enemy of God." Scripture also says: "God opposes the proud but gives grace to the humble" (see James 4:4–6). Pride is at the heart of worldly values, which are contrary to God. From the beginning, pride has been at the core of sin and resulted in our alienation from God. The first temptation began with "If you eat of the fruit, you will become like the gods" (Gen. 3:5). Our egos make us want to be God rather than to serve God. It is this pollutant that brokenness seeks to clean, eradicate, and cauterize.

When we initially accept Christ, we are really just responding to God's love, and we receive a portion of grace. But God "opposes the proud. He gives grace to the humble." A proper Christian life should receive more and more of God's grace over time. The problem is that so many believers live their lives with only the original portion. Pride thwarts this process. Most ministry and most Christian effort are done with human strength instead of by God's grace. Humility is a vessel through which we receive more grace. Humility is spurned in an untamed soul, so it can only be born in a broken one.

"The Christian life cannot develop without a deepening awareness of what we first recognized at the time of conversion: self-centeredness still runs deep within us, cannot be overcome with hard work and good intentions, and is both fatal and wrong."[3] "Self-pity, fear of suffering, withdrawal from the cross; these are some of the manifestations of soul life, for its prime motivation is self-preservation. Lowliness is not looking down on one's self; rather it is not looking at one's self at all."[4]

Pride pollutes our potential. "Therefore submit to God. Resist the devil and he will flee from you. Draw near to God and He will draw near to you. Cleanse your hands, you sinners; and purify your hearts, you double-minded. Lament and mourn and weep! Let your laughter be turned to mourning and your joy to gloom. Humble yourselves in the sight of the Lord, and He will lift you up" (James 4:7–10). This is the best self-help advice available. Too long we have tried to pull ourselves up by our boot straps. We strive to arrive and climb the corporate ladder tooth and nail, only to reach the top and discover it was leaning against the wrong wall. The paradox pops up again; humble yourself to be lifted. The way to get up in life is to get down before the Lord.

How do you "do" humility? Submit to God. Resist the devil. Come near to God by "washing your hands"—referring to our actions and deeds—and by "purifying your hearts you double-minded"—referring to our souls. Kierkegaard said, "Purity of heart is to will one thing." Mendell Taylor said purity is when "everything inside is on God's side." We "do" humility by repenting and being sorrowful. And we "do" humility by getting serious. There is a solemnity in brokenness as you confront your inability. It is not a laughing matter. Pride prevents us from fulfilling the picture God has of us in life.

Pride pollutes our perspective. "Do not speak evil of one another, brethren. He who speaks evil of a brother and judges his brother speaks evil of the law and judges the law. But if you judge the law, you are not a doer of the law, but a judge. There is one Lawgiver, who is able to save and to destroy. Who are you to judge another?" (James 4:11–13). One of the most common expressions of the sinful nature is building yourself up by tearing others down. Gossip, bickering, and judgment all reflect an unbroken spirit. In addition, our job is not to review the Bible and determine what we do and do not agree on. Scripture is not a movie we review and critique. We do not have the option of rating it like a meal. It is truth. In street language, James is saying, "Who died and made you king?" How egotistical to make ourselves judges over others and God's law. To break a law is to put yourself above it. The word *lawgiver* is used six times in the Old Testament and once in the New Testament, and each time it refers to God alone. When we have pride in our lives, we do not see things in their proper perspective. Conversely, you never see things more clearly than when humility fills your soul.

Finally, pride pollutes our future. "Come now, you who say, 'Today or tomorrow we will go to such and such a city, spend a year there, buy and sell, and make a profit'; whereas you do not even know what will happen tomorrow. For what is your life? It is even a vapor that appears for a little time and then vanishes away. Instead, you ought to say, 'If Lord wills, we shall live and do this or that.' But now you boast in your arrogance. All such boasting is evil. Therefore, to him who knows to do good and does not do it, to him it is sin" (James 4:13–17).

First of all, James talks about the sin of presumption. We think we can carry on without God. We start thinking we are hot stuff. James says, "You don't even know when you are going to die." Let that remind you how powerless you really are. We are temporary; here today, gone tomorrow.

He also talks about the sin of bragging. We feel we have our lives plotted out. We act like we know what achievements we are going to possess, most of them aside from God's will. Therefore we end up making bad career, financial, or relationship decisions because we think we know best.

Then he talks about the sin of omission. Our problem is that although we may know something in our heads, it does little good until we know it in our hearts. This is the secret to spiritual growth. Most truths never make it to our hearts, because we hear them in our heads, and we are too proud to change. "Hey, that was a good sermon. Those people today really needed that." We know scores of our friends who should apply the gospel, but the subtlety of pride causes us to believe that it really is not that important for *us* to live out. Like a mule, a stubborn person is one who will not do what he knows is best, just because a parent, boss, pastor or even the Spirit told him. He is too proud to kneel before God, to wash feet, to admit wrong, to humble himself. We must be doers, not merely hearers.

These hang-ups all revolve around the same point. We feel somehow that God really is not for us. Not many books on humility make the best-seller list. We think that if we fully submit to Him, we will be settling for second best. Submitting means hanging up our dreams and aspirations and living a life of perpetual disappointment. Most of all, pride pollutes our perceptions of God. It reminds me of the Dear Abby column which appeared in the June 5, 1990 issue of the St. Paul *Pioneer Press Dispatch*.

> *Dear Abby*:
>
> A *young man from a wealthy family was about to graduate from high school. It was the custom in that affluent neighborhood for the parents to give the graduate an automobile.*
>
> Bill *and his father had spent months looking at cars, and the week before graduation, they found the perfect car. Bill was certain that the car would be his on graduation night.*
>
> *Imagine his disappointment when, on the eve of his graduation, Bill's father handed him a gift-wrapped Bible!*
>
> Bill *was so angry that he threw the Bible down and stormed out of the house. He and his father never saw each other again.*
>
> *It was the news of his father's death that brought Bill home again. As he sat one night going through his father's possessions that he was to inherit, he came across the Bible his father had given him.*
>
> *He brushed away the dust and opened it to find a cashier's check, dated the day of his graduation—in the exact amount of the car they had chosen together.*
>
> Beckhah Fink, TX

God's word, and even the trials and testings we experience are often the wrappings of more valuable gifts the Father has in store for us. Taken at face value, they often represent what we do not want. But if we dare open them, and approach them in the right attitude, we find that God has given us our dreams. He ends up giving us ourselves, enlarged and developed beyond anything we could ever muster in our own strength.

■

TEMPERAMENTS

Brokenness produces similar fruitfulness among people. However, the breaking process takes different approaches according to different temperaments. The concept of brokenness sounds somewhat mystical, perhaps reserved for only the introspective and subdued. Regardless of your personality or emotional blueprint, the process takes on similar qualities. It works on areas of poor productivity, which often vary according to different personalities. In order to understand the results of brokenness, it may be helpful to highlight the areas in which the process takes place in various temperaments.

I suppose one reason I found myself so involved in this subject is that my basic temperament style probably resists the breaking process more than others. The choleric, "I-can-do-it" attitude of a visionary who sets goals and climbs the ladder of success can be one of the worst, unless it is tamed. It is an example of what happens when one's strengths become one's weaknesses.

The resolve and will of the person who is driven to achieve often obstructs God from moving in the manner He desires. Often, people with many talents and an abundance of God-given resources will earnestly attempt to do great things for God. Because these people have great degrees of ability, there is a strong temptation to achieve out of human strength and to fail to rely on God's strength.

These individuals will often experience brokenness in the areas of personal pride and independence. The element that keeps this type of soul untamed is the drive to achieve and accomplish great things through one's own intellect, skills, giftedness, and network. Although being driven and forwardly motivated can be strong qualities, they can supplant God's proper place in a person's life. Breaking for this person may come through a significant failure or the inability to achieve a certain goal. My two episodes of brokenness I referred to in the beginning of this book emerged out of times when all my personal efforts resulted in either declining or plateaued effectiveness. No matter how hard I tried, I could not accomplish my goals. Breaking may even come when you realize self-obtained goals, but then experience disillusionment when the results you hoped for do not materialize. Being broken in the right place for this temperament is not so much disillusionment as much as it is de-illusionment, a reorientation toward truth.

David wrote,

> I am poured out like water,
> And all My bones are out of joint;
> My heart is like wax;
> It has melted within Me.
> My strength is dried up like a potsherd,
> And my tongue clings to My jaws;
> You have brought Me to the dust of death. (Ps. 22:14–15)

This conveys the feeling of a doer who thrives on the power of self-confidence, but who finds himself in a state of utter inability.

Paul was this type of doer. He experienced numerous difficult situations and a thorn in the flesh so that his soul would remain tame before the Lord. He refers to his voluntary activities of disciplining his body so that he would not falter from the faith and from his ministry. The doer temperament often undergoes breaking in those areas which block full surrender to God. The areas of pride, ego-strength, ambition, and giftedness become sanctified if the breaking process is allowed to work as intended. The result of brokenness in this temperament is a more humble, compliant, relaxed achiever who gives God the final say.

The happy-go-lucky, sanguine, people-person temperament experiences brokenness in different areas than the doer. This personality thrives on relationships and attention from others. He or she tends to be the life of the party, a vibrant character who attracts people through charisma and good-natured demeanor. These traits are strengths, which again can become weaknesses in the unbroken heart. They become liabilities when a person is unable to obey God and step out with faith in areas that may risk the rejection of others. If God calls you to confront a person or situation, and your concern for how people think of you prevents full obedience, you need to be broken.

A person whose untamed heart exudes these qualities will usually experience the breaking process in specific areas that thwart God's Lordship, often in relationships. People may let them down. Divorce or separation may take place. Friends, for unknown reasons, begin to reprimand and alienate this attention-seeking person. Psalm 55:12–14 says, "For it is not an enemy who reproaches me; then I could bear it. Nor is it one who hates me who has exalted himself against me; then I could hide from him. But it was you, a man my equal, my companion and my acquaintance. We took sweet counsel together, and walked to the house of God in the throng." The result of David's broken relationship is found several verses later;

"As for me, I will call upon God, and the Lord shall save me." (Ps. 55:16). These are all opportunities for this personality to rely less upon relationship skills and more upon God. When human relationships take the place of the focus and contentment that the Holy Spirit desires, a person becomes less fruitful and unsurrendered to Christ.

As in all the temperaments, the breaking process unique to the sanguine may be hard to understand at the time. Here, the individual's response to the process will determine whether a person becomes broken in the right or the wrong place. A people-person broken in the wrong places will either dive into social events and try harder to gain attention or will become cynical and untrusting of others. The intention of this breaking is to create a personality dependent upon God and a person who is surrendered to God's use of his or her gifts and unique qualities. Being broken in the right place will result not only in this attitude but also in a freedom from depending so much on approval and acceptance from others.

A person with a melancholy, analytical temperament tends to be very thorough in activities and relationships. This person brings order to disorganized events and projects. He or she follows through, taking on an assignment only when it can be done with quality and completion. These traits are strengths. However, the very qualities that produce the strengths of this temperament can also become weaknesses which serve as targets of breaking. This temperament often depreciates one's own worth, resulting in low self-esteem. This warped self-image avoids the idea that we were created in God's image and therefore deflects the love, forgiveness, and acceptance of God vital to realizing who we are in Christ. Another potential barrier to the analytical trait is what I refer to as analysis paralysis. Some of the spies in the book of Numbers might have suffered from this when they reported back what they saw in the Promised Land. Their concern for fact kept them from faith. Faith often transcends logic and requires the believer to go beyond human feelings of comfort.

The person with a melancholy temperament usually experiences breaking along the lines of self-dependence and structure. At times the person may be confronted with the intensity of God's love and must, therefore, reject apprehensions of self-worth. This feeling of self-betrayal causes one to trust Scripture and the Holy Spirit instead of one's own thought processes.

This temperament is also prone to worry and introspection, which tend to be antithetical to the faith process. By worrying, you deny the existence of a good God who is in control. In essence you appoint yourself God. "If God is not going to do it, I'd better take over and worry about it." A melancholic likes a planned, methodical, orderly life. Spontaneity and surprises fray the nerves. The drive to order is an attempt to take things into one's own hands, even though it is a delusion. Therefore, the other major area of breaking processes involves the arena of faith, trusting God for the unexpected. An analytical personality will be required by God to transcend human logic and what is seen, to step out on faith. The breaking process provides a heart that is not stewing or working out of its own human comfort zone, but is able to surrender to God's leading and Lordship. The result is a melancholic who is free to affirm God's love, free to risk failure, and free to peacefully let God handle the loose ends.

The other major temperament type (according to Hippocrates) is the phlegmatic, the peaceful personality. The strengths of this personality include a calm and tranquil spirit. This person is good with people and responds well under pressure. She likes to feel accepted and usually does not get burdened down with worry and is not overly ambitious. This person tends to smell the roses and is often unencumbered by the pursuit of fortune or fame. This person is good with others and strives for peace and harmony. These fine strengths are esteemed by Scripture. Many of us in Western civilization, who tend to use people and strive for the golden ring, can learn a lot from these people.

However, even these strengths can also become weaknesses. The peace-loving nature of this temperament can be debilitating in moments when confrontation and standing up for justice are required. The unwillingness to "ruffle the feathers" can be contrary to what God requires at certain times. Justice and peace often are not passive processes. Therefore, God frequently uses situations requiring confrontation and loving antagonism to prune the unfruitful elements of this temperament.

Another target of the breaking process is visionary action. This temperament is sometimes susceptible to laziness and apathy. God provides missions, visions, and projects which require action and stepping out in faith. He will often bring these people into direct contact with situations which demand them to transcend their temperamental barriers. This breaking process is not comfortable, but the comfort sought by this type of person tends to thwart God's desires for them. When we let our temperament strengths determine the parameters of our faith and obedience to God, we reveal areas which need taming so that we may respond to the Father with submission. A phlegmatic, easy-going personality broken in the wrong places will become reticent at the chance to try new projects. She will tend to pull back from people and become an emotional hermit. This temperament, broken in the right place, will obey God in progressiveness and in seeking to fulfill ministry missions and goals, even when they are contrary to one's natural inclinations.

Breaking temperamental differences does not imply that God's goal is for all of us to act alike. Every individual is unique and His calling in our lives is equally unique. The common theme He seeks is for everyone to nurture a sensitive spirit of a surrendered will. God does not seek to change the choleric doer into a phlegmatic rester, or a sanguine people-person into a melancholy thinker, or vice versa. Rather, God wants all of us to come to a point of obedient neutrality. When we tell God "I won't do _____," because it goes against our temperament, we are not communicating a personality trait as much as we are purveying an unbroken spirit. We usually feel pain and pressure in the areas which resist change and push against God and His Spirit. We are likely to experience brokenness in the arenas of our strengths which, when untamed, eventually serve as our weaknesses. That is because we often rely on our strengths as our security and allow them to replace God's presence. The result of being broken in the right place is the fruit of the Spirit, produced with the unique imprinting of our own gifts and personalities.

When personality traits prevent us from responding to God obediently, and to situations appropriately, they become targets for breaking. Like a logger who breaks up the key logs that cause a jam, the Master Logger focuses on those barriers in our lives which impede our growth. A mature person responds appropriately to the situation at hand. Like Solomon said, "Everything is beautiful in its time." There are times to take charge and confront, times to laugh and have fun, times to be detailed and analytical, and times to be low-key and at rest. Maturity allows us the flexibility to wash feet, to carry a cross, to unleash sanctified anger, and to overturn tables.

Lord, make me an instrument of your peace.
Where there is hatred, let me sow love;
Where there is injury, pardon;
Where there is doubt, faith;
Where there is despair, hope;
Where there is darkness, light;
Where there is sadness, joy.
Divine Master, grant that I may seek
not so much to be consoled as to console;
to be understood as to understand;
to be loved as to love;
for it is in giving that we receive;
it is in pardoning that we are pardoned;
and it is in dying that we are born to eternal life. Amen."
(St. Francis of Assisi)

That is the embodiment of brokenness. Living out the faith. Your entire life becomes a paradox.

When we break out of the retaining wall of life, the shell of self-centeredness which seeks its own fulfillment, we discover a new freedom. This is the liberty which results from a paradigm shift, a new way of viewing the world. In my office, below the photograph of the bound sheep awaiting slaughter, sit beautiful, green marble bookends, each mounted with a brass eagle, majestic wings spread for flight. The paradox of the Christian life is represented here, that only when we submit as the lamb to the slaughter are we free to soar like an eagle.

A sort of reckless abandon comes over the attitude of the person with a tamed soul. This is not a thrill-seeking irresponsibility found in the world. It is more of a sense that "I don't have to survive. I don't have to control my own destiny; He does. I don't have to call the shots; He does. I am not able to accomplish all I need to accomplish; He is." We are more apt to respond as Esther did when God's people needed a clutch play to save the game: "And if I perish, I perish" (Es. 4:16). Our reck-lessness is a growing desire to do whatever God wants us to do, because we are not consumed with other tasks, like ego enhancement, reputation preservation, and making something of ourselves. Count Zinzendorf said, "I have one passion; it is He, He alone." We are like the bondser-vant in Exodus 21, who when freed to leave declares, "I love my master and do not want to go free."

Troubles appear dwarfed. We feel immune to the stress of events that are out of our control. We have a truer sense of what is and is not in our control. The roses smell sweeter and the birds sound happier to the person who has been freed from the incarceration of the old nature. Sometimes, one can make a jail break only by being bro-ken. But the fruitfulness of this freedom outshines even the finest outcome of the unbroken soul.

■

QUESTIONS FOR REFLECTION

1. How is maturity more a matter of growth than of age? Can you think of people who illustrate your ideas?

2. Think of someone you consider mature. What qualities in his/her life do you admire and would like to emulate?

3. Which of the characteristics of a mature person do you feel are closest to your strengths? Which do you feel are further from your life at this time?

4. List the pride pollution result which you believe is the most common and most detrimental.

5. Which of your strengths do you feel could become weaknesses? In what way?

When Christ calls a man, he bids him come and
die.

—Dietrich Bonhoeffer

CHAPTER
TEN

■

Being the Person
You Want to Be

■ ■ ■

*At the end of the first year of beginning Saddleback
Valley Community Church, I was completely worn out
emotionally and physically. I was trying to keep up with
the rapid growth and was working 18 hour days. While
speaking on the last Sunday morning of the year, I felt I
was going to faint and was unable to complete the message. Fear and depression overwhelmed me. I took a
month leave from the church, taking my family to Phoenix
for recuperation and reevaluation. This was my "desert"
experience. Out of spending intensive time with the Lord,
three convictions were burned into my heart: 1. It's God's
church, not mine. 2. Ultimately, it's His responsibility, and
3. By grace, I am God's man for this church at this point in
time. During the next 12 months, I battled depression as
the Lord taught me many, many truths that have shaped
my life and ministry. It was the most difficult year of my
life as I was physically unable to do much of what was*

*required of me. I was forced to learn total dependence on
the Lord for every area of ministry.*

—Rick Warren

*Shortly after resigning my banking career in order to
concentrate on ministry among young people, I was afflicted by a voice/throat problem that threatened to termi-
nate my speaking ministry before it had begun. I was most
upset about this. Then one day I sensed that I was being
asked by the Lord, "What is it you really love? Preaching
about Me or Me?" Once I was honest enough to admit it
was probably the former and got things in proper perspective, I learned through brokenness to submit to His
plans and discover the vast possibilities of doing His will.*

—Stuart Briscoe

■

PREPARING THE SOIL FOR A PRODUCTIVE LIFE

"Be all that you can be," says the slogan of Army re-
cruiters. This self-help theme fills the titles of numerous
books, magazine articles, and personal growth seminars.
On several occasions, I have taken informal surveys during conferences and asked people to think of someone
they highly respect, and to list the qualities in that person
which they admire most and would like to emulate. Consistently, nine times out of ten, the qualities include traits
like: positive, loving, confident, forgiving, honest, humble,
accepting, and encouraging. We put vast amounts of
energy into achieving, purchasing, and envying material
items, when by our own admission, we value character
traits over skills or possessions. We have a mental image
of the person we would like to become. We have a secret
awareness of the potential person in the mirror that others do not see.

Most of the time, the one in the mirror is more loving, more joyful, more peaceful, and more faithful than the one in the flesh. We try to communicate more kindness and more patience, but end up falling short. If we think about it, most of these traits are only available through spiritual nurturing. They are the manifestations of God's Spirit at work within us. These are not qualities that we can produce on our own. We can sow and water and cultivate, but God gives the increase. We are the bearers of fruit that He produces in us. The way to be the people we really want to be is to try harder not to try so hard.

Dirt generally has a bad reputation in our vocabulary. "You have a dirty mind" means that someone is ridden with lust. "You have a dirty mouth" means that someone uses bad language. "Have you heard the latest dirt?" means you are about to hear some gossip. We dislike dirt in our carpets, on our clothes, and in our children's ears. But if you are a farmer, dirt is good. In fact, dirt is usually called soil when it refers to growing things.

Iowa has 25 percent of the nation's Grade A soil. Having grown up on an Iowan farm, I can remember my dad taking samples of the soil and sending them to the United States Department of Agriculture office at Iowa State University for analysis. The analysis showed what type of soil was in the sample, what nutrients and chemicals it contained, and what crops would grow best in that type of soil. All soils are not alike. Shelby soil tends to have a high clay content. It is more dense, keeps out air, and lacks good humus necessary for growing crops. On the other hand, Sharpsburg is usually Grade A ground, full of humus and the nutrients necessary for plants to grow well. We would often supplement the soil nutrients by adding nitrogen, phosphorus, or other elements.

Jesus talked about the different soils. There was the rocky soil where the seed died. The hardened dirt did not provide for moisture, air, or fertilizer, and the seed was useless. But the good soil produced bountifully. A lot of work goes into preparing soil to yield a good crop. My dad would plow under the fields each fall, so that the plant stubble could decay and add nutrients to the soil below. Later in the year he would disc the fields, and finally harrow them to prepare for planting.

My daily chores after school consisted of cleaning out the stalls in the barn and hog house of our farrowing sows. Since hogs have short gestation periods, we had baby pigs almost all of the time. Twice a day we let the sows out to eat, and while they ate we restored a healthy environment for them to live. I would shovel the mess into the alley between the two rows of stalls. After the stalls were all cleaned, I scooped the manure and straw into a large a pile at the end of the building. Then I would open the door and pitch the pile into the manure spreader. Sometimes this equipment was referred to as the "honey wagon," partially as a tongue-in-cheek remark hiding its real purpose, but also because farmers know the benefit of manure. We would pull the spreader behind the tractor and spread it all over the hillsides, especially on the soil that needed fertilizer.

In our culture we are so fruit-oriented and production-focused that we fail to recognize the importance of "preparing the soil" of our lives. Proper soil analysis and preparation is crucial to bearing the fruit we desire in our lives. Galatians 5:16–27 talks about characteristics we seek to emulate, character traits of the type of person most of us would like to become: love, joy, peace, faithfulness, patience, gentleness. However, just concentrating on the fruit itself rarely produces much yield. What we need to understand is the process of preparing the soil. That is what brokenness is all about.

Brokenness is like manure in our lives. At first it seems

anything but appealing, but it fertilizes our souls so that they will bear much fruit. In the context of fruitfulness, Galatians 5:24 says, "And those who are Christ's have crucified the flesh with its passions and desires." The scriptures are teeming with similar verses, mandating the death of the old man, the deeds of the flesh, and the old self. Fruit of the Spirit grows out of soil fertilized by the decaying old nature. The very source of our frustration with a self-centered lifestyle actually becomes the humus for spiritual growth.

It is no wonder that the word *humility* has the same etymology as *humus*. Humility is one of the surest signs that a person has been broken in the right place and has put to death the sinful nature of the untamed soul. Humility is hard to fake, for false humility shows itself quickly under the stress of relationships and temptation. True humility has little in common with low self-esteem and self-degradation. It has everything to do with the death of selfish ambition and the working out of your own agenda and power. Proverbs 15:33 says, "Before honor is humility." It is a prerequisite to the things we seek most in our lives.

■

TESTS OF TRUE HUMILITY

There are several ways to detect humility, good character fertilizer, in yourself or in others. Here are seven common ways to spot a humble spirit.

1. **Humility does not demand its own way.** If you think "It's my way or the highway," or if you often feel the need to defend yourself a lot, chances are your humility level is low.

2. **Humility exudes an attitude of service.** You are there to help people, not to be helped. Jesus said, "I

came to serve, not to be served." It is not a consumer-oriented atmosphere where you shop around for who or what can give you the best deal.

3. **Humility does not seek attention or credit.** It is not concerned with having its name placed in the program, or on the dedicatory plaque, or even spelled correctly. There is almost a feeling of awkwardness that comes over humble people when the spotlight shines in their direction. This person often changes his or her name to "Anonymous."

4. **Humility forgives when offended, but is hard to offend.** Perhaps the best way to avoid being offended by others is to become humble. Humble people do not read into others' responses. Therefore, they are free to be honest and innocently naive to the hate generated by others. At the same time, when hate is overt and obvious, they are at liberty to forgive, to release others from a false sense of obligation to love a certain way. Thomas à Kempis wrote, "The humble person, when he is rebuked, is yet in sufficient peace; because he resteth on God, and not on the world."

5. **Humility does not criticize others.** Finger pointing, opinion giving, and condemnation rarely emanate out of a pure, selfless attitude. Most criticism is personally oriented and seeks to punish another. Yet, humble people are not confined by the fear of speaking up for truth. They can be authoritative without being authoritarian because God is their motivation for making suggestions.

6. **Humility produces a teachable spirit.** Good leaders are learners. That is why leaders need to learn humility. Humble people know that they do not know everything, and recognize the multiple nuances that operate when more than one perception is involved in a situation. Humble people practice one of the most important behaviors of learning—they listen a lot. Beware the proud leader

claiming to have all the answers. Humble people ask questions more than they give answers. Although Jesus was called Teacher, one of his favorite teaching styles was to answer questions by asking other questions.

7. **Humility is gracious and thankful.** Perhaps this is a lost quality in our culture. We are all too aware of our rights and demand them even beyond what normal law affords. If you received a coin with humility on one side, thankfulness would be on the other. It is very hard to be truly gracious and proud. Unthankfulness may just be the worst sin in the Bible. The Children of Israel were constantly being condemned for their unthankful attitudes throughout the years. Jesus told the parable of the ten lepers, where only one returned to say, "Thanks." The New Testament reminds us to give thanks, always.

Humility is the best soil test for showing us whether brokenness has occurred in the right place. It is good news that humus is present, because the decaying of the dead, sinful nature gives hope of a fertile soil for fruit-bearing. When, and only when, the soil has been prepared, can we go ahead and concern ourselves with further cultivation and nurturing of the plant.

■

THE INTERNAL TUG OF WAR

The main struggle for Christians is not in choosing between the sinful nature and the Spirit. It is in trying to do both. Galatians 5:17 says, "the flesh lusts against the Spirit, and the Spirit against the flesh." They are in conflict with each other. The essence of sin is not bad deeds such as murder, lying, cheating, gossiping, and the like. As we mentioned before, the primary core of our sinful nature, our flesh as it is called in the passage from Galatians, is the propensity to become our own god. This is the theme of countless cults and the New Age movement, "you are god," "you can become a god," "reach the god within you." The symptoms of this nature are self-centeredness, stealing, pride, etc. Even "good," moral people, who fail to allow the Creator to be Lord of their lives, fall prey to this sinful nature of self-lordship. Being our own god is the first sin and is at the root of every other sin and temptation.

The Spirit and the sinful nature are like opposite poles of a magnet, always repelling each other. Trying to keep the Spirit and the sinful nature inside one person is much like putting two cats in a pillow case. Farmers realize that all crops do not grow in the same type of soil. Trying to raise grapes and corn in the same plot of land will not bring good grapes and good corn. So it is with people who want to grow spiritual fruit from character soil which is not fertile. People who are not Christians really have little hassle with their sinful nature. They are not concerned with following God's way. But Galatians 5:17 also says you are to live by the Spirit, "so that you do not do the things that you wish." Now there's a conflict. Doing as you please requires no power, no spiritual discipline, and therefore no conflict.

The key to this spiritual life is to focus on living by the Spirit, not on trying to avoid the desires of the old nature. "Walk in the Spirit, and you shall not fulfill the lust of the flesh" (see Gal. 5). We are to "walk in the Spirit." The word translated "walk" refers to a marching step or a dance step. I remember in marching band, our instructor would remind the less coordinated members to keep in step, "Left, right, left . . . left . . . left." If we got off beat, we would look down at others' feet to regain our step. It is hard to hear the cadence when you are far from the drummer. Stay close so that you can keep in step.

Plato wrote an allegory called "The Cave." In the story, some people have been chained in a cave all their lives, confined so that they only face one wall of the cave. Behind them is a fire which shines light onto the wall. Objects representing trees, animals, and nature are moved near the fire, casting shadows onto the wall. Since these shapes were all these people had ever known, their whole world consisted only of shadows. This was their reality. Suppose one of the people is released from the chains. He is able to see the fire and he realizes that what he thought was reality was merely a shadow of objects behind the people. Then, if that person is taken out of the cave into the light of day, he would see real trees, birds, and animals, not just the icons. Then, if this person returned to the cave and talked with his friends facing the wall, trying to explain what he had seen and telling them that they were seeing only representations of reality, they could not believe him. Plato concludes by saying this man would never be able to happily return to his former way of living.

That story is a lesson in life and learning. It also serves as a wonderful illustration of spiritual growth. As our awareness of God's plan for us deepens, we find it more and more difficult to communicate fully with those who, in essence, are facing the wall. We come to identify with 1 Peter 2:11 where it says we are "aliens and strangers in the world." Galatians 5 informs us that life in the Spirit transcends what we are familiar with in our natural world. This spiritual fruit becomes abundant following a season of brokenness and humility (humus). Having been broken in the right place, we find the thought of going back to our untamed souls undesirable.

■

FALSE MATURITY

What is true spiritual maturity, and how is it different than perceived maturity? Legalism can appear to be mature Christianity, but it is not. The problem addressed in Galatians, as in several New Testament books, is the influence of Judaizers, people trying to get the new believers to follow legalistic practices instead of living by the freedom of the Spirit. Reliance on works is a weakness which often comes across as maturity and spiritual fruit, but is really immaturity and human religiosity. Legalism measures Christianity in terms of behaviors and appearances, and is often (but not always) a weakness of those older in the faith. Legalism is a person's way of avoiding suffering. Adopting external standards of behavior is easier than having a truly tamed soul, which requires internal growth and transformation. Every homemaker knows the difference between straightening up a house and deep cleaning.

Legalism develops when we associate our culture with Christianity. For example, we assume that democracy or capitalism is "Christian," just because we've come to know Christ in America. If we find God in a legalistic subculture, then surely such rules regarding smoking, drinking, hemlines, jewelry, going to movies, etc., must be biblical standards. It is easier to become legalistic than truly spiritual, because once we set moral standards, we don't have to wrestle with gray areas. Things become black and white, right or wrong. Since we are visually oriented, since we can measure our own or another's behavior, we feel we're making progress, when real character growth and spiritual maturity take time. Legalism also results in condemning others and producing spiritual pride.

I was raised in an environment where it was considered a sin to drink alcohol, smoke, gamble, dance, go to movies, or play cards. As for drinking alcohol, the only clear biblical mandate is against strong drink and being drunk. On the other hand, the Bible clearly states that gossiping and overeating are sins (Prov. 11:13, 18:7–8; 2 Cor. 12:20; 3 John 1:10; Rom. 1:29; 1 Tim. 5:13; Prov. 23:2, 21; 28:7; Titus 1:12). People were expelled from the Christian college I attended for drinking alcohol, but as far as I know, no one ever left because they gossiped or ate too much. Many churches have failed to distinguish between the healthy, artistic dancing of a culture and sexually provocative dancing, and have decided, therefore, that all dancing is bad. A man told me once that line dancing was wrong because it is done in bars. That line of thinking would also suggest that restrooms are immoral because they exist in saloons. I am not promoting these behaviors. I am defending biblical rationale. I am not suggesting all these guidelines are wrong. I am only saying that it is easy to make our personal culture and behaviors seem like God's, and that the temptation to take the easy road is ever before us. Brokenness does not follow the easy road to maturity.

We need to differentiate between principles and practices. It is easy to associate possible practices of Christianity with principles of Christlike living. Stephen Covey explains this concept in the context of a manager and his employees: "Principles are not practices. Practices are specific activities or actions that work in one circumstance but not necessarily in another. If you manage by practices and lead by policies, your people don't have to be the experts; they don't have to exercise judgment, because all of the judgment and wisdom is provided them in the form of rules and regulations."[1] Christ wants us to be mature and to respond appropriately to situations. He is not interested in robotic behaviors that simply look holy, but in reality are little more than impish replication. "If you are led by the Spirit, you are not under law" (Gal. 5:18).

The flip side to the weakness of legalism is license,

which is not true maturity either. License refers to a liberal response to God's grace. It tends to be a weakness of those who are younger in the faith. The problem is that exercising spiritual freedom often results in ignorant flirting with sin and insensitively offending others. When people flaunt their liberty, they make their freedom in Christ more important than ministry to others. Scripture says, "Do not cause your brother to stumble."

The primary reason my wife and I do not drink alcohol is that we know we could not minister to certain people if we did. In a society where alcohol adversely affects one out of four families, costs billions of dollars in treatment and thousands of lives annually, I must realize that many people are offended and troubled by this significant problem. This reason alone is enough for me not to want to be identified with such a social ill. In essence, for me to drink because it is "my right" would be placing my freedom over the needs of others, a selfish and immature attitude. (A secondary reason is because we have chosen to identify with a denomination which does not allow alcohol use by its clergy.) This is merely one of numerous possible examples.

When Christians vehemently defend their rights and freedoms as believers, and debate the limits which others impose on them or even themselves, it is a strong indication of an unbroken soul. Some people believe that liberty is true maturity, but it is not.

■

TRUE MATURITY

The entire law is summed up in a single command, "'You shall love your neighbor as yourself.' But if you bite and devour one another, beware lest you be consumed by one another" (Gal. 5:14–15). Paul is talking here about emotional cannibalism among Christians. When people of the same faith cannot get along in Christian love, they are not living in the Spirit. Interdenominational and intra-church hostilities deny God's intention of being of one mind. Only when we allow for spiritual fruit in our lives will we move from watching Plato's wall toward seeing God's light of reality.

The fruit of the Spirit is love, joy, peace, patience, kindness, goodness, faithfulness, gentleness, and self-control. These are the character traits which emanate out of a person filled with and led by God's Spirit, which results from being broken in the right place. Being broken in the wrong places often results in low self-esteem, anger, depression, hatred, and varying degrees of moral malpractice. Legalism and liberty are often Christians' forms of covering brokenness in the wrong places. Like wax fruit, they look like the real thing, but they have little substance. They do not help the body grow.

Spiritual character traits differ from their human counterparts. Only the names are the same. They are of a different nature because they are spiritual and not human in origin. They give us a new reality which transcends what most of us strive for and work toward. Many of us think that we should strive to love and concentrate on being joyous.

But we cannot achieve the beatitudes and the fruit of the Spirit out of human striving. Rather, they are descriptions of what we will be like when God's Kingdom truly reigns in our lives. The Bible calls it fruit of the Spirit versus fruits of the Spirit, because the person whose life is Spirit-led tends to emulate all of these traits. Think of them as different facets of the same jewel, appropriately manifested, (super)naturally under various settings and where they are needed.

A mature fruit tree is one which bears fruit. True maturity means the manifestation of spiritual fruit. Let's take a look at these character traits which emulate the person we would like to become.

Love

is treating others and yourself as incredibly valuable. The initiating concern behind human love is "what you do for me." As long as you are nice to me, or help me, or turn me on, or stimulate me, or love me, then I will love you. But the theme of spiritual love is your God-given value. Value-driven love is based on faith—what the Bible says—and not emotion—how I feel. Psalm 85:10 says "love and faithfulness meet together." Human love is based on personal self-image. If I think and feel good about myself, I can love you. If I do not value myself, I cannot love you sufficiently, for I cannot give what I do not possess. Spiritual love is determined by what is right and by obedience to God. It is based on the self-image that comes from recognizing that we were created in the image of God and that His love for us is demonstrated through His Son (John 3:16; Rom. 5:8).

Joy

is positive faith. I have never met a joyous person who did not basically see life in a positive way. People who do not have a positive faith do not have joy. When things are going well, it is relatively easy to put on a happy face and smile awhile. But what happens when things are not going well?

Human joy is based on what God has done for me. Biblical joy emanates from God's goodness and His expression of grace and love in our lives. It is faith-oriented, not emotion-driven. That is why James can write, "Count it pure joy when you face various trials and temptations." This sort of reality makes no sense to those in the cave, facing the wall, but it does to Christians.

Human joy is based on circumstances and external events, which are often out of our control. Spiritual joy is based on what God can do. This joy responds to the hope God always provides in every situation, regardless of what seems to be. Christians realize that circumstances are merely shadows and may not represent reality or at least the whole truth. People who have been broken in the right place nearly always have a cheerful disposition and a sanctified sense of humor. The unbroken take themselves too seriously which thwarts laughter and cheer.

Peace

is confidence in the midst of turmoil. The theme of human peace is the security we gain from self-confidence and our environment. As long as we feel in control and the world around us is somewhat stable and safe, we will have peace. But the theme of spiritual peace is knowing Who controls the future. Again, it is faith-driven and not emotionally-oriented. Human peace depends on others' responses and relational wholeness. As long as countries are amiable and pleasant, peace is possible. But when someone else's response is hostile or offensive, peace threatens to evaporate. Spiritual peace is based on our orientation to God. It comes out of internal wholeness, and therefore is not prone to the ups and downs of relationships and the responses of others.

Patience

is the peace of realizing God is in control of the important things in life. Patience is necessary to get to know God intimately. Psalm 37:7 says, "Rest in the Lord and wait patiently for Him; do not fret because of him who prospers in his ways." "I waited patiently for the Lord; And He inclined to me and heard my cry" (Ps. 40:1). Several scriptures talk about patient endurance (Rev. 13:10; 14:12,

2 Cor. 1:6). Patience comes from the word *patior* which means to suffer.

> The first thing Jesus promises is suffering. 'I tell you . . . you will be weeping and wailing . . . and you will be sorrowful.' But he calls these birth pains. And so, what seems a hindrance becomes a way; what seems an obstacle becomes a door; what seems a misfit becomes a cornerstone. Jesus changes our history from a random series of sad incidents and accidents into a constant opportunity for a change of heart.[2]

One of the most difficult qualities to obtain in life is the willingness to delay gratification. We tend to be an overnight delivery, fax, and ATM-type people who feel that waiting in the eight-item express lane at the supermarket approximates eternity. Eternal life is a concept we compare to waiting for our frozen dinner to thaw in the microwave. But brokenness anesthetizes the pain of waiting. Endurance refers to the quantity of commitment. Patience refers to the quality of commitment, our attitude while we endure.

The thought behind human patience is that things progress as we desire. As long as everything goes as planned, we have no trouble being patient. But, if there are hangups, hold-ups, or interruptions, patience dries up. Spiritual patience comes from committing what we cannot control to God. Life is full of things we cannot control: traffic lights, the economy, and, most significantly, people. We need wisdom to discern what we can and cannot control. Like the Prayer of Serenity says, "Lord teach me to know the difference between what I can and cannot change." Impatience is an emotional response to our feelings, not faith in God.

Human patience is based on our concept of timing.

Spiritual patience is based on God's timing. A man once went to God and said, "Is it true that 100 years is like a minute to you?" God said, "Yes, that is right." The man continued, "Then surely $1,000,000 is like a dollar to you." "You are correct, my child," God responded. The man smiled. "Then will you give me a dollar?" asked the man. "In a minute," God replied.

Those who have been broken have a tranquil patience. "All time belongs to you if you belong to Christ, the present and the future. Welcome the coming and going of time, for you do not belong to time, you belong to Christ and He is the same yesterday, today and forever, the unchanging, the unfading. He is not a sunset or evening star, He is the bright and morning star, a sunrise!"[3] He tames the "strive to arrive" impulsiveness.

Patience is not passive indifference or apathetic laziness. Rather, it is faithfully working according to God's schedule. We often think that faster is better and now is best. But God is not concerned about the amounts of time we spend. He is concerned that the timing is right. You can cram for a test, but you may not retain the knowledge you have gained. The good things in life do not come overnight. "Therefore, be patient, brethren, until the coming of the Lord. See how the farmer waits for the precious fruit of the earth, waiting patiently for it until it receives the early and latter rain. You also be patient. Establish your hearts, for the coming of the Lord is at hand. Do not grumble against one another, brethren, lest you be condemned" (James 5:7–9). "And we desire that each one of you show the same diligence to the full assurance of hope until the end, that you do not become sluggish, but imitate those who through faith and patience inherit the promises" (Heb. 6:11–12). "The Lord is not slack concerning His promise, as some count slackness, but is longsuffering toward us, not willing that any should perish but that all should come to repentance" (2 Peter 3:9).

Kindness

is responding to people with the intensity of good friends and the politeness of strangers. "Add to your faith . . . brotherly kindness. . . . For if these things are yours and abound, you will be neither barren nor unfruitful in the knowledge of our Lord Jesus Christ" (2 Peter 1:5–8). Human kindness says, "I want you to like me." We learn etiquette and manners so that we can be socially acceptable. Political behavior, networking, and "you scratch my back, I'll scratch yours," are typical. This is not to imply that these human traits are wrong, only that they are finite and temporary.

Doug Smith, a long-time center for the Los Angeles Rams football team and fine Christian man, shared with me one common response people have to professional athletes. While in a clothing store, dressed very casually, a salesperson appeared apathetic toward him and a friend. They asked for some help, and the salesperson eventually asked, "You're big. Do you lift weights?"

"I've done some lifting," Doug replied.

"Looks like you've played some football," the clerk continued.

"Yes, I've played some ball," Doug mentioned.

"What did you play?"

"I play for the Los Angeles Rams," Doug said. Suddenly, the salesman's face lit up and he got excited.

"Really! Who are you? I knew it!" he shouted. "What's your name?"

The man's kindness was not toward Doug Smith the person, but toward the image of fame and success behind a professional athlete. Such is the human attitude of kindness.

Spiritual kindness says, "I want you to like God." Here, kindness is born of one's desire to be a good ambassador for God. In Titus, Paul tells us to be good employees and churchmen so that we make the gospel attractive, not so that we make ourselves attractive. Human kindness is politically-driven, not faith-driven. Human kindness is concerned about "how you can help me." It says, "If you cannot help me, I have no reason to be nice to you. But if you can help me, or are a potential client, or can be a friend, I'll be kind to you." Spiritual kindness asks "how can I help you?" It sees kindness as an end in itself, not a means to an end.

Faithfulness

means unconditional loyalty. I remember the testimony of Terry Anderson, an American journalist held hostage for six-and-a-half years by Islamic terrorists. When a reporter asked if he desired revenge or wanted his captors to be arrested and prosecuted, Anderson replied, "I am a Christian, and as a Christian, I must forgive them." He went on to confess that his personal loyalty to God gave him the energy to go through the torture and captivity.

The Marine slogan is *semper fidelis,* always faithful. The theme of human faithfulness is mutual trust. When President Reagan began the end of the cold war, he said we should trust the Russians, but "trust verified," meaning let's be sure they prove their words of trust. That is wise, but it is nevertheless human trust. A man and wife have mutual trust when each goes half-way and they meet in the middle. But if one betrays the other, human trust ends.

The theme of spiritual trust is God's unchanging nature. "What if some did not have faith? Will their lack of faith nullify God's faithfulness? Not at all!" (see Rom. 3:3–4). God illustrated his faithfulness to an unfaithful Israel through His prophet Hosea, whom He told to take a prostitute named Gomer for his wife. Gomer ran away from Hosea, who in turn went out and bought her back. Lest we cast stones, let us all realize that we too have been spiritual Gomers. But spiritual faithfulness is based on God's sameness, not on our consistency or that of others.

Human faithfulness is based on perception. If I perceive someone is trustworthy, even if he is not, I will be apt to put faith in him. If I perceive someone is not trustworthy, even if he is, I will be apt to doubt him. Spiritual faith is scripturally-oriented, based on God's track record through time and what the Bible says about Him. Human faithfulness is based on my fulfillment. As long as I'm fulfilled in marriage, I'll stay married. As long as I'm fulfilled at my job, I'll stay employed there. As long as my friends and goals satisfy me, I will prove faithful. But faithfulness wanes when my fulfillment ebbs. Spiritual faithfulness transcends personal fulfillment and is based upon God's faithfulness.

Gentleness

is harnessed strength allowing empathy. When Jesus said, "Blessed are the meek, for they shall inherit the earth" (Matt. 5:5), He was letting us know that quiet, harnessed strength will always outperform loud, obnoxious energy. Human gentleness is typically seen as tranquilized temperament or repressed emotions. People who demonstrate gentleness are often considered wimps, not goal-oriented movers and shakers. A laid-back, phlegmatic temperament has little to do with the spiritual quality of gentleness.

Another source of human gentleness is repressed emotions. Some people remain calm amidst stressful situations by repressing their true feelings. This is similar to trying to keep a beach ball under water. Soon, it splashes to the top. Repressed emotions eventually emerge in the form of passive-aggressive behavior, migraines, high blood pressure, ulcers, or heart attacks.

Spiritual gentleness is disciplined sensitivity. Undisciplined sensitivity is sloppy agape. Flimsy sentimentality has hardly more affect than a mushy Valentine card. Tough love needs strong, deep gentleness. Biblical love is not for the weak-kneed pansy. Human gentleness is emotion-oriented, while spiritual gentleness is faith-oriented. The former is based on human disposition, how you handle your emotions and your temperament. The latter is based on spiritual confidence and loving strength.

In his first epistle, Peter directly addresses women about gentleness: "Do not let your adornment be merely outward—arranging the hair, wearing gold, or putting on fine apparel—rather let it be the hidden person of the heart, with the incorruptible beauty of a gentle and quiet spirit, which is very precious in the sight of God. For in this manner, in former times, the holy women who trusted in God also adorned themselves" (1 Peter 3:3–5). I have nothing against the plethora of beauty consultants or cosmetic products available. (The word *cosmetic* comes from the root word *cosmos,* literally meaning, "making order out of chaos.") But attitude is the beauty secret deeper than the skin.

The modern women's movement in America has greatly helped women in some areas, but in other areas, it has hurt them. It has hurt women when they feel a need to take on more masculine traits and deny the uniquely feminine traits God has given them. The loss of a gentle spirit makes even gorgeous women average, but gentleness makes average-looking women gorgeous.

Peter continues by addressing men: "Husbands, likewise, dwell with them with understanding, giving honor to the wife as the weaker vessel, and as being heirs together of the grace of life, that your prayers may not be hindered" (1 Peter 3:7). The phrase "weaker vessel" can cause some women to lose their gentle attitudes. The beauty of the context is that women need to be treated as more delicate people, in that their spirits can be crushed more easily. Men can say things to each other in ways that do not offend each other, but which can damage the emotions of a woman. Instead of treating women like beer steins, deal with them like fine crystal. In essence, Peter is telling us not to take sandpaper to a marble countertop. Men, we are to be gentle.

Self-control

means the power to say no to the wrong things, and the freedom to say yes to the right things. The word for self-control comes from the word for power, and discipline means a safe and sound mind. We might say that this concept is the power of a sound mind. The human view of self-control is "how do I feel?" If we feel like running, we'll run. If I feel like turning down the donut or extra piece of pie, I will do it. Although that may be a weak position, our human concept of self-control tends to be emotionally based. Our natural tendency is to be disciplined primarily in the areas where we have emotional motivation.

Spiritually, self-control is "what's right?" As Paul discoursed about "righteousness, self-control, and the judgment to come, Felix was afraid and answered, 'Go away for now; when I have a convenient time, I will call for you'" (Acts 24:25). That is a typical human response, do something only when it is convenient. Human self-control comes through gritted teeth. Spiritual self-control comes through surrendered will. Human self-control is based on, "I can do it if I try." Spiritual self-control is based on, "I can't do it; God can".

Galatians 5:22–23 says, "But the fruit of the Spirit is

love, joy, peace, longsuffering, kindness, goodness, faithfulness, gentleness, self-control. Against such there is no law." Laws bind, restrict, chafe. Christianity is intended to free us from ourselves, not bind us to another system. Only when we die to the sinful nature, and through brokenness allow God to do all He wants in us, can we ever reach our true potential. Until then, we will never become the people we really want to be. We will always want to try harder and be better. When these qualities emerge from a life of brokenness, they are true character traits and not efforts. They come from focusing on God, and seeing His Spirit work in our lives, surrendered out of brokenness.

God never intended us to become believers by faith and grace, only to end up trying to reach our potential on our own. It is our striving that so often gets in the way. Only by simple faith can we let go of our earnest but vain attempts at reaching sainthood and striving to become all we can be for the glory of God. Think about what power is released when a single tiny atom is broken.

All too often, we put on seminars and conferences designed to produce spiritual fruit, without addressing the core issues. It is similar to sponsoring a gold-mining convention, complete with seminars on how to pan for gold and the latest pan technology. However, the real work is getting to the river. The chief goal in producing spiritual fruit is the abiding. If you abide, you will bear fruit. Psalm 66:10–12 says,

> For You, O God, have tested us;
> You refined us as silver is refined.
> You brought us into the net;
> You laid affliction on our backs.
> You have caused men to ride over our heads;
> We went through fire and through water;
> But You brought us out to rich fulfillment.

The land of milk and honey follows the wilderness. Light follows darkness. Fruit grows as seeds die. The shell becomes the fertilizer for its own new shoot.

The life of the Spirit is wings to help us soar, not handcuffs or a straightjacket to keep us from hurting ourselves. Only in the freedom that comes through brokenness can we gain the character traits that we so eagerly desire and so passionately admire. Only then will we transcend the frustrations of knowing what we want in our lives, but being unable to make it happen. As a child, I learned the shortcut of remembering the difference in spelling desert and dessert. Desert (with one *s*) has sand, and dessert (with two *s*'s) includes strawberry shortcake. The way to make a dessert out of your desert is by adding an *s*, which stands for surrender. It may be corny, but it's a good thing to remember.

"Humility does not rest, in final count, upon bafflement and discouragement and self-disgust at our shabby lives, a brow-beaten, dog-slinking attitude. It rests upon the disclosure of the consummate wonder of God. Humility rests upon a holy blindedness, like the blindedness of him who looks steadily into the sun."[4]

■

QUESTIONS FOR REFLECTION

1. Describe some of the "humus" events/episodes in your life which you now recognize as potentially enriching your life and making you more fruitful.

2. Which of the signs of humility do you see somewhat evident in your life? Which do you see lacking?

3. In Plato's allegory of the cave, do you see times in your life when you were able to see a new angle, a new perspective, so that it changed your life and you would not go back to the old way of thinking? If so, how are you different? How do you approach those still chained to the old perspective?

4. As you look at your life, what signs (past or present) do you see of legalism? What signs (past or present) do you see of flaunting your freedom?

5. What spiritual fruit do you see more prevalent in your life? Which are more scarce?

In order to be a servant leader, you must first learn servanthood.

—Robert Greenleaf

CHAPTER ELEVEN

■

Servanthood

■■■

Unity is the high water mark of spirituality, and there is no unity without humility, and there's little true humility without brokenness. The John 17 paradigm declares unity to be the goal of all believers. Pride, arrogance, ignorance and culture keep believers from following the pattern of the Trinity. Brokenness leads to repentance which issues into reconciliation. Reconciliation releases the power of God. God wrestles with all of us and cripples us even as he crippled Jacob. Pain plants the flag of truth in a rebel heart.

Yes, God has used brokenness as a powerful tool in my life. It is in those dark hours that God becomes vital and real, and character is forged in the process.

—Joe Aldrich

Awhile ago, I went through a process of breaking which is creating great freedom in my life. Over the years, I have gotten a lot of justifiable criticism from staff, pastors, and others. People would say through other people to me, "You're not personable. You shut people out. Your whole life is shallow. You always talk about yourself. You always seem to be the center of your conversation. You're not sensitive to people." I found myself over the years not able to say "no" to requests. I was always saying "yes" to people on the outside, but on the inside I was saying "no". I got to the point of resentment and bitterness. I felt used and unappreciated.

Psalm 139:23–24 says, "Search me o God, and see if there is any unclean way in me." One day I was giving a testimony, sharing my vulnerability about my dad, when a couple came up to me afterward and thanked me. They told me how they too were adult children of alcoholics, and that they were learning to deal with dysfunctions in their lives. For the first time, I realized I had some of the traits they were speaking about. I had grown up with all my theology teaching me that the only way to be a loving person was to say "yes". As a result, I became a very controlling person. It was a defense mechanism. I call it less than a godly response pattern. Almost every dysfunction is a truth out of balance.

I had lost hope of ever being in control of my life. The dominant childhood feeling for me was to be important. My dominant fear was the fear of dying without being important. I believe it motivated me in a lot of the books, videos, films, to say "yes," and talk about myself. 2 Corinthians 12:9 says, "And He said to me, My grace is sufficient for you, for power is perfected in weakness". That gave me courage. If I always do what I've always done, I'll always be what I've always been. I've asked God to bring me to the point where my outer "no" will be an inner "no", and my outer "yes" will be an inner "yes".

God showed me I need to live this out, so that I can be a healthy person. I must deny myself, those patterns of response that are unpleasing to God. In the last few years, I've seen more things in my life that I don't like, but I've never been more excited because I'm growing. I'm really becoming free. If we're all supposed to be perfect, we wouldn't need unconditional love. So often in the church, when you look good, when you have no problems, they applaud you. When you go to Alcoholics Anonymous, if you have a problem, they applaud you. In the church we often look good and get worse. In Alcoholics Anonymous you look worse, and get better. I'm getting better. It's my response to mature in the Holy Spirit. I thank God that He's alive and working in my life.

—Josh McDowell

Servant Leaders

Don't give us blessings—give us grace to be unquestionably obedient to Your every last command and desire.

Don't give us status—give us a place to serve.

Don't give us things for our use—use us.

Don't give us a mansion to live in—give us a springboard to take Christ's love to the whole world.

Don't give us good jobs—put us to work.

Don't give us pleasure—give us perspective.

Don't give us satisfaction—teach us sacrifice.

Don't give us entertainment—enable us.

Don't give us good salaries—give us strength to do Your will.

Our great joy in life is in pleasing our Lord—and there is no other joy comparable.[1]

When we think of leadership, we often think of a General Patton, the President of the United States, or a demanding but confident CEO of a Fortune 500 corporation. There are many different types of leading. There is benevolent dictatorship, political manipulation, charismatic persuasion, empowerment, networking, and authoritarianism. Often these forms are blended and intermixed as needed. "Men who harp on authority only prove they have none. And kings who make speeches about submission only betray twin fears in their hearts: They are not certain they are really true leaders, sent of God. And they live in mortal fear of a rebellion."[2]

But when we think of leadership, we are not often drawn to the mental image of a man in his T-shirt, washing the filthy feet of his friends and pupils. Little, if anything, about this image would remind us of leadership, success, or personal achievement. Some Christian leaders try to rationalize their human approach to leading a service-oriented group by saying, "I serve by leading." This is not the same thing as a servant leader.

Footwashing, a duty not even required of slaves in His day, is the example Jesus gave us to emulate. While the disciples maneuvered for power and prestige, Jesus showed them powerlessness and humility . . . or did He? No conquest is so worthy as victory over self. Therefore, Jesus displayed incredible power and ability by voluntarily submitting to the Father through service to others.

A story from Indian folklore illustrates how a servant can be like Jesus. There was once an old man who meditated early every evening under a large tree on the bank of the Ganges River in India. One morning he saw a scorpion floating helplessly in the current of the river. As the scorpion was pulled closer to the tree, it was caught by long tree roots that branched far into the river. The scorpion struggled frantically to free itself, but only became more entangled.

When the old man saw this, he immediately stretched himself onto the extended roots and reached out to rescue the drowning animal. The scorpion jerked wildly and stung him and the man withdrew his hand. After regaining his balance, he once again stretched to save the panicked animal. The scorpion struck again. Every time the old man came within reach, the scorpion stung him, so often that his hands became swollen and bloody and his face distorted by pain.

At that moment, a passerby saw the old man stretched out on the roots, struggling with the scorpion. He shouted, "Hey, stupid old man, what's wrong with you? Only a fool risks his life for the sake of an ugly, useless creature. Don't you know that you could be killed trying to save that ungrateful animal?"

Slowly the old man turned his head, and looking calmly in the stranger's eyes, said, "Friend, just because it is the nature of the scorpion to sting, why should I ignore my own nature to save?"[3]

This story helps us understand why Jesus was able not only to wash feet, but also to die on a cross for a sinful, thankless race. It also explains the disciples' motivation when they faced martyrdom for their beliefs. It had become their nature to serve, to love, and to live for Christ, regardless of the circumstances.

Brokenness changes our nature. It frees us from the dictatorship of pride and self-will. The world watched in amazement as the Berlin Wall fell, freeing millions from the bondage of communism. When God's Spirit breaks the walls of our soul, we are set free to live a Christlike lifestyle. The Mother Teresas of the world evoke admiration and pique our curiosity. We see them as both saints and oddities. The world's system does not produce selfless people like this. God's system does.

True service is self-giving and comes out of brokenness. This is healthy. Unhealthy service stems from self-centeredness. Service which emanates from a need to be needed, a desire to please, a seeking for attention, or low self-esteem, is unhealthy. It does not result from being broken in the right place. True brokenness never mars one's self-esteem. The only part of self that dies during our breaking processes is the old self—the sinful nature. Brokenness overcomes the self-defeating part of us that works contrary to the Spirit (Gal. 5:24–26) and to self-surrender. That part of our being is no friend. It is a traitor who promises to fulfill and love, but who consistently undermines our progress toward purity and wholeness.

"The greatest peril for us in Christian service is to lean upon ourselves and to draw upon our soul power—upon our talent, gift, knowledge, magnetism, eloquence or cleverness. The experience of countless spiritual believers confirms that unless our soulishness is definitely delivered to death and its life at all times inhibited from operation, it will be most active in service."[4]

Ministry is therapeutic. It takes one's attention off of oneself. However, neurotic service indicates a desire for attention and may be the result of guilt or a need for approval rather than selfless love. Service that flows out of a spirit which has been healed and made whole by brokenness is sensitive to the welfare of others and desires to glorify God.

■

SELF-ESTEEM AND BROKENNESS

We should discuss in more detail the relationship of self-esteem and brokenness. There are basically two schools of thought about self-esteem theology. One view says that we are worthless worms, deserving only destruction as punishment for our sins. But because of God's loving nature, He has given us grace—unmerited favor—and although we are nothing, He saved us for Himself.

The other view says that we were all created in the image of God, and although sin marred that image, it is still there. Therefore, every human has incredible value, and God's love and grace are sought to renew this tarnished image. Although we are not deserving, we are not worthless. Christ would not die for what is worthless.

Although I was raised in the former theology, I have come to believe and preach out of the latter belief system. The bottom line is that we have incredible worth, whether it comes from His love for us as worthless creatures, or because we were made in His image. The Bible says that we are to love our neighbors as we love ourselves. The Greek translation of this action is the well-known word *agape.* It is the same unconditional love with which God loves us. Self-esteem is merely a psychological term for recognizing God's love for us.

Agape is defined in much greater detail in 1 Corinthians 13:4–8. This love-yourself-love-others concept is possible only when your psychology and theology are in tune with each other. People with low self-esteem have a very difficult time loving others effectively. They tend to be proud, self-centered, easily angered, and impatient. They harbor grudges and ridicule others while lifting themselves up. People with a poor self-image have a harder time producing faith. They love only in response to love and find hope more difficult, which explains why depression—hopelessness—is so rampant in low self-esteem victims.

You see, all of the qualities I just mentioned are taken directly from scripture (1 Cor. 13:4–8). The self-centered person is really not in love with himself. He loathes himself. He has lost his self-value and is striving to gain attention and value from others. He cannot see beyond himself. He is obsessed with himself. Pride and narcissism have little to do with *agape* love. They are a caricature of self-esteem, a false love trying to fulfill a lack of the real thing.

The person who truly loves (agape) himself is able to love his neighbor. He is free to reach beyond himself to others. We cannot give something we do not possess. We cannot love others sufficiently if we do not love ourselves. God loves us from the inside out. That is self-esteem.

People with low self-love rely on external sources for value. They are concerned with achievement and symbols of success and applause and attention. All of these things are antithetical to the attitude of brokenness. True self-esteem—true self-love—cuts our need for external love from others. I am not saying that we do not like it, or even want it, but when we require love from someone else, we place demands on them that they are not able to meet consistently. And when we need love and they cannot supply it, we develop unhealthy relationships and all that they entail.

Hopefully, you can see that servanthood, humility, and being broken in the right place help restore our self-image. They raise our self-esteem by refining our sense of personal value. Our value is intrinsic. It is not determined by our educational degrees, how much money we have in the bank, how many parishioners attend our church, or what people say about us. Brokenness seeks to release us from frantic mind games that leave us scurrying to and fro for tidbits of ego-stroking praise. It ties us into God's love, which in turn helps us love others as they need to be loved.

This is the theme of servanthood. Being a servant in the truest sense can only occur when a person has a healthy self-esteem. I believe this to be possible only by being broken in the right place. It purifies our self-image, releasing us from the need for external love and the longing for value from others and from achievements.

Brokenness in the wrong places demeans, ridicules, and diminishes self-esteem. It prevents us from emulating healthy servanthood. Those who have been broken in mind, body, or relationships alone tend to withdraw from others. The older we get, the more likely we are to see people becoming cynical and negative. That is because life gives us ample opportunities to become broken in the right or the wrong places. And when we respond improperly to the breaking process, our self-image will be damaged.

"When you surrender to Christ, all self-hate, all self-loathing, all self-rejection drops away. How can you hate what he loves? By no known process or method can the self be eliminated. It is a part of us, a very important part—it is us! Put the self out of the door, it will come back by the window, usually dressed up in religious garments, but the same self still. Love simply cannot spring up without self-surrender to each other. What happens to the self when surrendered to God? He wipes it clean of selfishness. The problem is the same everywhere—the self, the self-centered self, the self-preoccupied self, the unsurrendered self. When we ask, 'Is self-surrender workable?' the answer is, nothing else is workable."[5]

■

THE ULTIMATE POWER

Everyone is called to be a servant, but not everyone is called to be a leader. On the other hand, most of us have situations where we need to display leadership behaviors, whether in the home, with our children, at church, in ministry, at work, or in the community. In Colossians 1:23 Paul calls himself a servant of God. "Many men pray for the power of God. Hidden under such prayer and fervor, however, is ambition; a craving for fame, the desire to be considered a spiritual giant. Even as men pray these prayers, they are hollow inside. Prayer for power is the quick and the short way, circumnavigating internal growth."[6]

Stephen Covey writes, "The great servant leaders have that humility, the hallmark of inner religion. I know a few CEOs who are humble servant leaders—who sacrifice their pride and share their power—and I can say that their influence both inside and outside their companies is multiplied because of it. Sadly, many people want 'religion,' or at least the appearance of it, without any sacrifice. They want more spirituality but would never miss a meal in meaningful fasting or do one act of anonymous service to achieve it."[7]

Jesus said, "You have heard that it was said, 'An eye for an eye and a tooth for a tooth.' But I tell you not to resist an evil person. But whoever slaps you on the right cheek, turn the other to him also. If anyone wants to sue you and take away your tunic, let him have your cloak also. And whoever compels you to go one mile, go with him two. Give to him who asks you, and from him who wants to borrow from you do not turn away" (Matt. 5:38–42).

Servants demonstrate a force which transcends traditional power. Romans 12:21 tells us to overcome evil with good. The French word for *power* means literally, "to be able." Power provides freedom. And freedom is not the ability to do as we want, but the ability to do what we ought. However, before we focus on the "ought," we must focus on the "is." The "is" precedes the "ought." That is, when we become spiritual people and allow God freedom in our lives, we therefore become enabled to do what we must to obey Him. Obedience is primarily an attitude of the heart, and secondarily a response of the body.

The Bible says to turn the other cheek when someone hits you on the right cheek. Since most people are right-handed, especially in earlier cultures where left-handedness was seen as something sinister, a slap on the right cheek would have to be done with the back of the hand. This scripture implies an insult more demeaning than an open slap to the face. This is an attack on your very personhood. When Jesus says to turn the other cheek, He is suggesting that we respond instead of react. Servants express self-control. Reactors give up the most important power they possess, the power to choose.

When Jesus told us to "give up our outer cloak," he was referring to the Mosaic Law, which granted an inalienable right to possess one's outer cloak. No lawsuit could force a person to give up his outer cloak. And no Jew would be caught in public wearing only a loincloth. Jesus was telling us that servanthood goes beyond the comfort zone. Our society is thrown off-guard by sacrificial actions because they are unnatural.

Roman soldiers had a practice of commandeering civilians to carry luggage. The farthest a civilian could be forced to carry a soldier's gear was the distance of a Roman mile. But Jesus said that if someone interrupts your plans and forces you to go one mile, also go the second mile. In essence, Jesus was saying that servants should deliver more than is required. They should give—and then give some more. I do not think He was promoting a masochistic lifestyle of feigned martyrdom. Rather, He was talking about motives of love.

Servanthood purifies motivation.

Servanthood is only possible after a person has been broken in the right place and surrenders with humility. We have so many mixed motives that we sometimes have difficulty knowing our true intentions. Serving others sacrificially not only comes from an attitude of brokenness, it also often replicates the experience which caused it. It keeps us humble and focused on God.

One of the greatest examples of servanthood is in the story of Ruth. Ruth lost her husband, her brother-in-law, and her father-in-law. The easiest thing Ruth could have done at that point was return to her homeland and family, whom many believe were wealthy. Instead, Ruth committed to Naomi, her mother-in-law, saying, "wherever you go, I will go. . . . Your people will become my people" (Ruth 1:16). This is the statement of one who has been broken, who has surrendered her will. Ruth's comment is repeated often in wedding ceremonies, the intent being to communicate selflessness and dedication. Ruth became a field worker, picking up grain droppings in the hot sun. In her brokenness, she turned to service.

When we go through a period of breaking, we are very tempted to focus inward and center on our own pain. Ruth's most natural response would have been to go home and be consoled as her sister-in-law, Orpah, did. It was only natural. Few would have blamed her. Instead, Ruth ministered to Naomi. Her service helped heal Naomi. She became broken in the right place, and God used her life as an ancestor of the Messiah.

Servanthood also clarifies our objective.

One of the most difficult things to discover is what we are supposed to do with our lives. Although the specific will of God is not revealed here, the general will of God is. We are to serve others. If our actions cannot be done in the attitude of a servant, we are outside of Christ's intentions. Jesus said that He came to serve, not to be served (Matt. 20:28). Paul uses the word *slave*. Slaves do not have any rights of their own. Their identity is centered around serving others.

Servanthood does not allow us to fall too far if we fail.

I am amazed at how often my little boys fall, get right back up, and run off. If I were to fall like that, I would need a longer recovery time. But, they are much closer to the ground than I am.

The higher we are, the harder we fall. History books and newspapers are full of stories about people falling in their careers, marriages, and lives in general. Servants do not usually fall, but when they do it isn't far because they are already on their knees.

Servanthood gives us quality relationships.

As servants, we become sensitive to others. Perfect people have a hard time relating to others. No one meets their expectations and therefore, people frustrate them. They are forever feeling let down and betrayed. Servants realize their own imperfections and are much more patient with others and their imperfections. They have a hard time looking down on people because of their own low vantage point.

Servanthood allows us to model by example.

The tools of servanthood are simple: a towel and basin. Max DePree said, "The first responsibility [of a leader] is to define reality. The last is to say thank you. In between the two, the leader must become a servant, a debtor."[8]

We can learn to say "thank you" out of etiquette, but a true attitude of thanksgiving is the fraternal twin of humility. We cannot possess humility (humus) and not express gratitude. One of the surest ways to detect a humble spirit is by spotting a gracious attitude. Brokenness expands our capacity for grace. Gracious people merely exhibit what fills them. Pride keeps us from learning, from healing relationships, and from seeking God because we have made ourselves our own god. The smallest package is a man wrapped up in himself. Servants are perpetually thankful.

■

AN ATTITUDE OF GRATITUDE

We live in a society which demands a lot and thanks little. Yet, the Bible constantly tells us to be givers of thanks. Those who are broken in the right place exhibit an attitude of gratitude. Although it may seem a simplistic overview of the trait, here is an outline on thanksgiving, spelling the word THANKS.

The "T" stands for *telling God and others the difference they've made in our lives.* In Luke 17:11–19, Jesus healed ten lepers. Only one of them came back to express his thanks for what Jesus had done for him. Being healed from leprosy made a big difference in his life, not only healthwise, but socially, financially, and psychologically. No longer would he be an outcast. He could return to his family and friends and his trade. The man's thankfulness expressed the difference Jesus had made in his life. Thankfulness is a major exercise of godliness that we should practice our entire lives. Gratitude is the heart of the Christian life.

When we thank others, we are recognizing the positive changes they have made in our lives, large or small. This is also true of our spiritual lives. The Heidelberg Catechism says, "Why do Christians need to pray? Because prayer is the most important part of the thankfulness God requires of us." It is recognizing the change God has made in our lives.

The "H" stands for *humbly responding as if we do not deserve anything.* On more than one occasion in the Bible, we see people at Jesus' feet. This represents a position of humility and submission. The leper threw himself at Jesus' feet. The woman with the issue of blood was healed by touching the hem of Jesus' garment. The woman with long hair anointed Jesus' feet with costly perfume. Jesus himself washed his disciples' feet.

There is a natural humility involved in an attitude of thanksgiving, a recognition that what was received was not deserved. This is the attitude of one who has been broken. Brokenness teaches us the spiritual lesson that we are fortunate not to get what we deserve. If our sins were rewarded as deserved, all of us would immediately perish. The unbroken heart feels it deserves good things and often expects and demands certain positive rewards. A growing problem in our nation is the attitude that society owes us jobs and financial security. Many people now consider employment their right and fail to recognize that they need to work hard and find a suitable job. "Those who are not grateful soon begin to complain of everything," said Thomas Merton.

The "A" stands for *accepting our need for others.* John Donne wrote, "No man is an island." The person who expresses gratitude has come to realize that he or she cannot survive alone. Our independent spirit tries to delude us into believing that we can make it on our own, but this is untrue. Nearly everything we do involves the need for others. For example, actors, salesmen, and bankers need others to buy their skills or products. We depend on others to make our clothes, to grow our food, to distill and transport our fuel. The list is endless. Humble people acknowledge their need for others. Calvin referred to thanksgiving in biblical terms as a sacrifice of praise. We praise God for His nature and for His sustenance.

The "N" stands for *not taking things for granted.* The healed leper returned to thank Jesus because he wanted Him to know he did not take this gift lightly. We so easily take things for granted once they become familiar to us. Among the most thankful United States citizens are those who have recently returned from a third-world culture, because they become aware of how much we have in America. Abraham Lincoln understood brokenness and, as President, he authorized Thanksgiving Day as a holiday. He wrote, "We have forgotten the gracious hand which preserved us in peace, and multiplied, and enriched, and strengthened us. And have vainly imagined in the deceitfulness of our hearts that all these blessings were produced by some superior wisdom and virtue of our own.

Intoxicated with unbroken success, we have become too self-sufficient to feel the necessity of redeeming and preserving grace, too proud to pray to the God that made us."

You may have heard the story of the man who was betrayed by a friend. He went to his friend and asked, "How could you do this to me? Who picked you up out of the gutter? Who gave you your first job? Who lent you money and bailed you out of jail?" The supposed friend replied, "You did, that's true. But what have you done for me lately?"

When times were good, the children of Israel notoriously took God's past provisions for granted and began failing in their spiritual walk. How often do we forget the things God has done for us? Instead of counting our blessings, we count our trials and wants. Only in times of brokenness do God's children repent and turn again to the God who has provided so many times in the past. John Calvin said, "We are surrounded by God's benefits. The best use of these benefits is an unceasing expression of gratitude." Gratitude takes nothing for granted.

The "K" stands for *killing our enemies and problems by adjusting our attitude.* James tells us to "consider it pure joy" when we experience trials and testings. Likewise, people often say that the best way to get rid of our enemies is to turn them into friends. An attitude of thanksgiving is perhaps the best way to deal with difficult people as well as tough circumstances, for it changes our perceptions and therefore our response toward them. Paul understood brokenness. He wrote, "Giving thanks for all things to God the Father in the name of our Lord Jesus Christ" (Eph. 5:20); "Rejoice always, pray without ceasing, in everything give thanks; for this is the will of God in Christ Jesus for you" (1 Thess. 5:16–18); "For I have learned in whatever state I am, to be content" (Phil. 4:11).

In his letter to the Philippians, Paul used the words *joy* and *rejoice* thirteen times.

When you are grateful, you are able to see the good that God's testing and trials produce. I am learning to write genuine and loving thank-you notes to people who have offended me in some way, because their actions help produce character traits in me that allow me to reach my potential.

William Law said, "If anyone can tell you the shortest, surest way to all happiness and perfection, he must tell you to make it a rule to yourself to thank and praise God for everything that happens to you, for it is certain that whatever seeming calamity happens to you, if you thank and praise God for it, you turn it into a blessing."

Helen Keller wrote, "I thank God for my handicaps. Through them I have found myself, my work and my God." John Wesley added, "Thanksgiving is inseparable from true prayer. It is most essentially connected with it. He that always prays is ever giving praise, whether in ease or pain, both for prosperity and for the greatest adversity." The set of the sail, not the wind, determines a ship's destination.

The "S" in thanks represents *standing out in the crowd.* Ten lepers were healed, but only one said thank you. An attitude of gratitude gets noticed: Philippians 2:14–15 says, "Do everything without complaining and arguing, so that you may shine like stars." Stars shine brightest when the night is darkest. Regardless of position or power, gracious people consistently write thank-you notes, make thank-you calls, and say "thank you" often. They remember the little things and do not take others' gestures for granted. In so doing, they stand out in the crowd, for there is nothing so common as the man or woman wrapped up in his or her own world. Those who emanate a gracious attitude born out of a broken, tamed spirit will be remembered for their fresh, unique perspective. Servants do not demand or assume life owes them and that is precisely why they are thankful.

■

GOODNESS GRACIOUS

Brokenness introduces us to a new measure of God's grace, as well as a new awareness of God's mercy in our lives. A strong correlation exists between experiencing God's grace and displaying a gracious attitude. In fact, a study of four related Greek words reveals a prevailing theme for Christian living. The words *chara* (joy), *charis* (grace), *charisma* (gift), and *eucharist* (thanksgiving), all evolved from the same root. Although the Bible, ancient secular Greek, and the first century church used these terms in various ways, an overview of them might help us discover an often overlooked core principle within our Christian walk. *Chara* refers to the joy we experience in our relationship with God. Philo referred to it as religious intoxication. It is a "supreme good mood," available only through God. Paul uses the word often in reference to joy in suffering (Col. 1:11; 2 Tim. 1:4). This is "the joy of the Lord" which transcends circumstances.

The word *charis* is often translated "grace." Grace is commonly defined as "unmerited favor," but it goes beyond such a simplistic reduction. *Charis* is the state causing or accompanying joy. Literally, it refers to having favor with our Creator. Just as a child rejoices when he finds favor with his parent, we experience joy (*chara*) in knowing our Father favors us. "Noah found grace [*charis*] in the eyes of the Lord" (Gen. 6:8).

Charis denotes a gracious disposition which finds expression in gracious action. It is the process whereby one who has something turns graciously to one who is in need. Recipients of this favor respond with *charis*, which means "thanks." Grace often occurs in the context of forgiveness and mercy, and thanks is to be given for expressions of it (Ps. 5:7; 107:43). In turn, people who experience grace from another are to respond in kind to others they meet. In essence, *charis* is the basis of the salvation experience, the realization that God freely gave to us when we did not deserve it (Rom. 3:23–24, 5:8; Gal. 2:21). Grace is divine favor shown in Christ (Eph. 1:6–7).

Charisma refers to the result of *charis* as an action. For example, it is the proof of our favor. The benefit. The gift. Paul refers to it as the gift of salvation (2 Cor. 1:11, Rom. 5:15–16). The popular version of *charisma*, referring to personal magnetism, vibrance, and even sex appeal, grew out of the belief that certain people were gifted by God and so attracted attention because of His divine touch. The plural of the word, *charismata*, of course gave birth to the title "charismatics," which commonly refers to those believing in and promoting the spiritual gifts of tongues and prophecy. However, it literally refers to spiritual gifts in general and God's endowments to the believer.

Finally, the word *eucharist* means, basically, "thanksgiving." The Eucharist is the name commonly given to the sacrament of Communion or the Last Supper. Eucharist is meant to be practiced whenever we eat. Thus, when we "say grace" before dinner, we are expressing thanks for God's mercy in providing our food and sustenance. In the literal sense, *eucharist* means "to show favor," but this imposes a duty of gratitude. The Greek culture held thanksgiving in high esteem, whether it was thanksgiving to the gods or to other people.

Hopefully you can see by this brief review of the words referring to joy, grace, gift, and thanksgiving, that all are a central part of our spiritual relationship with God. They originate from a single theme. The gracious person is one who has both experienced and come into an awareness of

God's grace. The person's response to God's favor is joy, resulting in a gracious attitude of thanksgiving and in forgiveness of others.

In Matthew 18, Jesus relates the parable of the unmerciful servant in response to a question on how often one should forgive. The servant represented one who was financially broken (18:24–25) and emotionally broken (18:26), but who failed to be broken in the right place (18:28–30). The result was a lack of thanksgiving and forgiveness.

Brokenness reveals the grossness of our depravity at a deeper level, and establishes a fresh dependence on God. In essence, it expands our reservoir of grace by helping us see God's great mercy in our lives. Only then, when we have recognized our own favor from God in light of our original condition, can we respond with a lifestyle of forgiveness and thanksgiving. Forgiveness is our response to grace demanded; thanksgiving is our response to grace received. Both emanate from a heart which recognizes its favor with God and the joy thereby created. As I said previously, the person with low self-esteem usually finds mercy and thankfulness difficult. In essence, this person does not feel in favor with the Creator, and thus develops a self-image which does not reflect God.

Perhaps one of the most God-like attributes we can express is a gracious spirit—a spirit of mercy and thanksgiving. God is well-versed in it. The person who lacks in this area lacks being broken in the soul. The Christian who has been broken in the right place reflects the image of God, who is full of grace. Brokenness deepens our joy, and expands our capacity for mercy and thanksgiving.

Servanthood relies chiefly on character rather than skill, position, or giftedness. One of the most frustrating realizations in Christian ministry today is that, although God grants various kinds of gifts in varying degrees, He usually does not choose to bless people according to their giftedness. The natural world seeks the talented, people-skilled, experienced individual. It heralds the superstar who can out-run, out-jump, out-sing, and out-sell the competition. But when God hangs a medal around someone's neck, He does not look for the best groomed and highest degreed person. God seeks the person whose character is most developed and who is most able to handle His blessings. God utilizes the gifts and resources He avails people, but He prefers a tamed soul. Watchman Nee said, "Our Lord never asks how much is done. He only inquires from whence it is done." Which is to say that His dominant concern is for character development, not talent or intellectual growth. The latter traits are not very usable if the former is not in place.

After all is said and done, servants outperform non-servants. After all of the accomplishments are tallied up, the only ones that will have eternal benefit are those performed by servants. Is it fair? Is it right? I might say that I do not know, but it *is* right. Society denies this truth. My own mind tempts me to believe it is not so. It is only in a state of brokenness that we come to realize the scriptures are true and that Jesus was right when He exemplified this pattern of living. It is only through the breaking of our spirits that we are willing to let go of our strong yearning to be served instead of to serve, and to rely on character instead of charisma. Thus we learn to walk "in His steps," and fulfill both our mission and our ultimate potential.

Amy Wilson Carmichael wrote,

> God, harden me against myself,
> The Coward with pathetic voice
> Who craves for ease and rest and joy.
> Myself, arch-traitor to myself,

My hollowest friend,
My deadliest foe,
My clog, whatever road I go.

Someone said that you know whether or not you're really a servant by the way you react when you're treated like one.

■

QUESTIONS FOR REFLECTION

1. How can a leader be a servant while maintaining responsibilities of a leader?

2. What aspects of I Corinthians chapter thirteen do you feel you express somewhat effectively now? What aspects do you feel you are lacking at this time?

3. Which of the servanthood characteristics did you find most beneficial for you at this time in your walk?

4. What can you do to enhance your attitude of gratitude quotient on a daily basis?

5. What can you do to enhance your servanthood quotient? With your family, church, and work associates?

The central sin is the sin of trying to make yourself God. The word "evil" is the word "live" spelled backwards. It is an attempt to live life against itself. Self-surrender is more of an offer than a demand.

—E. Stanley Jones

CHAPTER
TWELVE
■

The Commencement

■ ■ ■

One of the most painful experiences of brokenness in my life came when beloved Christian teammates seemed to devalue me and minimize my importance to them and to our shared mission. The pain was exquisite! I would not want to go through that again.

I realized what the problem was. I had been putting my trust in people. The Bible tells us to put our trust in God and to love people. There is no biblical basis for putting our trust in other people. We are to love them as Jesus loves us, which is totally and unconditionally even though we fail Him continually.

Since then I know the price of love. We will be hurt. You can expect it. But the withholding of love leads to spiritual death. So, the pain of brokenness in relationships is always a possibility as we extend the costly kind of love which Jesus demonstrated and which He urges us to practice if we are to be His disciples.

—Bruce Larson

■

NOT-SO-FINAL FINAL THOUGHTS

Sometimes, after a long day or a stressful event, my wife and I like to steal away to a local coffee shop. We sit and unwind and sip gourmet coffee as we watch small waves lap against the lake shore. We feel no pressure to impress each other, so we are able to just relax. The journey of writing this book has been much more emotional than cognitive, more personal than professional. Therefore, I'd like to take a moment to put my feet up and "debrief" what we've discussed. As I conclude, I'm reminded of C. S. Lewis when he said, "Think of me as a fellow-patient in the same hospital who, having been admitted a little earlier, could give some advice."

Although this book was written out of the context of personal brokenness, I see larger societal trends which reflect the results of being broken in the right place. I see cultures like the Koreans, who exhibit an attitude of brokenness. War and the threat of communism have shaken their culture such that Christianity has spread like wildfire through the nation. Some of the largest local churches in history are now alive and well in Korea. Korean believers often pray for hours and through the night, depending on God as their sole sustenance. People cannot do this without a sense of brokenness.

I am concerned for my generation of Americans—the "baby boomers." We are the best educated and most affluently raised generation in history. But as a whole, we have been spared character-building events like a depression or world war. I am not wishing these catastrophes upon us, but I am reminding us that we have had it relatively easy versus building character. We are also experiencing the highest crime and drug-abuse rates in our history, in addition to other moral maladies like rape, child abuse, and abortion. I cannot help but believe that a good amount of our moral decay is happening because we have not been broken in the right place. Ray Brown, professor of popular culture at Bowling Green University said of the 1990s, "The concept of shame may be gone. Beliefs like that don't come back unless something really drastic happens. And right now I can't imagine what that could be."[1] As a result, we continue to be broken in the wrong places, and the walking wounded are all around us. When a society does not experience corporate breaking, it must rely on individual brokenness for character building. We may not be far from such a broad experience, when an economic crisis, AIDS, or some other catastrophe shakes us to reality.

But this is a book of hope, not of despair. Hope is always God's goal and is sometimes shrouded in events leading to brokenness. I pray I have not made a mockery of the process I have described. The concept stands on its own merits without my help. I do not wish to insult the hallowing process by poorly documenting and describing it. I do not say that in feigned humility. I am old enough to know that I am too young to adequately take on an explanation of such a deep and potent principle. I would never assume or hint that I have written a definitive work on this subject. I sincerely hope that in thirty years or so, Lord willing, I might rewrite this book, looking at my adult life through the rearview mirror.

I would like to think I would only add an array of more detailed illustrations and firm up some of the more saggy statements. There are scores of other stories, ideas, and statements which could be added to anyone's file on brokenness. In reality, this sort of book should be published in three-ring-binder form, so that new pages could be easily added.

Hopefully, you can now start a personal file on brokenness. You will want to add other articles, scraps of papers with personal ideas, illustrations, scriptures, prayers, and anecdotes. Such a file would be a resource for great ministry both for those experiencing brokenness and for those fighting the process. And of course, the file can help you sort through your own pain and questions as you experience your own breaking. Hopefully it will guide you in voluntary brokenness, the self-promoted discipline of availing yourself to the Spirit on a regular basis. My goal was to touch on the historical ideas of the subject, yet provide practical ways for you to relate to your own experience.

I also wanted to provide something of substance, without making anyone sift through a lot of wrappings to get to the meat. This book was written primarily for those who are presently being broken. If pain and emotional blood are oozing out of your spirit, you may be tempted to pursue instant relief. "Scab theology" seeks to cover hurts quickly, and I don't believe that is healthy. This book is intended to help you heal from the inside out. I wish I had had a book like this to help me understand sooner that my pain and suffering and disillusionment were okay, that my times of breaking had a meaning and purpose, and that they represented a common and necessary process in life.

I also wrote this book for the rest of us, those of us who remember a significant time of breaking in our past and will likely experience another episode in the future. As I have surveyed various nationally-known Christian leaders, most of them witnessed to times of private breaking. Only a few did not recognize such episodes in their lives.

The breaking process tends to be episodic. It has a beginning and an end. It is best to see it as a threshold, a temporary passage which takes us into a new condition. It is the cocoon stage of the metamorphosis from caterpillar to butterfly. It is the ugly duckling transition to beauty. The result of this process is greater wisdom, more fruitfulness, and expanded capacity for the Spirit in your life.

Personally, I feel the word *brokenness* conveys too many elements of pain and suffering for me to feel comfortable using it on a regular basis. I do not wish to communicate a negative theology that makes people feel they need to be oppressed. I am all for joy and exuberance. Being broken in the right place purifies the soul and releases such rejoicing. It is the dying of the seed so that new life can sprout. I like the vision of fresh shoots better than that of dead seed casings. I would recommend that the terms *broken* and *brokenness* be reserved for those times when they best fit, when the process involves pruning, cutting back, refining, and the like. It would do a disservice to come out with buttons, bumper stickers, and slogans on the concept. Reserve it for appropriate times and sequences. Brokenness is a process which requires a sense of awe, quiet respect, and sensitivity, especially for those going through it. It seems more like a graveside ceremony than a baby shower.

I read a simple story a father told about his two-year-old daughter. On their walks, she would often wrap her little hand around her father's little finger. One day, she became discontent with this arrangement and interrupted her normal chatter. "Daddy, I don't want just your finger, I want your whole hand." So the father opened his whole hand and, for the first time, allowed her to "hold" his hand in hers. A part of spiritual growth is coming to a place where you are no longer satisfied with the finger of God and you desire His whole hand. This process repeats itself through life. During this transition, events and circumstances which formerly seemed disruptive, burdensome, and painful now seem developmental, necessary, and enhancing. This is not to say the pain diminishes.

Rather the suffering produced by the frustration of not understanding the intended benefits evaporates. Pain does not seem quite so bad when it appears to serve a purpose. So it is with brokenness.

In C. S. Lewis' book, *The Screwtape Letters,* Screwtape wrote Wormword this warning about God: "When He talks of their losing their selves, he only means abandoning the clamor of self-will; once they have done that, He really gives them back all their personality, and boasts (I am afraid, sincerely) that when they are wholly His they will be more themselves than ever."[2]

■

REACHING OUR POTENTIAL

When we realize that God ultimately seeks to release our potential through this process, we can accept the pain much better. Among the few articles and books I discovered in my search for material on brokenness, I came upon a rich book called *A Tale of Three Kings* by Gene Edwards. The book, in a narrative, poetic style, addresses one of David's character-making episodes prior to his kingship.

David went through a time of brokenness when King Saul sought to take his life (1 Sam. 18–26).

> David had a question: What do you do when someone throws a spear at you? Does it not seem odd to you that David did not know the answer to this question? After all, everyone else in the world knows what to do when a spear is thrown at them. Why, you pick up the spear and throw it right back!
>
> And in doing this small feat of returning thrown spears, you will prove many things: You are courageous. You stand for the right. You boldly stand against the wrong. You are tough and can't be pushed around. You will not stand for injustice or unfair treatment. You are the defender of the faith, keeper of the flame, detector of all heresy. You will

not be wronged. All of these attributes then combine to prove that you are also, obviously, a candidate for kingship. Yes, perhaps you are the Lord's anointed.

There is also the possibility that some 20 years after your coronation, you will be the most incredibly skilled spear thrower in all the realm. And most assuredly, by then . . .

Quite mad.[3]

So what do you do when you have a spear-wielding king or person in your life? Do you let this person or circumstance injure you? Edwards continues:

You have your eyes on the wrong King Saul. As long as you look at your king, you will blame him, and him alone, for your present hell. Be careful, for God has His eyes fastened sharply on another King Saul. Not the visible one standing up there throwing spears at you. No, God is looking at another King Saul. One just as bad—or worse.

'God is looking at the King Saul in you.'[4]

Why did God allow David to go through this time of brokenness?

David the sheepherder would have grown up to become King Saul II, except that God cut away the Saul inside David's heart. The operation, by the way, took years and was a brutalizing experience that almost killed the patient. And what were the scalpel and tongs God used to remove this inner Saul?

God used the outer Saul.

King Saul sought to destroy David, but his only success was that he became the handmaiden of God to put to death the Saul who roamed about in the caverns of David's own soul.[5]

David ran away from Saul and hid in hollows of the rock ravines. He went from hero to homeless, all without apparent reason. But . . .

There in those caves, drowned in the sorrow of his song, and in the song of his sorrow, David very simply became the greatest hymn writer, and the greatest comforter of broken hearts this world shall ever know.

Suffering was giving birth. Humility was born.

By earthly measures he was a shattered man; by heaven's measure, a broken one.[6]

■

THE END IN PERSPECTIVE

One of the beauties of brokenness is that it ultimately prepares us for death. Death is the final result of living in a sinful world. It is not a victory. We say things like that because we are insecure with our own mortality and try to mask death's insult. God is the Creator of life. Death was never His plan. But, the breaking process makes us ready for death at any given spot along the journey. Paul said, "Oh death where is your sting?" Brokenness is the de-stinging process. I like to think of it in terms of declawing the cat. We often hear of people mourning the "premature" loss of a person. "Oh, they were so young. What a shame, they had so much of life before them." We look in the mirrors and watch the wrinkles come and the hair turn gray (or fall out). We ponder our own mortality. Do you ever get ready for death? Don't you always die with music still left in you? If you asked most people, they would admit they're too young to die. But that's because we tend to be product-oriented instead of process-oriented.

We see life as a series of achievements, milestones, and marker events. However, God is process oriented. Achievement and fruitbearing are parts of the process. They are important. But it is by abiding in Him that we discover what Christianity is all about. God does not allow us to be broken just so we'll be bigger producers, but so we'll be bigger people. He is in the people-building business. As we experience brokenness, we come to see life as a journey instead of a destination. Really, the destination is the journey. We are so arrival oriented that when someone dies without arriving at certain train stops, we mourn for them. When we see life as an ongoing journey, we trust God with our dreams and aspirations. We worry less, if at all, about when He will decide to take us off the train. Any time is all right, if He decides at ten or twenty, seventy or eighty years, it makes little difference.

It has been noted that the story of life begins in the garden, the Garden of Eden. Another significant landmark is the Garden of Gethsemane, which ultimately leads to a final garden, the garden tomb. But it is in the last garden that we experience the resurrection, the hope of eternal life.

The taming of the soul through brokenness brings great rewards.

Near our home is a lake, backdropped by a mountain. In the early morning, as I jog around the lake, I see what appears to be two mountains, one pointing up, the other pointing down. It is hard at times to see where the mountain separates from its reflection in the water. On windy days, the turbulent waters resist a clear reflection of the mountain's beauty. The waves call attention only to themselves. A calm lake demonstrates the peak's majesty. Brokenness is designed to tame the soul, so that in its smooth tranquility it can reflect the glory of God. We were made in His image, and He seeks for us to mirror His likeness.

Psalm 131:1–2 says,

Lord, my heart is not haughty,
Nor my eyes lofty.
Neither do I concern myself with great matters
Nor with things too profound for me.

Surely I have calmed and quieted my soul,
Like a weaned child with his mother,
Like a weaned child is my soul within me, once it has
    been tamed.

I always thought it peculiar that to celebrate graduations we hold commencement exercises. Graduation signifies the finish, the completion of a journey. Commencement announces the start. Unfortunately, none of us Christians on earth ever graduate from God's school. We just keep commencing. Although you are nearly through with this book, and hopefully have a better grasp of the concept of brokenness, I trust you will also see yourself in a new start. I congratulate you for taking this journey. Oliver Wendell Holmes said, "I would not give a fig for simplicity this side of complexity, but I would give my life for simplicity on the other side of complexity." Now you know the solution. It's simple. "Thy will be done."

Since a majority of this manuscript was written during a time I spent at the Manresa Retreat Center near Azusa, California, in between lectures, prayer, meals, worship, solitude, sleeping, and running, I think it would be appropriate to end with a prayer by Ignatius Loyola, who experienced brokenness at Manresa in Spain. It is the prayer only a tamed soul can say with veracity.

■

THE GIFT OF SELF TO GOD

Take, Lord, and receive all my liberty, my memory, my understanding and my entire will—all that I have and call my own. You have given it all to me. To You, Lord, I return it.

Everything is Yours; do with it what You will. Give me only Your love and Your grace. That is enough for me.

God rarely uses a man greatly, until he hurts a man deeply.

—A.W. Tozer

■

A Special Message to Leaders

INCARNATIONAL LEADERSHIP

■ ■ ■

All the writers who wrote about prisons but who did not themselves serve time there considered it their duty to express sympathy for prisoners and to curse prison. I . . . have served enough time there. I nourished my soul there, and I say without hesitation: "Bless you, prison, for having been in my life!"

Looking back, I saw that for my whole conscious life I had not understood either myself or my strivings. What had seemed for so long to be beneficial now turned out in actuality to be fatal, and I had been striving to go in the opposite direction to that which was truly necessary to me. But just as the waves of the sea knock the inexperienced swimmer off his feet and keep tossing him back onto the shore, so also was I painfully tossed back on dry land by the blows of misfortune. And it was only because of this that I was able to travel the path which I had always really wanted to travel.

The meaning of earthly existence lies not, as we have

229

grown used to thinking, in prospering, but . . . in the development of the soul.[1]

—Aleksandr Solzhenitsyn
(describing what he learned from his years
in a Russian labor camp)

■

GOD'S FAVORITE TOOLS

Most of us throw away our broken tools, or at least try not to use them. But not God. If you were to go to God's tool shed, you would find something very interesting. God's favorite tools are those which have been broken. They may be taped up and nailed together with splints, but they have obviously been broken in the past. This is not to say that God does not use new, unbroken tools. He can bless anyone He chooses. But God's favorite tools for cultivating and growing His garden are those which have been broken. "I've yet to see a leader that God has used tremendously who has not been broken," wrote Rev. Paul Cho.

As you study different leaders, you will find that many of them rose out of personal tragedies and overcame personal barriers, such as poverty, or physical or relational challenges. Tough times are necessary for the production of strong personality traits. Fred Smith responded to the question of why we seemed to be in a leadership crisis. He said that because this new generation has never gone through an economic depression or world war, it lacks confidence. We have plenty of visionary, gifted people, but they lack the confidence needed to feel secure about their leadership.

Brokenness has a lot to do with leadership, especially from a Christian standpoint. Much of my own motivation for researching this subject grew out of the desire to understand how God develops leaders so that they become useful for His purposes. I have devoted much time and energy, academically and casually, to the study of leaders, as is reflected in the testimonies in this book, and believe it is important to explore brokenness in the life of a leader. Most of us are involved in the leadership process in some way, because we are either leaders or followers. As followers, we need to be concerned about the character development and attitudes of those who lead us. Most of us wear many hats, and our roles vary from situation to situation. You may not see yourself as leader material. But if you have wondered why certain gifted people are never used by God more than they are, or why some leaders who glean success often crash and burn in their careers, I believe this chapter will satisfy some of your curiosity.

Ignatius Loyola, who founded the Jesuit order in the Catholic Church, sought the Lord at Manresa in Northeast Spain. Loyola spent nearly a year there, praying and meditating. Loyola, a soldier, was wounded in battle in 1521. He hobbled to a monastery and before he was finally healed, he dropped his sword at the altar. As one author said, "At Manresa, he became a sword." That is a concept I call incarnational leadership. Brokenness is where trustworthy, enduring leadership is born.

■

LEADERSHIP POWER

There are several different types of power resources that leaders use. Typically, seven categories emerge in leadership discussions: coercion (force), information (what you know), expertise (talent/skill), personal power (charisma), position (hierarchy/authority), reward (what you can do for me), and association (who you know). As we look at the spiritual implications of these power resources, we are able to see that none of them are inherently evil or good in themselves, (although coercion is perceived by some as always bad). Power is energy, and can be a tool for destruction or construction. As you study the Bible, you see all of these power resources used in various places throughout Scripture. Although certain ones tend to lend themselves to more unethical uses than others (i.e. coercion), we need to consider them neutral in and of themselves.

Because each of these power sources can be utilized in the appropriate places for good, and in other places for evil, we should be concerned that those people who come into power have had proper character development and are operating out of godly motives. Although brokenness and its fruits do not make a person a leader, people who function as leaders without this process in their past should be esteemed lightly in that role. Unbroken people have the propensity to become inconsistent or even dangerous. That is exactly why the concept of incarnational leadership and the process of brokenness are so important to effective leadership. Tommy Barnet said, "You must be broken before your spirit can get out." "The rock must be smitten before the living waters can flow. The alabaster box must be broken before the odor of the ointment can fill the house. It would be dangerous for God to empower an unbroken man."[2]

"What makes the temptation of power so seemingly irresistible? Maybe it is that power offers an easy substitute for the hard task of love. It seems easier to be god than to love God, easier to control people than to love people, easier to own life than to love life. Jesus asks, 'Do you love me?' We ask, 'Can we sit at your right hand and your left hand in your Kingdom?'"[3]

As I have mentioned, spiritual humus (humility) is perhaps the most important result of the process of brokenness. It is necessary for the healthy emergence and use of leadership. The breaking process shows the potential leader his or her inabilities to handle life's situations with human strength. The intended outcome is for the person gifted with potential power resources to seek God's power and wisdom. A lack of humility before God is the root of nearly all leadership dilemmas and may be the main reason He chooses not to use many apparently gifted people in leadership functions. "Christian leadership is not a leadership of power and control, but a leadership of powerlessness and humility in which the suffering servant of God, Jesus Christ, is made manifest. I, obviously, am not speaking about a psychologically weak leadership in which the Christian leader is simply the passive victim of the manipulations of his milieu. No, I am speaking of a leadership in which power is constantly abandoned in favor of love."[4]

■

LEADING OUT OF WHO YOU ARE

An ancient adage says, "Every man has three names; one his father and mother give him; one others call him; and one he acquires himself." Incarnational leadership means one must lead primarily out of who one is, not what one knows, who one knows, what one can do, or how one can do it. The individual who has access to power resources, but who lacks humility and full surrender to God, is similar to a sixteen-year-old behind the wheel of a car. The teen has the feeling that he can handle all that power, but more often than not, he discovers only too late that he cannot. When our power resources transcend our character strength, we are bound to fall.

The Bible refers to about 300 people who functioned in various leadership processes. Of these, 100 are listed in more detail, and half of them are listed with enough information that we can basically determine how they finished their careers as leaders. Robert Clinton reports that only about 30 percent of leaders in the Bible finished well.

It is interesting how enamored we are with the power, glory, honor, and mystique that accompanies leaders. But it is also interesting how few of those individuals end up as winners. The papers are full of daily examples of leaders in business, politics, sports, and even organized religion, who finish poorly. Most leadership positions create a picture of the person that is bigger than life. They distort reality. Brokenness is reality therapy. Welcome to the real world. When leaders start believing in their press clippings, or in their own immortality, they are destined for a fall.

Brokenness must not only be a part of a person's formative times, but must continue during crucial growth periods for its foundational effects to be realized. There is often a period of character building during a leader's early ministry, before God significantly blesses his latter ministry. During this time in a leader or potential leader's life, the priority is not the individual's ministry, but the development of the leader's character. Various challenges or opportunities arise which serve as opportunities to grow or shrink in character. These help determine how God will use this person in the future.

A part of this process is the concept of brokenness. The Spirit led Jesus into the wilderness prior to His great messianic ministry. God revealed His promise to Abraham, but then waited many years to fulfill it with a son. Those were years when God waited for Abraham to become impotent. God does not work through us greatly until we recognize our impotence. And in some cases, He has to wait for many years. "Prayer has no value before God, if it does not arise out of a recognition of our impotence."[5]

Then, God called Abraham again to give up the dream

when He called him to sacrifice Isaac. "Some people give up their Ishmaels, but not their Isaacs. The gift that God gave them they have begun to use to glorify themselves."[6] It is interesting that at the same location, Mount Moriah, David later purchased land to set up an altar, and Solomon later built the temple there. The bottom line is, God always and only builds His Church on the sacrifices of His people. John and James wanted positions next to Jesus, but they were not willing to drink the cup. Brokenness counteracts the temptation to get something for nothing. Albert Einstein said, "Sometimes one pays the most for the things one gets for nothing."

New visions often emerge from times of brokenness. At forty, Moses appeared to be an arrogant, self-willed man. But by eighty, after years in the desert, he was a broken man whom the Bible refers to as "the meekest man who ever lived." Here was a man who could be trusted with the awesome power and responsibility necessary to lead an entire nation out of slavery and into the Promised Land. The Children of Israel wandered in the wilderness forty years before they entered the Promised Land. Only then were they willing to cross the Jordan and enter the land. The enemies still inhabited Canaan. The only thing that had changed was their attitudes, and that was everything. By Joshua chapter three, the Ark of the Covenant was at the head of the procession. Brokenness in the right place clearly defines our priorities and puts God out front.

Time after time, we see events in the lives of leaders which indicate that God is processing or building the men and women. This pouring of the foundation is crucial for later construction of any sizable structure. Large structures built on shaky soil end up falling. The higher up the edifice, the deeper the excavation for the anchors. Short structures require only shallow footings. Just as most leaders have many years of silent, quiet character-building activities prior to being used greatly, Paul spent thirteen years growing between his conversion and his first missionary journey. People whose ministries or endeavors flourish quickly do not often last a lifetime.

■

THE LEADERSHIP CRUCIBLE

"Leaders grow through mastering painful conflict during their early years, confronting experiences that cause them to turn inward and examine themselves and their motives. They have been literally, 'born again.' I'm not talking as much of the spiritual process as I am of the breaking and crushing that happens in life, allowing a new person to emerge from the rubble. Leaders endure major events and crises that lead to a sense of separateness—estrangement from their environment. Having been broken, either by their own mistakes or the persecution of the world, they turn inward in order to re-emerge with a created, rather than inherited, sense of identity."[7]

In 1902, Harvard psychologist William James popularized the concept of being twice-born from English scholar Francis W. Newman, who wrote, "God has two families of children on this earth, the once-born and the twice-born." This was sort of a derivation from the biblical passage on the second birth (John 3). James sought to apply the concept to business and beyond, suggesting that those who encounter difficulties in life and experience alienation, are forced to look inward (instead of outward) for a redefined sense of identity.

Seventy years later, Harvard's Abraham Zaleznick picked up the twice-born notion in differentiating leaders from managers. So, now we do a full circle to suggest that Christian leaders are born again again. The first second birth has to do with salvation. The "third" birth has to do with one's separateness, taking nothing for granted, seeking vision and guidance beyond current organizational resources. This is the realm of character development, of brokenness.

Again, attitude is the soil which nourishes the character fruit necessary for leadership. Anyone who wants to grow a crop, plant an orchard, or start a nursery must understand the specific plants. Climatic needs, water, light, season duration, disease and pest vulnerability, and soil requirements are all vital for healthy growth. Brokenness is a necessary element for effective spiritual leadership. Nouwen said, "The great illusion of leadership is to think that others can be led out of the desert by someone who has never been there." The breaking process produces a leader that can be trusted.

■

PASTORAL SUCCESS

Since many reading this book are pastors and lay leaders, and because I am a pastor, I want to talk a moment about success in the ministry. It is often tempting for us to disguise unhealthy ego issues under the banner of church growth techniques. It proves an effective camouflage because no one can argue against adding more souls to the Kingdom. The problem of being fascinated with size and growth rates is that it sets into motion, or at least feeds the flames of, our desire for personal success. This in turn tends to promote the unhealthy aspect of competition. I have witnessed several church growth-oriented pastors touting their church as, "the fastest growing church in _____," "the largest church in the _____." Others do not include numbers, but add that, "I want my church to be the most influential in _____." I could never judge the hearts or motives of these men. Only God knows our intentions. I believe for the most part their ministries are anointed. Truly they are flourishing. But statements like these do not reflect an attitude of brokenness.

One pastor of a large church stood before a group of pastors and said, "I'll admit it, I have a coat of many colors." Although that might be true, how does that make the other brothers feel who wear plain old sheep skin? This attitude sounds very similar to those of the disciples, jockeying for position, to see who would be the greatest in Jesus' kingdom. Robert Bellah writes, "Few people ask, What does it mean to be Number One in an interdependent world? And what would be the moral purpose of being Number One?"[8]

We read that Jesus was intensely frustrated with these desires. These attitudes create a silent fallout from loving leaders who feel they just do not match the abilities and anointing of those who appear to be enjoying "success" in ministry. An inherent weakness in the ministerial success syndrome is that it tends to raise up certain leaders as human heroes, letting others know "how I did it," implying that "you should do it that way too."

The implication is that wherever we see growth, God favors one person over another—a good leader. We fail to understand scriptures that tell us the rain falls on the just and the unjust. Bad things will happen to good people and bad people. Good things will happen to bad people and good people. We cannot reduce God's blessings and circumstantial growth to a matter of who is good and who is not. Some growth is cancerous growth. On the other hand, even Jesus was not able to persuade some people. We run the old Apollos and Paul scenario, to which Paul reminded the followers that he planted, Apollos watered, but God gave the increase. Somehow, we often suggest that formulas, styles, and people give the increase.

We tend to fire coaches, managers, pastors, and CEOs

when things are not going well, because we have accepted the myth that everything rises and falls on a personality. In doing this, the individual becomes the scapegoat, symbolically taking the sins and deeper problems of the organization outside of the camp. I am all for quality leadership, but leadership should not be seen as the cure-all in an organization. Such a view is overly simplistic. In the same note, we of the leader cult pay great salaries to and esteem those leaders who find themselves with organizations which excel, and pay little attention to the rest of the team involved in the leadership process. Humble leaders understand that like the turtle seen on top of the fence post, they did not get there by themselves.

Ironically, a danger exists in a leader who shoulders the blame for a lack of growth or outward success. This neurotic introspection can cause a leader to become emotionally fatigued and guilt ridden. A recent poll showed that pastors have one of the lowest personal satisfaction ratings among professionals. How do you rate success in the ministry? A broken leader realizes God gives the increase. If He can use a donkey, His success does not depend upon you or me. To say an organization's failure is the sole responsibility of a single leader is to make God out to be a small God. Many pastors beat themselves by asking, "What am I doing wrong? What's improper in my life? Why isn't God blessing my ministry more?" The person who believes he or she is the sole cause for the lack of productiveness of an organization is the same person likely to take credit for the success of an organization if it excels.

Many great leaders do great work and are never heralded, never see crowds breaking down their doors, but yet are doing fine and are often leading better than those experiencing incredible growth and numerical increase. We have succumbed to the goddess of success and relinquished our belief that God is God and can do what He wishes, as He wishes, when He wishes, wherever He wishes, as long as He wishes, with whomever He wishes. This is not to deny the importance of good leading and incarnational leadership. God always prefers to use those who lead out of character strength and spiritual intensity, but His blessing does not necessarily equate with incarnational leadership (i.e. King Saul).

As a church leader, I have done more than my share of comparing. "How big is your church?" you ask, appearing not to care that much, but feeling relieved that for the number of years you have been there, your church is bigger. Playing the numbers game can be a serious fault in that it tries to measure spiritual fruit in physical manifestations. We so desperately seek tangible verification for our faith, ego, and ministry, that we rationalize the process to vindicate ourselves and prove our worth and anointing. The problem with playing the numbers game is that it pits church against church, leader against leader, and man against his own apparent success or failure. Then there are the jealous feelings which emerge when you meet the man whose stellar success glows from glossy magazine covers, book jackets and three ring seminar notebooks. Is all this really worth all the carnality it stirs up? For me, I am not sure, but the more I study brokenness, the more I have my doubts. I guess the bottom line is that if it stirs up carnality, it only shows that carnality was there all along.

D. L. Moody experienced a breaking when he met George Mueller. Mueller listened to all the great things Moody said he had done for God. Mueller then said, "I have heard about the great things you have done for God. But what about all the great things God has done for you?" Watchman Nee wrote, "To have God do his own work through us, even once, is better than a lifetime of human striving."

It is so easy as leaders to cast our own golden calf under the good intentions of leading the people in worship. People can be sincerely wrong, and sincerely partially wrong. We run the risk of implying that numerical growth reflects spirituality. We fail to realize that leadership is complex, and so is spirituality. How is it we justify the tremendous growth of some cults and worldly corporations? Or is the church merely another corporation to be run effectively with superior leadership? The copycat mentality is dangerous, as we try to clone our styles and our ministries after another who has become so "effective." We deny our unique creativity by trying to "be" just like a more successful endeavor.

Eugene Peterson points out the danger of ministerial leadership which focuses too much on know-how and skills. It is easy as leaders, especially Christian leaders, to fall into our culture's emphases of knowledge gathering and program and activity implementation. God is not opposed to these processes in proper order, but He is opposed when they become the primary focus over soul development. As leaders with knowledge, we run the temptation of the Messiah-syndrome, the "you-need-me" mentality. "My parishioners are dependent on me teaching them and showing them the right way to live." This attitude can become addictive and often leads to anger toward people when they fail to do "what I told them to do," and we burn out because we feel that everyone depends on us.

As leaders with right behaviors/skills, we run the temptation of becoming ministry managers. We run programs well and smoothly perform pastoral behaviors. Here we run the risk of thinking of ourselves as CEOs instead of servants. We eventually find ourselves bored and dis-illusioned. A problem with most ministerial success syndrome materials is that they emphasize these two aspects—having better knowledge and performing better actions. If we don't say it overtly, we communicate by its absence that soul development and spirituality are not the most important aspects for Christian leadership. Even prayer and worship become techniques which can help the church grow, instead of being ends in themselves. We naturally assume that the alternative to knowledge and skill is ignorance and incompetence, but such an assumption overlooks the thrust of leading out of who we are and the abilities God has given us.

E.M. Bounds said, "The Church is looking for better methods; God is looking for better people. What the church needs today is not more machinery or better, not new organizations or more novel methods, but people whom the Holy Spirit can use, people of prayer, people mighty in prayer. The Holy Spirit does not flow through methods, but through people. He does not come on machinery, but on people. He does not anoint plans, but people—people of prayer."

Eugene Peterson points out that the problem with the tasks of ministry is that many of them can easily become habit-forming. Informational and motivational approaches to ministry can be addictive. Unlike other addictions where people can separate themselves from food, or pornography, or drugs, a Christian leader does not have the freedom to separate himself or herself from the very things that can become addictive. That is why Christian leadership is such a dangerous occupation, and why so many fall. It is similar for Christian leaders in secular settings. "At the heavily trafficked crossroads of my will and God's will, everything is at issue—the way I work, talk, love . . . The relationship of God's will and my will is not a specialized religious question, it is THE question. How we answer it shapes our humanity in every dimension."[9]

■

BROKEN LEADERS PRODUCE WHOLE PEOPLE

How refreshing it is for a leader to say, "We did not do anything to manipulate this growth in our church. God did it." These words often go unheard, because they produce frustration for the ambitious, growth-oriented technician. They do not provide formulas or recipes. But isn't that really how the Holy Spirit tends to work, sporadically as He chooses, in spite of our efforts and our abilities to manipulate Him. A broken person does not care who gets the credit, and avoids the implication that he is responsible for the success. God uses people, as He chooses, when He chooses, to the degree He chooses. Our primary goal must not be to manifest results, but to remain available. This is assertive passivity. This must not be an excuse for mediocrity or a "we're not big but we sure are holy" mentality. Brokenness says "I want to be available for whatever God has for me, large or small, popular or unpopular."

I do not want to dismiss the need to grow quantitatively or qualitatively. But the rat race of the success syndrome tends to chew up and spit out a lot of well-meaning, capable leaders and potential leaders, because we get caught in its allure. Like the wisdom in Proverbs suggests, we must avoid prostituting ourselves for the temporary satisfaction that success and fame offer.

Brokenness also helps us cut the emotional umbilical cord many pastors have with their churches. Dr. Paul Meier, of the Minirth-Meier counseling centers, notes that a large percent of people "called" into ministry have co-dependent tendencies. As a result, they fail to grow the church and the people because they need to be needed. They unconsciously create an unhealthy body which depends upon their personal talents and ministry, instead of releasing church members to be mature and do ministry on their own. This subtle problem is why many people are drawn to ministry-type careers, out of their needs, not others'. It may be a major reason most churches in America remain so small and plateaued. When we break in the wrong place due to a dysfunctional family life or other past imprinting situations, we tend to live out a lifestyle of insecurity, emotionally needing others to depend on us. This may appear saintly from the outside, but is in fact neurotic.

Brokenness creates a dependency on God, not upon the needy people who need us. It frees us from the emotional string-pulling co-dependent relationships produce. The broken pastor is free to take risks, to model vulnerability, to hold and be held accountable, to confront sin and game-playing with love, and without the fear of losing relationships. Paul says, "Am I now trying to win approval of men, or of God? Or am I trying to please men? If I were still trying to please men, I would not be a servant of Christ" (Gal. 1:10). It is only when we are free from emotionally depending upon others that we can objectively provide quality ministry which in turn frees and matures those we shepherd. As leaders, we must be sensitive to people, but not controlled by them as people pleasers, tempted to tickle ears. Brokenness frees us from the strings of popularity and the need to be liked.

What we need to recover in leadership training is the idea of evangelical spirituality and character development. In our pantry sits a can of chili soup with a label that reads, "chili con carne," meaning chili with meat. The incarnation refers to God in the flesh, Jesus Christ, God "with meat." According to God, leadership which tends to be knowledge oriented, and skill and giftedness oriented, versus incarnate, isn't worth beans.

A story is told of a young preacher who went to preach his first sermon. He had done so much work on this masterpiece that he was full of his own importance. He entered the pulpit with tremendous confidence, but once up there, he blanked out and couldn't think of a thing. Finally he came down from the pulpit utterly humiliated. As he slumped down the steps, an old preacher said to him, "If you'd gone up the way you came down you'd have come down the way you went up."

Nearly all of the power resources, knowledge, and skills can be used with or without incarnational leadership. But when God desires leaders, He desires them to be genuine, real, leaders who are developed from the soul outward. The reason many leaders do not last long and fail to finish well is because the pressures finally get to them.

I thoroughly enjoy chocolate. I always have. I remember my disillusionment as a child after receiving my first chocolate Easter bunny. "Wow, look at this, a whole rabbit made of milk chocolate," I thought. When I unwrapped it and bit off an ear, I sadly discovered it was hollow. You can buy cheap and expensive chocolate Easter bunnies. The cheap ones often look like the expensive ones. But the cheap bunnies are hollow. The expensive ones are solid milk chocolate.

We have all met people who were solid, real, spiritual. They did not have to tell you they were real. You saw the same person whether they were "on" or just relaxing. You felt a refreshing sense of security being around this person and an appreciation in knowing them. That is what God is looking for, not for people who can manipulate and work a crowd, not for gifted orators who persuade and turn on the emotions, and not for managers of ministry.

God wants men and women who lead out of who they are as people.

Incarnational leaders influence people to win souls because they are sharing their faith. If you give, people will tend to give. If you love, people will love. If you forgive, people will forgive. If you worship, people will worship. Brokenness is the process by which our mixed motivations become purer. Out of the humus, we grow to be the people we need to become and we minister out of our overflow. Our ministry emerges from our integrity and our wholeness.

■

MAINTAINING THE EDGE

Although brokenness is an important part of the leadership development process, a person who rises in leadership because of incarnational growth can also lose this edge if he or she fails to respond appropriately to breaking processes in the future. As we have mentioned earlier, brokenness tends to be episodic. It has a beginning and ending. It also tends to be cyclical. Many leaders can target a time in their lives when they experienced significant pruning and passed through a personal wilderness. However, these historical testimonies can become meaningless monuments unless the results are in present tense. Memories which are not incarnate today are worth little.

I believe that is why so many Christian leaders, who appear at one time to have an anointed ministry, fall from their positions. There is no guarantee that those who endorsed or gave testimonies for this book, or this author himself, will finish the course well in spite of past periods of breaking. Ministry that initially comes out of incarnational leadership and a spirit of brokenness can often continue on its own, due to its own energy and the synergism of the people drawn into the leadership process. However, if the effects of brokenness fade away, and new breaking does not occur, a leader is susceptible to temptation and falling to evil. It happens all the time. Remember King David? At times we are amazed to watch a ministry so blessed by God and led by such a strong leader, and yet see what appeared to be sudden character failure. I have also seen a fence built. The strong wood posts are placed in the ground to hold up the fencing wire attached to them. Then water begins eroding the dirt from around the base of the fence post, or the post starts rotting in the ground. After awhile, the fence ceases to be held up by the post, but the post is held erect by the fence. Erosion and root rot often go on with few outward symptoms, until the "sudden" demise.

The basis for all sin is making yourself into your own god. We are never immune to the temptation to rely on our own knowledge, experiences, network, and God-given gifts. We are always prone to the temptation of believing our own press releases, unless we retain the attitude of brokenness. When the influence of brokenness ceases to remain in our lives, we will resort back to a reliance on ourselves and not on God.

It is possible to grow in brokenness and also to grow out of brokenness. The latter remembers the process as a historical memory versus a present reality. An unattended orchard soon is overgrown with weeds, its unpruned trees producing inferior fruit. Henri Nouwen points out that Paul grew in his brokenness. Although it may be straining the unique context of each passage, you see a refining response from Paul in his ministry. Around twenty-five years after his conversion, Paul wrote, "I am the least of the apostles" (I Cor. 15:9). Nearly five years after that he wrote, "I am less than the least of all the saints" (Eph. 3:8). And a year later he said, "I am the chief of sinners" (1 Tim. 1:15). Notice the progression in humility of ranking himself among the apostles to the head of the sinners. His concern was present, not past. As we grow in holiness, we become more aware of our inadequacies and the gravity of our sin condition. "Leadership, for a large part, means to be led. You all know the third temptation of Jesus. It was the temptation of power."[10]

■

BENEFITS OF BROKEN LEADERSHIP

The world applauds the person who can take control. We handsomely reward those who can control their own bodies (athletes, models), corporations (CEOs, entrepreneurs), information (professors, media), speech (lawyers, politicians), and other people (military, etc.). May the best controller win. Losing control is negative. "He's out of control," (mad/angry). "She's lost control," (of a class). "Get control of yourself," (self-discipline). "The world is out of control," (chaos, anarchy). But the way of the cross is one of giving up control to God.

Unbroken leadership seeks to take charge. As broken leaders, we recognize that God is in charge. Because I am not in charge, I do not have to worry about manipulating circumstances. James 4:14 reminds us that "we do not even know what will happen tomorrow, in spite of all our plans. We are but a mist that appears for a little while and then vanishes. Instead, we ought to say, 'If it is the Lord's will.'" Matthew 6:25 reminds us that we cannot even add a single hour to our lives, so why worry? Psalm 127:1–2 says that "unless the Lord builds the house, its builders labor in vain. In vain you rise early and stay up late, toiling for food to eat, for he grants sleep to those he loves" (NIV).

Leaders and their people will never understand stewardship of time, money, talents, and relationships, until they understand that those are sovereignty issues. When we think we are in charge, we will have a problem letting go of the time, money, and energy God desires. The person who realizes the sovereignty of God does not have to rely on the political maneuvering that others use. Kelly writes, "Instead of being the active, hurrying church worker and the anxious, careful planner of shrewd moves toward the good life, we become pliant creatures, less brittle, less obstinately rational."[11]

One of the inherent challenges in the first stages of brokenness is "What will others think? They'll consider me a loser. How will I save face? They will think I am untalented, or spiritually weak, or inferior." Accepting brokenness frees me from the expansive energy of worrying about what others are thinking. Likewise, it sanctifies my ambitions. To deny ambition is pseudo-humility resulting in repressed anger and/or apathy. We must face our drivenness and surrender it. It is alright to possess ambition, but not to be possessed by it. Realizing that the torrid stream of ambition ultimately leads nowhere without God's constant direction, we must be willing to let go and avoid the "bigger and better" syndrome. We all have unique niches in life, and when we compare and compete, we run the high risk of pride or burnout and depression. "Once I have found that in my total brokenness I am still loved, I become free from the compulsion of doing successful things."[12]

Because I am not in charge, I don't have to fight for my rights. A lot of energy goes into saving face and making sure that justice is carried out on those who betray us. A board member approached me once about someone who was spreading some negative talk about me. He asked, "So what do you intend to do?" I smiled and said, "Probably nothing. God is sovereign." When He is in control, you know that justice will ultimately be served. When leaders fail to heal from past hurts, and to forgive those who have betrayed them, they are revealing unsurrendered rights.

Because God is in charge, I don't have to survive. When we are in charge, we ultimately end up in the survival mode. The survival mode involves clinging to our limited resources, clutching to our job and nervously releasing our time and money. When you own a business, you tend to be tighter with your money than those who work for you. When God owns our world, we are freer to dream, to risk failure, to step out on faith, to trust Him financially. At the core of leading is vision, risking to change, grow, to go for it. The survival mode comes out of the belief that God is not sovereign and that if I am going to make it, it is up to me. "But there is something about deepest humility which makes men bold. For utter obedience is self-forgetful obedience. Out of utter humility and self-forgetfulness comes the thunder of the prophets, 'Thus said the Lord.'"[13]

Since God is in charge, what is my responsibility? That is a logical question since much of our activity comes out of the belief that life is up to us. If God is in charge, I can trust Him, even when I don't understand Him. Every day we trust people or situations we know little to nothing about, like who is piloting the plane I am flying on and how was it maintained? Who built my car and how do I know the person driving toward me is not going to swerve and hit me? No, we don't have to understand in order to behave. When people say they do not have faith in God because they do not understand Him or His ways, they are more often admitting they would rather not repent of their sins and yield to God. Faith is rarely a matter of information or rationale, but one of surrender and obedience. When you realize God is sovereign, you can trust Him without always understanding Him.

If God is in charge, I can have peace, even when circumstances do not comply. The great hymn, "It Is Well," was written by a man who had lost his family to a shipwreck. The words sung so often were penned during a time of death, of brokenness. Christians are known for dying well. Even in the most dramatic circumstance, a cessation of life as we know it, we can have peace, because He is sovereign. As I write this, I have no guarantee I will wake up in the morning. As you read this, you cannot be certain that you will finish this book. Life is too fragile, too unstable. But we can still have peace.

If God is in charge, I need to obey Him, even when I do not feel like it. The sovereignty of God is not a rationale for lying down and doing nothing. A fatalistic, existential view is not the result of God's sovereignty. Because He is in charge, I have responsibilities, but they are different from the ones when I think I am sovereign. What is important is doing His will, not being successful. Although God would consider faithfulness and success as the same, most of us consider them separately. Brokenness and realizing the sovereignty of God release us from the unceasing drive to make things happen, even with our God-given gifts, even for His service. Great rationalization goes on in the name of ministry when we try to do great things for God instead of striving only to do His will. When we are self-sufficient Christians, we try to use God. But when we are broken Christians, we make ourselves available for God to use us. No one is indispensable in Christ's church. "Too many well-intentioned people are so preoccupied with the clatter of effort to do something for God that they don't hear Him asking that He might do something through them."[14]

Brokenness helps us confront the blind spots in our lives. When our lives seem to be going well and appear fruitful, it is easy to develop blind spots. We can ignore these weaknesses and deny them when others confront us or hint at them. It is as easy to excuse our blind spots as "other people's problems," "their carnality," and "you can't please everyone." One of the beautiful things about brokenness in leadership is that it keeps you in tune with those areas where you need personal growth and provides an attitude that is receptive to seeing areas of concern. Often the blind spot itself is an inability to see a lack of brokenness and its results in one's life.

Broken people are not interested in things, in numbers, in fame or attention. They are very interested in pleasing God, glorifying Him, and being sensitive to the Holy Spirit. I once met with a local politician who has received a significant amount of national attention. During the discussion I asked, "Have you considered running for governor?" He responded, "I am not interested in that position." I smiled, "That's probably a good reason for running." Holy ambition comes forth as a calling. Unholy ambition comes forth as drivenness. Tozer said, "A true and safe leader is likely to be one who has no desire to lead, but is forced into a position of leadership by the inward pressure of the Holy Spirit and the press of the external situation. Such were Moses and David and the Old Testament prophets. I believe it might be acceptable as a fairly reliable rule of thumb, that the man who is ambitious to lead is disqualified as a leader."

"The Christian leader of the future is called to be completely irrelevant and to stand in the world with nothing to offer but his or her own vulnerable self. The long painful history of the Church is the history of people ever and again tempted to choose power over love, control over the cross, being a leader over being led."[15]

■

LEADING AND FOLLOWING

"It is the nature of God to make something out of nothing. Consequently, if someone is nothing, God can make something out of him. Men make something into something else. But this is vain and useless work. Thus God accepts no one except the abandoned, makes no one healthy but the sick, gives no one sight except the blind, brings no one to life except the dead, makes mercy upon no one except the wretched, and gives no one grace except those who have not grace. Consequently, no proud person can become holy, wise or righteous, or become the material with which God works, or have God's work in him, but he remains in his own works and makes a fabricated, false and simulated saint out of himself, that is a hypocrite." (Martin Luther from a Lenten Meditation)

The need to be needed, to be in charge, to be up front, to receive attention, and to take charge are not the sort of motivations which reveal incarnational leadership. These are not healthy responses of a heart set to do God's will. Eugene Peterson wrote, "The moment I begin exercising my will, I've put a fox in charge of the hen house. My will is my glory."[16] The mind games of success in ministry and reaching your potential tend to take the focus off of God being God in one's life. If you are a leader or potential leader, take periodic times of introspection and listen to criticisms from friends and enemies. As we grow in holiness and grow toward God, we become more and more aware of our own mixed motives and selfish intentions. The worst kind of evil is evil which appears as good. Remember, most evil is not of the satanic ritualistic type. Most evil appears as light.

A great statesman once made a speech that turned the tide in national affairs. "May I ask how long it took you to prepare that speech?" asked an admirer. "All my life has been a preparation for what I said today," he replied. That is the truth about incarnational leadership. It is the type which flows out of the years of character building process. It cannot be capsulized in a "how to" seminar or a book of traits to emulate.

Oswald Sanders tells the story of a young man who was beginning his work with the Coast Guard and was called early to take part in a desperate assignment. A great storm had arisen and a ship was signaling its distress. As the men began to move the big vessel to the rescue, the young man, frightened at the fierceness of the gale, cried out to the captain, "We will never get back!" Above the storm the captain replied, "We don't have to come back, but we do have to go out."[17] Answers like this only come out of a character built by persistent challenges. Meister Eckhart said, "There are plenty to follow our Lord half-way, but not the other half. They will give up possessions, friends, and honors, but it touches them too closely to disown themselves."

> When God wants to drill a man
> And thrill a man
> And skill a man,
> When God wants to mold a man
> To play the noblest part;
> When He yearns with all His heart
> To create so great and bold a man
> That all the world shall be amazed,
> Watch His methods, watch his ways!
> How He ruthlessly perfects
> Whom He royally elects!
> How He hammers him and hurts him,
> And with mighty blows converts him
> Into trial shapes of clay which
> Only God understands;

While his tortured heart is crying
And he lifts beseeching hands!
How He bends but never breaks
When his good He undertakes;
How He uses whom He chooses
And with every purpose fuses him;
By every act induces him
To try His splendor out—
God knows what He's about![18]

That may sound like pretty negative theology—no doubt it appears very harsh. But when you are in the midst of a period of brokenness, those words ring surprisingly familiar.

If you are a part of a leadership process as a follower, seek wisdom regarding the selection of leaders. Look at the motives and attitude of potential leaders, not in a judgmental manner, but with a discerning spirit. Thomas à Kempis wrote, "We inquire whether he be courageous, rich, handsome, skillful, a good writer, a good singer, or a good laborer; but how poor he is in spirit, how patient and meek, how devout and spiritual, is seldom spoken of." Follow the leader who follows the Leader. Take great caution in giving support to a leader who exudes giftedness and vision, but who does not seem to live it out in his or her personal life. When you find a man or woman who expresses an attitude of brokenness and whose influence comes out of who he or she is, get in line behind that person. You will usually discover that you end up in front of him or her, because incarnational leaders are servant leaders.

If you are a pastor or other Christian leader, look for lay leaders and staff who have been broken in the right place. No amount of talent, charisma, or experience will make up for an unbroken associate.

Keep in mind that some of the men who have been given the very power of God have raised armies, defeated the enemy, brought forth mighty works of God, preached and prophesied with unparalleled power and eloquence. . .
And thrown spears,
And hated other men,
And attacked other men,
And plotted to kill,
And prophesied naked,
And even consulted witches.
What does this world need: Gifted men, outwardly empowered? Or broken men, inwardly transformed?"[19]

I hope by now we would agree, it is the latter.

Notes

Chapter Two
1. Gordon MacDonald, *Rebuilding Your Broken World* (Nashville: Thomas Nelson, 1988), dust cover.

Chapter Three
1. Charles Colson, *Born Again* (New York: Bantam, 1976), 124, 128.
2. Clarence Hall, *Portrait of a Prophet* (1933), 175.
3. Quoted by Robert Bellah, et.al., *Habits of the Heart* (Berkeley: University of California Press, 1985), 21.
4. Henri Nouwen, *Out of Solitude* (Notre Dame, IN: Ave Maria Press), 42.
5. Roberta Hestenes, "Personal Renewal: Reflections on 'Brokenness'" *TSF Bulletin* (Nov.–Dec., 1984), 24.

Chapter Four
1. Brian Fay, *Critical Social Science* (Ithaca: Cornell University Press, 1987), 29.
2. Ibid., 30.
3. Reinhold Neibuhr, *Discerning the Signs of the Times* (New York: Charles Scribner's Sons, 1946).
4. Donald McCullough, *Discipleship Journal* (1989), 49.
5. Watchman Nee, *The Spiritual Man* (New York: Christian Fellowship Pub., 1968), 121.
6. Quoted in Oswald Chambers, *My Utmost for His Highest.*
7. MacDonald, *Broken World,* 140.

Chapter Five
1. Philip Yancey, *Christianity Today* (September 8, 1989), 25.

2. Ibid.

3. Thomas à Kempis, *The Imitation of Christ*, 92.

4. Larry Crabb, *Men and Women* (Grand Rapids, MI: Zondervan, 1991), 68.

5. Ibid., 76.

6. W. Phillip Keller, *A Layman Looks at the Lord's Prayer* (Chicago: Moody Bible Institute, 1976), 95.

7. Peter M. Senge, *The Fifth Discipline* (New York: Doubleday, 1990), 95.

Chapter Six

1. Henri J.M. Nouwen, *In The Name of Jesus* (New York: Crossroad Pub., 1990), 62.

Chapter Seven

1. Crabb, *Men and Women*, 86,29.

2. Ibid., 80.

3. Dennis Kinlaw,

4. Ernest Becker, *The Denial of Death* (Free Press, 1975), ix.

5. Nee, *Spiritual Man*, 76.

6. Oswald Chambers, *Disciples Indeed* (Fort Washington, PA: Christian Literature Crusade, 1960), 85.

7. Henri Nouwen, *Seeds of Hope* (New York: Bantam), 47, 49.

8. Crabb, *Men and Women*, 76.

9. J. Oswald Sanders, *Spiritual Leadership* (Chicago: Moody Press, 1967), 16.

Chapter Eight

1. Richard Foster, *Celebration of the Disciplines* (San Francisco: Harper and Row, 1978), 4–5.

2. MacDonald, *Broken World*, 47.

3. Foster, *Celebration*, 84.

4. Ibid., 88.

5. Stephen Covey, *Principle-Centered Leadership* (New York: Simon and Schuster, 1991), 85.

6. Foster, *Celebration*, 70.

7. Ibid., 74.

8. Ibid., 76.
9. Dallas Willard, *The Spirit of the Disciplines* (San Francisco: Harper and Row, 1988), 175.
10. Foster, *Celebration*, 58.
11. Ibid., 30.
12. C. S. Lewis, *The Screwtape Letters* (New York: MacMillan, 1961), 41.
13. Foster, *Celebration*, 118.
14. Ibid., 134.
15. Willard, *Disciplines*, 224–225.

Chapter Nine
1. E. Stanley Jones, *Victory Through Surrender* (Nashville, TN: Abingdon Press, 1966), 42.
2. Ibid., 31.
3. Crabb, *Men & Women*, 53.
4. Nee, *Spiritual Man*, 185,175.

Chapter Ten
1. Covey, *Leadership*, 1991.
2. Nouwen, Henri, *Out of Solitude* (Notre Dame, IN: Ave Maria Press, 1974), 55.
3. E. Stanley Jones, *Victory Through Surrender* (Nashville: Abingdon Press, 1966), 44.
4. Thomas A. Kelley, *A Testament of Devotion* (New York: Harper and Bros., 1941), 62.

Chapter Eleven
1. Gordon Aeschiman, *World Christian Magazine*, as quoted by Paul Cedar, *Strength in Servant Leadership* (Waco, TX: Word Pub., 1987), 47.
2. Gene Edwards, *A Tale of Three Kings*, (Auburn, ME: Christian Books, 1980), 47.
3. Henri J.M. Nouwen, "Compassion in the Art of Vincent Van Gogh" *The Catholic Worker* (August 1976).
4. Nee, *Spiritual Man*, 190.
5. Jones, *Surrender*.
6. Edwards, *Three Kings*, 39.
7. Covey, *Leadership*, 85.

8. Max DePree, *Leadership Is An Art* (New York: Dell, 1989), 11.

Chapter Twelve

1. Ray Brown, quoted in "Is There No More Shame?" *Orange County Register,* January 5, 1992.
2. C. S. Lewis, *The Screwtape Letters* (New York, MacMillan Pub., 1961), 59.
3. Gene Edwards, *A Tale of Three Kings* (Aburn, ME: Christian Books, 1980), 15–16.
4. Ibid., 21.
5. Ibid., 22–23.
6. Ibid.

Appendix

1. Aleksandr Solzhenitsyn, *The Gulag Archipeligo Two,* (New York: Harper and Row), 613–615.
2. Zac Poonen, *Beauty for Ashes* (Bombay: Gospel Literature Service, 1973), 40.
3. Nouwen, *Name of Jesus,* 63.
4. Ibid., 63.
5. Poonen, *Beauty,* 56–59.
6. Ibid., 69.
7. Howard Haas, *The Leader Within* (New York: Harper Collins, 1992), 74.
8. Robert Bellah, *The Good Society* (New York: Knopf, 1991), 222.
9. Eugene Peterson, "Growth: An Act or Will?" *Leadership* (Fall, 1988), 34–39.
10. Nouwen, *Name of Jesus,* 57.
11. Kelly, *Testament,* 96.
12. Source unknown.
13. Kelly, *Testament,* 64.
14. Ibid., 97.
15. Nouwen, *Name of Jesus,* 17,60.
16. Peterson, *Leadership,* 34–39.
17. Sanders, *Spiritual Leadership,* 85.
18. Source unknown.
19. Edwards, *Three Kings,* 41.